PREFACE

It is claimed that there are probably 1000 different definitions of communication, none agreeing with the other in its entirety. However, everyone would agree with what theo Haimann once said, "The success of all managerial functions depends on successful communication." In the simplest sense, 'Communication is the conveying of information from one person to another.' However, in the Broad sense, communication is made up of huge complexities of dimensions, coverage, effectiveness and so on. Volumes can be written on each aspect of communication.

This Book, 'Communication Management' is a very humble attempt to present the voluminons subject in a very simple, brief yet innovative way for complete learning experience of the reader. The Book provides a large number of illustrations, diagrams, tables etc. to supplement the subject matter for easy and better understanding. Chapter outline at the beginning of each chapter indicate at a glance the topics covered therein. References and study questions including University and Professional examination questions (upto June 2009) at the end of each chapter enhances its utility for the students.

The Book covers the most contemporary technological advancements in the realm of Business/ office communication like Tablet Pc, Pen Drives, Voice Mail, i-phone, g-phone, broadband spectrum, LCD and Plasma TVs, Tele and Video-conferencing, NEC Vivid 2020 and several other gadgets. The Books also discusses the most popular of SMS Abbreviations, Management Terminology, Abhreviations of words and Terms in Appendices for practical use in communication. Three special chapters on 'Art of speech Making', 'Art of listening', and 'Office etiquette' have been specially written for the book.

While the Book is geared specifically for the university and professional students, it is equally suitable for teching community and practicing Managers.

Any ideas for the improvement of the book would be appreciated and thankfully acknowledged. I express deep gratitude to Mr. Neeraj Panday, Director, as also to the team of Mr. Sudher Joshi, particularly Mr. V.S. Rawat and Mr. Parmod Kumar, of the Himalaya Publishing House and Mr. B.K.Bhatt of M/S Elite-Art, the printers who have helped in the execution of this book with remarkable speed and excellence.

I am also grateful to a large number of subject-teachers, colleagues, friends and students who have directly or indirectly contributed in the preparation of the Book, Special thanks are due to my wife, Mrs. C. K. Chapra, Associate Professor in Commerce, Vivekananda College, Delhi University, Mrs. Ankita Bhatia, Assistant Professor in commerce, Laxmi Bai College, Delhi University, Mrs. Priyanka Gauri, Assistant Professor (Guest) in Commerce Shri. Ram. college of commerce, Delhi University and Mr. Ashish Chopra for their invaluable support in the preparation of this text.

DR. R.K. CHOPRA
627, Dr. Mukherjee Nagar,
Delhi-110 009

July 2009

COMMUNICATION MANAGEMENT

COMMUNICATION MANAGEMENT

(A Textbook of B.Com (Hons.), B.A. (Prog.), B.A. (V.S.), M.Com., M.B.A. and a reference manual for I.C.W.A. (Inter.), C.S. (Prel.), C.A. and other Professional and Competitive Examinations)

DR. R.K. CHOPRA
M.Com., LL.B., D.C.L. (I.L.I.), D.L.L., L.F.I.I., Ph.D.
Associate Professor, Deptt. of Commerce,
College of Vocational Studies,
University of Delhi
NEW DELHI - 110 017

Himalaya Publishing House

• Mumbai • Delhi • Bangalore • Hyderabad • Chennai
• Ernakulam • Nagpur • Pune • Ahmedabad • Lucknow

First Edition : 2009

Published by : Mrs. Meena Pandey
for HIMALAYA PUBLISHING HOUSE,
"Ramdoot", Dr. Bhalerao Marg, Girgaon, Mumbai-400 004.
Phones : 23860170/23863863 Fax : 022-23877178
Email : himpub@vsnl.com
Website : www.himpub.com

Branch Offices

Delhi : "Pooja Apartments", 4-B, Murari Lal Street, Ansari Road, Darya Ganj, New Delhi-110 002
Phones : 23270392, 23278631 Reliance : 30180392 to 396
Fax : 011-23256286 Email : hphdel@vsnl.com

Nagpur : Kundanlal Chandak Industrial Estate, Ghat Road, Nagpur-440 018
Phone : 2721216, Telefax : 0712-2721215

Bangalore : No. 16/I (old 12/1), Ist floor, Next to Hotel Highland, Madhava Nagar, Race Course Road, Bangalore-560 001
Phones : 22281541, 22385461 Fax : 080-2286611

Hyderabad : No. 3-4-184, Linampally, Besides Raghavendra Swamy Matham, Kachiguda, Hyderabad-500027
Phone : 040-655501745, Fax : 040-27560041

Chennai : No. 2, Rama Krishna Street, North Usman Road, T-Nagar, Chennai-600 017
Phone : 28144004, 28144005 Mobile : 09380460419

Pune : No. 527, "Laksha Apartment", First Floor, Mehunpura, Shaniwarpeth, (Near Prabhat Theatre), Pune-411 030
Phone : 020-24496333, 24496333, 24496323

Lucknow : C-43, Sector C, Ali Gunj, Lucknow - 226 024
Phone : 0522-4047594

Ahmedabad : 114, Shail, 1st Floor, Opp. Madhu Sudan House, C.G. Road, Navrang Pura, Ahemdabad-380 009
Mobile : 9327324149

Eranakulam : No. 39/104A, Lakshmi Apartment, Karikkamuri Cross Road Eranakulam, Cochin-622 011, Kerala
Phone : 0484-2378012, 2378016

Typeset at : Elite-Art, N.S, Marg, Daryaganj, New Delhi-110002

Printed at : A to Z Printers, Daryaganj, New Delhi-110002

CONTENTS

Chapter **1**

COMMUNICATION MANAGEMENT

CONTENTS

Chapter 1

COMMUNICATION MANAGEMENT

> ***"The success of all managerial functions depends on successful communication."***
> **—THEO HAIMANN**

The term 'communication' is derived from Latin word 'COMMUNIS', which means common. The process of communication which takes place between one human mind and another establishes a common meeting ground for understanding. Communication is any means by which a thought is transferred from one person to another. It involves receiving information and giving information.

Communication is one of the fundamental functions of an office, and a process essential for all forms of business. It is the process of conveying information from one person to another through the post, by telephone, by messenger service or by any other means. The term *communication* has been defined as, "an exchange of facts, ideas, opinions or emotions by two or more persons".[1] Shurter defines it as, "imparting or exchanging thoughts or information". Pitman, the British inventor of the shorthand system, defines 'communication' as transmitting a message in order to evoke a discriminating response. It involves a systematic and continuing process of telling, listening and understanding, and forms the basis of understanding among the members of an organisation". According to Theo Haimann[2] : "Communication, simply stated, means, the process of passing information from one person to another. It is the process of imparting ideas and making oneself understood by others. Thus, in its simplest sense, communication is the conveying of information from one person to another".

IMPORTANCE OF COMMUNICATION

Communication is a two way channel of transmitting ideas, plans, commands, reports and

1. Newman and Summer, *The Process of Management*.
2. Theo Haimann, *Professional Management*, p. 406.

suggestions, that influence attitudes towards an organisation and its objectives. It is said that, 'the success of an organisation depends on the adequacy of communication'. The importance of communication may be highlighted thus :

Importance of Internal Communication

1. Communication and Management Control : A business organisation consists of people and net work of decisions affecting them. Managing an organisation is getting things done through others, a task which requires a manager to communicate with other people. Communication serves the management in the sense that it makes everyone aware of what the organisation wants to achieve. Knowledge of attitudes and feelings of subordinates towards the job, firm, supervisor, and environment is of immense importance to a manager in exercising *'control'* over the operations of the organisation. This establishes the importance of upward and downward channels of communication.

2. Communication and Coordination : Since office function is a service function, to facilitate the performance of other functions, it cannot be envisaged in isolation of them. The problem of organisation and *coordination* is vital to the success of scientific office management and communication helps in attaining this success by making communication effective.

3. Communication and Integration : Communication is vital to the function of *integration*. Effective communication results in better presentation of information and creates awareness among the workforce of their working conditions. It is thus responsible for mutual understanding and promotes good relations.

4. Communication and Motivation : The office workers are to be motivated to work. The process of stimulating willingness to work among the workers is largely a process of communication.

5. Communication and Training : "In modern times, every organisation realises the importance of training. An increase in skill usually results in an increment in both quality and quantity of output. To understand increasingly technical nature of modern jobs, it is absolutely essential to undergo systematic training. Training is facilitated through a proper and efficient system of communication".

Importance of External Communication

External Communication implies the transmission of information to people outside the organisation (*e.g.*, customers, investors, suppliers, debtors, creditors, etc.) and its receipts from outsiders. Importance of external communication can be studied thus :

1. Communication and External Environment : It is very essential for a business enterprise to keep in touch with external business environment as it influences its functioning and results a great deal. A manager cannot decide wisely on whether to offer a new product line, if he has no knowledge of market potential, organisational changes involved and capital required etc. Similarly, he cannot decide upon inventory levels without knowledge of sales programme requirements, production and shipping schedules, availability prospects and price trends etc. His ability to get results depend primarily upon adequate and timely information.

2. Communication and Competition : Modern business is highly competitive in nature. Lots of information is gathered in the office to meet the challenge of competition. Such information is useful only if it is pr operly transmitted to the right persons for proper assessment of the state of competition so that steps may be initiated to meet the challenge of competition.

3. ***Communication and Public Relations :*** Communication is a tool for building human relationships. Businessmen are aware that the ability to get along with people, to advance in their jobs and to sell their goods, depends on clear communication. Good communication is another name for good public relations. Good public relations promote the interest of the enterprise.

The Purpose of Communication

In its broadest sense, the purpose of communication is to effect change — to influence actions towards the goals of an enterprise. In the *internal* functioning of enterprises, communication is essential as it integrates management functions. Communication is especially needed to :

(i) establish and disseminate goals of an enterprise;
(ii) develop plans for their achievements;
(iii) organise human and other resources in most efficient and effective way;
(iv) select, develop and appraise members of the organisation;
(v) lead direct, motivate and create a climate in which people want to contribute; and
(vi) control performance.

Communication also relate an enterprise to its *external* environment. It is only through communication, that managers become aware of :

(i) the needs of the customers;
(ii) the availability of suppliers;
(iii) the claims of stockholders,
(iv) the regulations of Governments; and
(v) the concerns of a community/society.

It is only through communication that any organisation becomes an open system interacting with its environment as shown in the following figure.

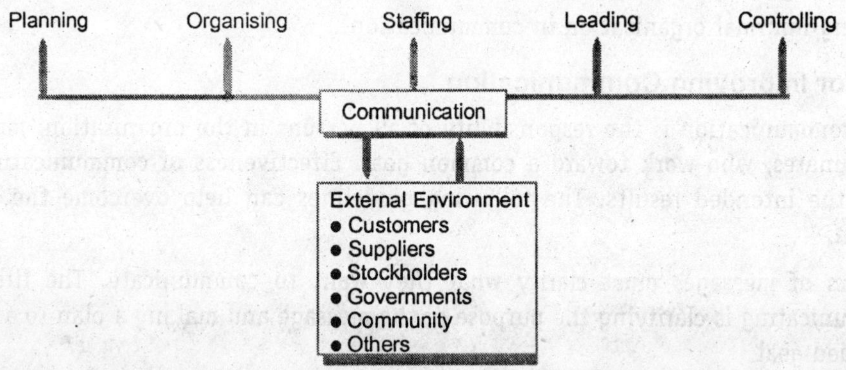

Fig.1.1. The Purpose and Functions of Communication[3]

3. Adopted from Koontz etc. : *Principles of Management*

COMMON BARRIERS TO COMMUNICATION

The common barriers to free flow of communication are those created by (i) departmentation, (ii) Geographical division of the organisation and (iii) multiplicity of staff and service groups. Group loyalty, lack of understanding of common organisational objectives and undesirable rivalry between different work groups are also some factors responsible for hindering the free flow of communication. These barriers can be overcome by orientation of the employees with the enterprise objectives, simplification of organisation structure and authority-responsibility relationship among the work force of the organisation.

Apart from the above, the following are the other barriers to the process of communication which are commonly encountered :

1. Defective system of transmission of messages.
2. Loss of message by transmission at successive levels and poor relation of information.
3. Lack of clarity and precision in delivering messages.
4. Wrong assumption or mis-interpretation of messages communicated.
5. Evaluating communication prematurely leading to stoppage in transmission of message.
6. Fear of consequences of a full and frank disclosure.
7. Lack of trust in oral communication of those who are in the habit of modifying original communication.
8. Lack of attention or failure to take note of instructions, notices, orders, or reports.
9. Failure to deliver important messages due to lathargy, carelessness or guilty consciousness.
10. Ambiguity or vagueness of the message delivered.

How to Overcome these Barriers?

The above barriers to the process of communication may be overcome by :

1. Paying proper attention to the quality of the message;
2. Creating adequate conditions of receiving messages;
3. Maintaining integrity of organised effort; and
4. Utilising informal organisation in communication.

Guidelines for Improving Communication

Effective communication is the responsibility of all persons in the organisation, managers as well as subordinates, who work toward a common goal. Effectiveness of communication can be evaluated by the intended results. The following guidelines can help overcome the barries to communication.

1. Senders of messages must clarify what they want to communicate. The first step in communicating is clarifying the purpose of the message and making a plan to achieve the intended goal.
2. Effective communication requires that encoding and decoding be done with symbols that are familiar to both the sender and receiver of the message. Avoid technical jargon which only experts in the particular field can understand.

3. The planning of the message should not be done in vacuum. Instead other people should be consulted and involved to (i) collect the facts, (ii) analyse the message (iii) and select the appropriate media. The content of the message should be according to the level of knowledge of the recipient and the organisational climate.
4. It is important to consider the needs of the receivers of the message. Whenever appropriate, one should communicate something that is of value to them.
5. It is said that the tone makes the music. Similarly, in communication, the tone of voice, the choice of language and the relation between what is said and how it is said influence the reactions of the reader of the message.
6. In most cases, information is transmitted without communicating. Communication is complete only when the message is understood by the receiver. One never knows whether communication is understood unless the sender gets feedback. This is accomplished by requesting a reply to the letter, asking question's or by encouraging receiver to give their reactions to the message.
7. The function of communication is more than transmitting information. Communication is vital for creating an environment in which people are motivated to work towards goals of the enterprise while they achieve their personal aim. Another function of communication is to exercise control on the staff.
8. Effective communication is the responsibility not only of the sender but also of the receiver of the communication.[4]

EFFECTIVE COMMUNICATION

Communication is a major function of an office. All office work, whether performed in one department or in separate departments, is inter-related and inter-dependent. An efficient performance of office work necessitates a regular exchange of information and messages among individual executives, different departments and within the same department. Communication is said to be the life blood of a commercial and industrial enterprise. The success of an organisation depends to a very large extent upon its ability to communicate effectively with its employees and customers. The Office Manager has, therefore, the responsibility of maintaining an effective communication service as part of the office organisation. Effective communication takes place when a thing is understood in the sense in which it has been communicated.

Selection of Communication System

A communication service must be accurate, speedy and economical. The Office Manager should be familiar with the various devices of communication and the different factors which should be considered before adopting a particular communication system. These facts are :

1. Speed : The time taken to transmit a message to its destination and the speed of the communication system should be considered on the basis of the urgency of communicating the message.

2. Distance : The distance between various persons or departments, who are in need of a communication service should be considered, and communication media, suitable for covering the distance, should be selected.

4. *Adapted* : Koontz etc. : *Principles of Management*

3. Accuracy : The communication medium which is selected should ensure accuracy in the transmission of messages. If figures are spoken over the telephone, they are liable to be misheard. In such cases, written communication is desirable.

4. Secrecy : If it is desired that persons other than the intended recipient of the information should not become aware of the information communicated, the medium that is selected should ensure secrecy; there should be no leakage of information.

5. Safety : The risk of losing the communication in transit should be considered. If an important legal document is to be mailed, it is advisable to send it by registered post.

6. Records : If it is necessary to keep some record of a communication, it would be better to use written communication.

7. Impression : A communication should be in such a form that it produces the desired reaction from the person receiving it. In some cases, a form letter is adequate while in others it might result in the communication being thrown unread into the waste-paper basket.

8. Cost : All elements of cost should be taken into account. The relative costs, both of installation and running the different systems of communication, should also be considered. For instance, the cost of labour and material expended on preparing and posting a letter generally far exceeds that of the postage.

9. Expansion : The flexibility and scope for future expansion of the communication device to be adopted should be considered.

10. The effect of peak load periods : The selected communicative means must have the capacity to satisfy the peak loads.

11. Responsibility : It may be important that responsibility for receipt of communication is fixed by having it in writing with a copy of it retained. In such cases, speed and cost may not be considered. Speed may be sacrificed, a little additional cost may be incurred for the sake of fixing responsibility of receipt of communication.

The Communication Process

According to Louis A. Allen[5] Communication is a four-way process. It involves :

(i) Asking;

(ii) Telling;

(iii) Listening; and

(iv) Understanding

According to Ernest Dale[6], the communication process implies :

(i) A sender;

(ii) A receiver;

(iii) A message; and

(iv) A motivating climate.

5. Louis A. Allen *The Management Profession*, p. 274.
6. Ernest Dale, *The Management and Organisational Behaviour*, p. 152.

The communication process is composed of the following :

(i) **Perception :** Assignment of meaning by an individual to the stimuli he receives from his environment.

(ii) **Encoding :** Putting thoughts into communication symbols.

(iii) **Transmission :** Conveyance of communication symbols to the receiver.

(iv) **Receiving and Decoding :** The receiver assigns meaning to the communication symbols.

(v) **Responding :** Receiver translates idea in action.

Communication may be internal or external. It may also be oral, written or mechanical.

THE COMMUNICATION FLOW IN THE ORGANISATION

In almost every organisation, communication flows in various directions : Downward, Upward and crosswire communication. Traditionally, **downward** communication was emphasised, however, one may visualise that if communication flows only downward, problems may arise. It may be argued that communication should also move **upward** from the subordinate. Communication may also move **horizontally or diagonally** *i.e.* within the same organisation levels or between different levels in the organisation, who are not in direct reporting relationships with one another. Such communication is called **cross wire** communication. These different communication flows are shown in the following diagram :

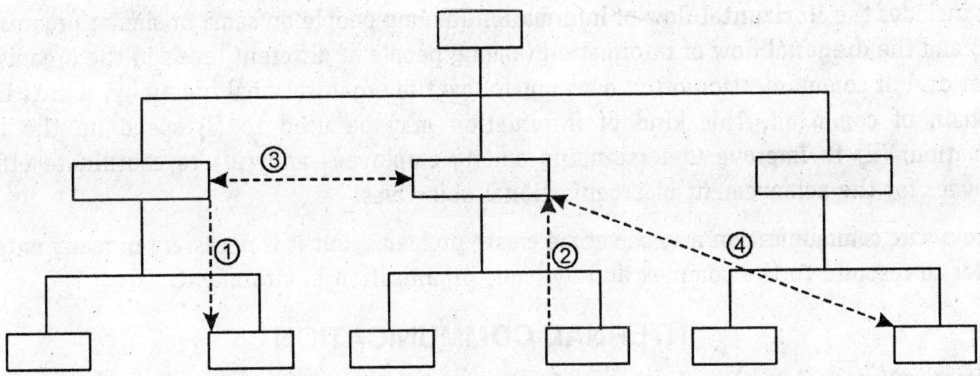

Fig.1.2 Communication flows in an organisation
1. Downward; 2. Upward; 3. Horizontal; 4. Diagonal Communication

Downward Communication

It flows from people at the higher level to those at lower levels in the organisation hierarchy. It exists specially in organisations with autocratic/authoritarian atmosphere. The kinds of Media used for **downward oral** communication include instructions, speeches, meetings, telephone, loudspeakers and even the grapevine. Examples of **written downward communication** are memorandum, letters, pamphlets, policy statements, procedure hand books and electronic news display etc.[7]

7. As quoted by Harold Koontz etc. (*Ibid*)

Downward flow of information through the different levels of the organisation is time consuming. Moreover, information is often lost or distorted as it comes down the levels of hierarchy. Often, many directives may not be understood or even read. As such, a feedback system is essential to find out whether information reached the recipient in the form, it was intended to.

Upward Communication

It travels from subordinates sup to superiors in the organisational hierarchy. Like downward, upward communication may also get distorted or filtered by superiors for unfavourable news to their losses. Upward communication is generally found in participative and democratic organisational environment. Upward communication may take the form of suggestion systems, appeal, complaint and grievance procedure, counselling sessions, groups meetings, exit interviews, morale questionaires, the grapevine etc.

Upward communication may be essential for upper management to know about production performance of employees, marketing feedback, financial data, the motivation and morale level of employees and so on.

Effective upward communication requires an environment in which subordinates feel free to communicate. It is therefore the responsibility of Top Management to create an atmosphere for creating a free flow of upward communication.

Cross Wire Communication[8]

It includes the **Horizontal** flow of information (among people on same or similar organisational levels) and the **diagonal** flow of information (among people at different levels in the organisation). A great deal of communication often does not follow the organisational hierarchy, it cuts through the chain of command. This kind of information may be used to (i) speed up the flow of information; (ii) to improve understanding among employees and (iii) to coordinate efforts of employees for the achievement of organisational objectives.

Cross wire communication may sometime create problems, but it is necessary in many enterprises in order to respond to the complex and dynamic organisation environment.

INTERNAL COMMUNICATION

Effective internal communication is fundamental to the existence of any office. Internal communication, also known as inter-communication, is a major function of an office. In a small organisation having upto ten employees, there may be no problem of internal communication, for these employees can easily communicate with each other. But as the organisation grows and the number of employees increases, the problem of effective communication[9] within organisation becomes more accurate and difficult. In a big organisation having a number of departments or sections, internal communication may be :

(i) Inter-departmental—that is, communication between the employees of the same department; or

8. *Adapted* : Koontz etc. : *Principles of Management*

9. Littlefield observes, "The number of messages communicated with maximum effectiveness is far lower than the number that miscommunicate because they are vague, incomplete, confusing, poorly adapated to the receipient, curt or late", (*op. cit*., p. 111).

(ii) Intra-departmental—that is, communication between different departments of the organisation.

Moreover communication may either be upward or downward. Upward communication is that which passes from a subordinate to the superior (as from a clerk to an officer, from an officer to the manager and from the manager to the Board of Directors). Upward communication may include reports, statistics, opinions suggestions, complaints, attitudes, ideas, rumours, etc., submitted by the lower level employees. Some companies have introduced the suggestion system for written upward communication. Employees are invited to submit their ideas and proposals under this system. Downward communication is that which flows from the top to the bottom, *i.e.*, from the manager to the assistant manager, or from a superior to a subordinate. It refers to directives and other messages that originate with officials at the higher levels of the organisation. Orders, policies, manuals, directives, instructions, procedures, circulars, bulletins, handbook, employee magazines—these are the most widely used channels of downward communication. The process of delegation is also a form of downward communication. "Downward communication helps to the different levels of hierarchy together and is the instrument by which an executive puts his delegated authority to effective use". Lastly, internal communication may be :

(i) Oral;

(ii) Written;

(iii) Mechanical; and

(iv) Through the use of the staff location device.

1. Oral Communication

Oral communication may take place in a face-to-face conversation or through mechanical devices.

(a) Face-to-Face Conversation: Theo Haimann says : "The human voice can impart a message with a meaning and a shading which even long pages of written words simply cannot convey'. Studies have shown that face-to-face communication carries the message better than any printed medium. Daily contact between subordinates and superior is the most important and frequently used method of effective communication. It is most effective because the superior can clearly explain his point of view to the subordinate, who can understand it quickly and clearly. Often, the quickest and the best way of ensuring co-operation is to talk the matter over with the people concerned. This is the most natural and perhaps the most important method of communication because, in conversation, ideas are conveyed not only by speech but by gesture and expression as well. A face-to-face conversation offers the following advantages and disadvantages :

Advantages : The advantages of a face-to-face communication are :

(i) It is immediate and helps in projecting the urgency of the matter.

(ii) It is the most suitable type of communication for confidential matters.

(iii) It makes for a personal approach which helps to resolve misunderstandings, irons out differences and develop a sense of belonging.

(iv) It fosters a friendly and co-operative spirit.

(v) It is very flexible; for decisions can be modified on the spot and without delay.

(vi) It provides an immediate response and feedback.

(vii) It allows both parties to participate in a situation—this is important for motivation, and offers a fertile ground for new ideas.

Disadvantages : The disadvantages of a face-to-face communication are :

(i) It may be less accurate and, being informal, may carry less weight.

(ii) It is unsatisfactory when Plan and policy decisions, requiring lengthy explanations, have to be communicated to employees.

(iii) By having direct personal communication, much of the time of office employees is wasted in making movements from one place to another.

(iv) Face-to-face communication may not be possible where the same information is to be conveyed to different parts of the organisation, particularly, when these are situated in different places.

(b) Mechanical Devices : The mechanical devices used for oral communication in the office include the telephones, the intercom system, the electric paging system, dictating machines etc.

TELEPHONES

The telephone is the most common and effective mechanical device used for oral communication. Telephonic communication may be classified according to whether they are internal—for example, between persons working in the same building—or external; for example, between the caller and some other subscriber to the telephone service.

In planning the telephone service for the office, the Office Manager should keep in mind the following points :

1. Sufficient Telephone and switchboard connections should be provided so that business outside the firm may be transacted without delay.
2. Inter-office calls should be freed from the switchboard, that is, connected without sidelines by either purchasing or renting a separate internal, automatic dialing system.
3. Well trained switchboard operators should be employed.
4. Modern and up-to-date switchboard should be installed.

Telephone connections may be divided into the following categories :

1. Direct Exchange Line : This form of communication is so widely used that it requires no general description. Under this system, there is one receiver to one exchange line. The telephone which is connected direct to the public exchange is known as the main instrument. In a large office, additional lines or connections to the exchange may be taken to cope with the increasing demand for telephone service. In such case, additional lines will have separate numbers, for instance, 25784861/4, which indicates that there are four lines which connect the particular subscriber to the "2578" telephone exchange—and these are numbered 4861, 4862, 4863, and 4864.

2. Direct Exchange Line with Extensions : With a growing business, the need for telephone connections may expand. In such a case, the direct exchange line may be provided with extensions. The main line and the extensions can both be used for internal as well as external communication. This system is cheap to install and run, and is adequate for a small office, but is unsuitable for a large organisation whose needs for inter-communication are extensive.

3. Private Branch Exchange System (PBX) : The Posts and Telegraphs Department provides a PBX (Private Branch Exchange) system which may be installed in an office to facilitate internal and external communication. Under this system, the internal telephone extensions are brought together on a private switch board and controlled for inter-communication. The switchboard is operated manually and controlled by the telephone operator employed by the office. The extensions

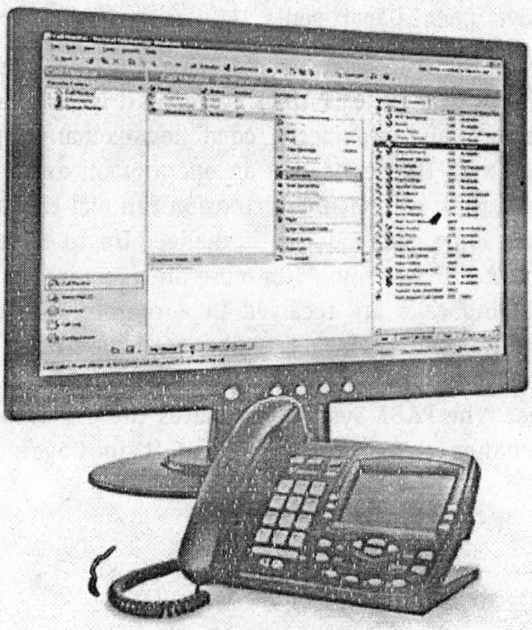

Fig.1.1. Private Branch Exchange

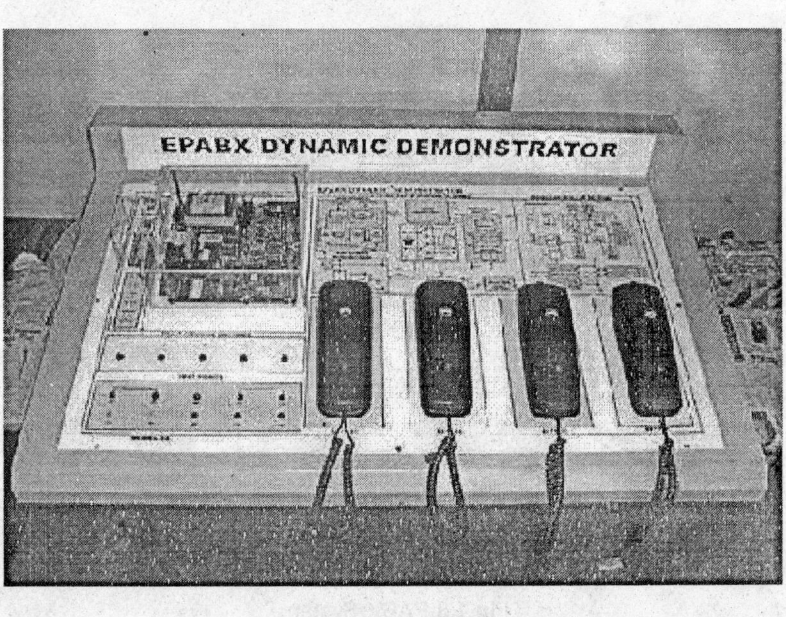

Fig.1.2. Expandable EPABX (By Syntel)
Source : Google Image Search

to the different departments of the organisation are connected with the PBX. Whenever the receiver is lifted on any of these extensions, this fact is indicated on the switchboard, the operator asks for the number which is required, dials it and connects it with the person who originally asked for the number. Similarly a call from outside is received by the switchboard operator, who puts it through to one or other of the departments, and then transfers it to a different department if the caller wishes to speak to more than one person. The PBX system has been quite popular with the Government Departments, Universities, Hospitals, and many commercial organisations.

4. Private Automatic Branch Exchange (PABX) System : It is installed with the help of the Posts and Telegraphs Department and provides a combined exchange and private automatic telephone service. It dispenses with the services of an operator on extension to extension calls and on outgoing exchange calls. Staff calling from extension can dial the extension required, and when an external call is required, a code number is dialled. Up to 50 extension lines can be provided under a PABX system. A PABX having 25 or more lines requires an operator for receiving the incoming calls. The incoming calls are received in a cabinet; the operator connects the required extension lines by dialing their extension number with the help of the digit keys or push buttons. Transfer or call back facility can be provided on a PABX to facilitate the transfer of calls from one extension to another. The PABX system eliminates the disadvantages of the manually operated private branch exchange and is fast replacing it in Government and Commercial Organisations.

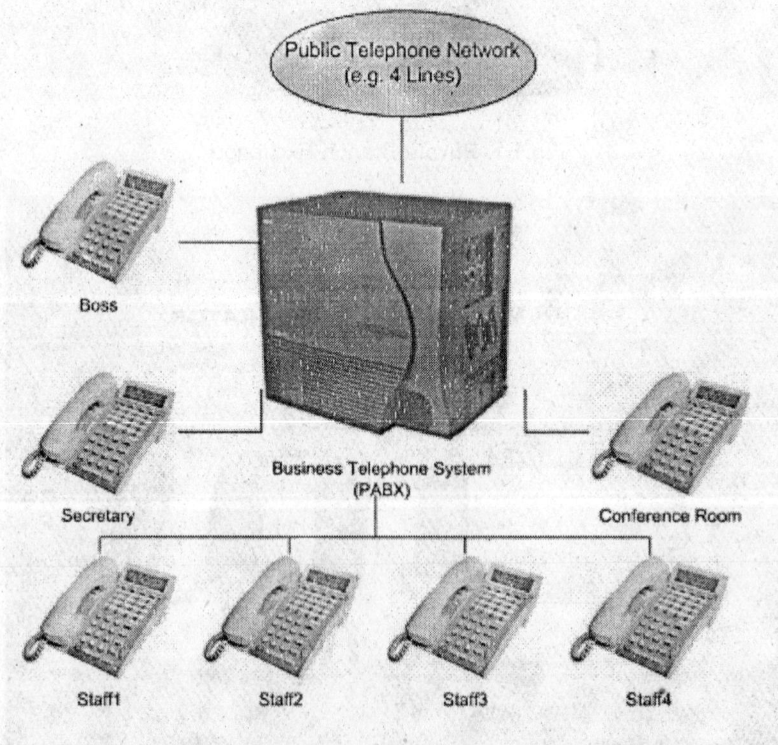

Fig.1.3 PABX System
Source : Google Image Search

HOW TO COMMUNICATE EFFECTIVELY ON TELEPHONE

Telephone manners are very important. It is the voice that is often the first or only impression a person receives of the speaker and of the organisation represented by him/her.

Tips for Telephone Talking

1. Speak slowly and clearly into the mouthpiece. Do not chew gum, eat or drink while talking.
2. Let your voice communicate that you are interested in the caller. Be friendly; but do not waste time.
3. Get to the point of the call. Be a good listener and pay attention to the person on the other end of the line.
4. Turn off background noise such as the TV or cooler etc. Remain calm during the conversation, even if the person at the other end is not.
5. Consider whether the call is important from your point of view or from receivers' point of view.
6. If the call is important from receivers' point of view, one should structure the information accordingly. First begin with what is important from receiver's angle. Talk about your interest later.
7. Keep the duration of the conversion as short as possible. The other person may not be free to spare time for your call.
8. End the conversation with a courteous comment such as 'Thank you' or 'Good-bye'. Then replace the receiver softly.

Tips for placing a call

1. Identify yourself, (*e.g.*, "Hello, this is Aishwarya Rai from Film City")
2. If the person you are calling sounds busy, ask if you can call back at a more convenient time.
3. if you have several points to discuss, make a list before hand so that you do not forget anything. Have all necessary information near you.
4. Try to answer the telephone by the second or third ring.
5. If your call is not answered even upto 10 rings, it is advisable to cut-off. Try some other time, unless it is very urgent.
6. If the telephone line suddenly gets disconnected, the courtesy demands that the dialer should redial immediately and say, "Sorry, the call got disconnected."
7. Identify yourself with the organisation you represent.
8. If the call needs to be transferred, politely ask, who is calling and do not leave the caller on hold for long time.
9. If you want your call returned, give your name, telephone number of the organisation and the time when you can be contacted.
10. Keep a slip pad and a pen near your telephone for taking down any message from the caller. Be complete and accurate also.

Tips for Writing Telephone Messages

Telephone messages must be taken carefully and delivered promptly. Here are 5 W's as a checklist:

1. What is that message and when was it taken?
2. Who is the message from and for?
3. When is the meeting or appointment mentioned in the message?
4. Where is the receiver of the message to go or call back?
5. Why is the message important? What is the purpose?

After the message is taken, it must be delivered promptly. A standard message form may be used by hand or the message may be e-mailed, depending on the situation.

Common Telephone Courtesies

1. In Business calls, use polite words like **'Thank you' 'please' 'nice of you'** etc. When you make a request or get something done or for a favour.
2. While making a request, use interrogative words like, "May I....", or "Could I....." or "Could you please...."
3. Use of direct categorical statement amounts to 'order'. Instead say, "May I request you to.....".

Telephone Precautions

1. Confidential or personal matters should never be discussed over telephone, as they could be overheard/tapped during conversation.
2. If at all, confidential or personal matters need to be discussed on phone, one may ask, like: "Are you free ? Can we talk about ...." "Can we discuss............."
3. Good etiquette on Telephone amounts to good manner and creates good business relations between the caller and the receiver (individual or company).

5. Private Exchange System : For very large organisations, particularly where there is extensive internal communication, it is advantageous to instal a private exchange system. Under this system, from 10 to 600 lines can be provided on a private exchange, and extensions may number several thousands. It is an automatic internal exchange system. A caller can get the required number by just dialing it. The system is ideal and economical only for a large organisation.

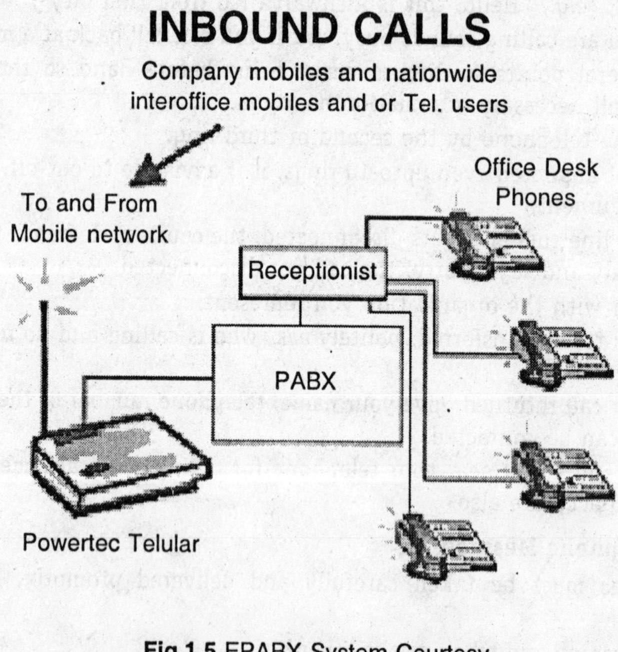

Fig.1.5 EPABX System Courtesy
Courtesy : Google Image Search

6. Inter-Communication System : Known briefly as intercom, this system has become very popular in India. Various types of intercom instruments are available up to a maximum of 40 lines. The system is not connected with the external telephone system and has to be installed by

Fig.1.6 Inter Communication (10 lines) System

the organisation itself. It facilitates quick verbal communication. In an organisation, various individuals or departments are equipped with a speaking-talking unit. By turning the switch or pushing the button, instant connection is obtained with any one on the circuit, and conversation can be conducted with great clarity of tone. The incoming calls are shown by lighted signals and are announced by buzzers. The conference key gives simultaneous contact with several persons.

An intercom system offers the following advantages :

(i) It may be installed as and when required and need no sanction of the Posts and Telegraphs Department.

(ii) It does not burden the external telephone lines and offers an ideal system for internal communication.

(iii) It is cheap to instal and run.

(iv) Time is saved by the use of intercom installations.

(v) It cuts down inter-office visiting.

7. Computerised Intercom : Computerised intercom (popularly known as 'Intellicom' works like an intercom but thinks like a computer. Outstanding features of this are :

(i) It can be expanded to 80/100 lines.

(ii) If the person called is with someone else, his calls can be transferred to that person's instrument, automatically.

(iii) If the person called is busy, his calls can be transferred to his 'Secretary', automatically.

(iv) If the party being called is busy, the exchange will call the caller once his line is free.

(v) At the touch of a button, it allows the operator to hold a conference by including up to 10 persons.

(vi) 'No disturb' and Group call 'pick up' facilities are also incorporated in the system.

Intellicom is the micro-processor based intercom with a self-diagnostic L.E.D. indicator to tell if something has gone wrong so that it can be put right instantly.

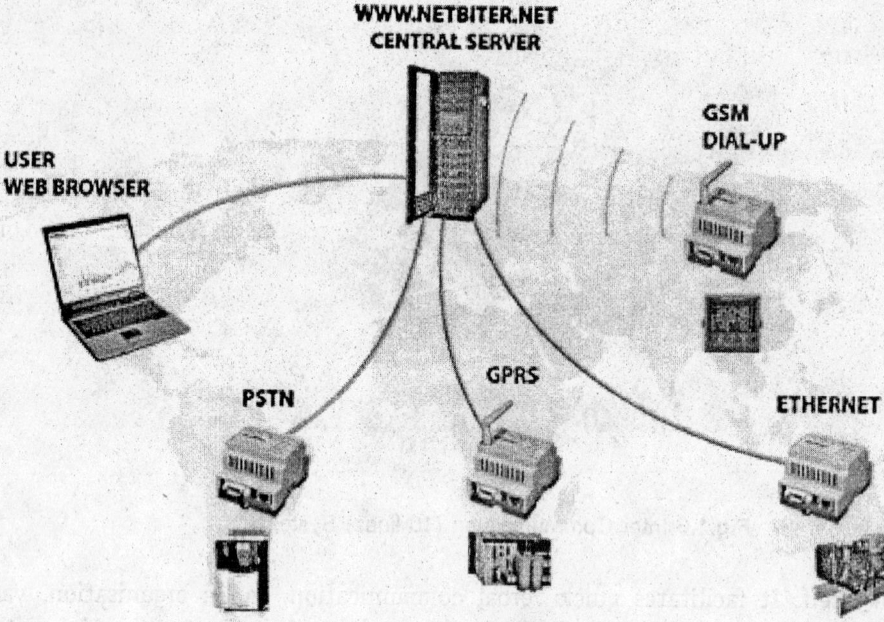

Fig.1.7 Intellicom
Source : Google Image Search

8. Executive or Loudspeaker System : It is a modern development of the intercom system, the essence of which is that a number of extensions radiate from a central instrument. These telephones are fitted with loudspeakers which enable persons to speak without having to lift the receiver. The amplifying instrument fitted to it allows a person to speak from a distance of up to 10 feet from the instrument.

Fig.1.8. Public Conference System

This system is particularly useful for :

(1) Holding joint consultations;

(2) Calling staff; and

(3) Providing means of inter-communication.

9. Radio Telephone : In Western countries, radiophones are used for business purposes, though in India, these are used mainly by the police and army services. For instance, in London, the General Post Office has now provided a radiophone service which enables a businessman to make ordinary telephone calls from a moving vehicle with the help of a wireless instrument. Under the system some select spots and moving vehicles have wireless sets from which messages are passed from headquarters to a particular vehicle and back. In India, the wireless system is recently opened to private business. We now have Radio Taxis in Metropolitan Towns in India.

10. Telephone Recording and Answering Sets : A telephone recording machine, when attached to a telephone, records the external incoming calls in the absence of the receiver himself. At the same time, a telephone answering set automatically answers an unattended telephone, and may :

(1) Transmit a recorded message to the caller;

(2) Invite the caller to record a message;

(3) Be used as a remote dictating machine; and

(4) Automatically repeat any messages recorded by callers when required to do so by a secret code word spoken over the telephone by an authorised person.

11. Dictating Machines : Dictating machines are used to deliver messages. A dictating machine is, in essence, like a tape-recorder. The message is recorded and the tape is sent to the person concerned, who plays it back. The dictating machine can be put to numerous business uses. It may :

(1) Give instructions to subordinates;

(2) Dictate correspondence in the absence of the stenographer.

(3) Send orders or taped reports by travelling salesman;

(4) Record the conversation of an executive with an outsider.

12. Electric Paging System : This is another system of internal communication, which may be used by larger enterprises—by departmental stores, insurance companies, head offices of banks, manufacturing plants, etc.,—where the executives generally move about from department to department. When an urgency arises, telephoning the various departments to locate a particular executive may be a very cumbersome and time-consuming job. This difficulty is overcome by the electric paging system, which is operated through a telephone switchboard. Under this system each executive is allotted a number. Whenever, he is called, the operator makes the electrical connection for this number. The number will sound throughout the premises. The moment the concerned executive hears his number, he picks up the nearest telephone, calls the switch-board operator, and receives the message.

2. Written Communication

Written communication may take the form of individually written letters, memoranda or reports, or may be formalised, as in orders, invoices or stereotyped letters. Internal written communication is concerned with the distribution of inter-office or intra-office letters or inter-departmental memoranda, and the routing of special reports or any other kind of papers or documents.

Tips for Improving Written Communication[10]

Effective writing may be the exception rather than the rule; nor do education and intelligence guarantee good writing. Many people fall into the habit of using technical jargon that can be understood only by experts in the same field. Common problems in written communications are that writers omit the conclusion or bury it in the report, are too wordy, and use poor grammar, ineffective sentence structure, and incorrect spelling. Yet a few guidelines may do much to improve written communication:

- Use simple words and phrases.
- Use short and familiar words.
- Use personal pronouns (such as "you") whenever appropriate.
- Give illustrations and examples; use charts.
- Use short sentences and paragraphs.
- Use active verbs such as "The manager plans...."
- Avoid unnecessary words.

John Fielden suggests that writing style should fit the situation and the effect the communicator wants to achieve. He recommends a,

(i) **Forceful style.** When the writer has power however the tone should be polite but firm.

(ii) **Passive style** is appropriate when the writer is in a position lower than that of the recipient;

(iii) **Personal style** is recommended for communicating good news and making persuasive requests for action.

(iv) **Impersonal style** is generally considered appropriate for conveying negative information.

(v) **Lively or Colourful Style** is suitable for good news items, advertisements and sales letters.

(vi) **Less colourful style** combining the impersonal with passive styles may be appropriate for common business writing.

Advantages : Written communications offer the following advantages over oral communications :

(i) Written messages are more accurate and exact.

(ii) They provide detailed instructions. The length and form of correspondence can be easily adopted to the subject matter and situation.

10. Koontz etc. : Principles of Management

(iii) Because they are formal, they carry greater weight than oral messages.

(iv) They serve as a permanent reference for the future.

(v) They have the widest possible coverage. Messages can be prepared and sent to any part of the world.

(vi) A written communication does not require the personal presence of an individual, as is the case in a face-to-face conversation.

(vii) It is an ideal means of conveying plans and policies, etc.

(viii) Sometimes, a written communication is necessary to satisfy legal and tax requirements.

(ix) Written communication is often less expensive than all other media of communication.

(x) It allows opportunities for adequate forethinking and is therefore free from ambiguity and vagueness.

(xi) It provides a written record or evidence of all transactions between the parties.

(xii) It is more convenient to send unpleasant communication through correspondence than to deliver it under oral communication.

Disadvantages : A written communication suffers from the following disadvantages :

(i) It can become excessively formal and a source of dispute.

(ii) It may encourage redtapism in the office.

(iii) It does not offer an opportunity for an immediate response.

(iv) Being formal, it fails to convey the feelings of the person sending it and does not foster a co-operative spirit.

(v) It may be difficult to keep written communications up-do-date.

Types of Written Communication

Written communications may be sent by a messenger or by a mechanical device.

(a) Messenger Service : It involves the appointment of messengers or office boys or peons to carry the memoranda, drafts and inter-departmental letters from different departments to their destinations. When it is essential to have written evidence of a communication between different departments or sections, the memoranda may be sent by these messengers. An internal messenger service, however, should be properly controlled, and collections and deliveries should be in accordance with a carefully drawn out schedule.

If properly supervised, such a system would be invaluable to the organisation. But the following drawbacks may be noted :

(i) It may result in wastage of time and money on unnecessary memoranda and envelopes;

(ii) The messengers may sit idle in the absence of messages; and

(iii) The service may not be useful if the organisation is well spread out.

(b) Internal Office-Mail Service : It is an improvement over the messenger service system. Under this system, a messenger collects the message and papers from different executives or departments and delivers them to their destinations at regular and stated intervals. "In" and

"Out" trays are generally provided on each desk for incoming and outgoing mail. Special messengers may be used for an urgent communication of written messages. If the timings of collection and delivery are properly regulated, this system may prove to be the most economical one.

(c) Mechanical Devices for Written Communication : When the volume of business is sufficiently large and its frequency more, some mechanical devices and aids may be used to deliver the letters and messages. The following are some of the mechanical devices used in modern offices :

Pneumatic Tubes

Pneumatic tubes are easy to instal and no special skill is required to operate them. These tubes carry the papers quickly and accurately to their destination. Under this system, a cylindrical pipe connects the various offices by means of which cylinders containing papers and documents, etc., are conveyed by suction from one department to another. These can be pre-set to deliver their contents at a certain stage as required. Such systems are of great use when a messenger service is difficult to maintain and when space is limited for human messengers to move from department to department. Unfortunately, **this system is not popular in India.**

Conveyors

Mechanical conveyors are used to convey papers and messages when the volume of work is large and fairly constant and when the destinations are fixed. Different types of belts and conveyors are used with advantage in offices in European countries. The main types of conveyors are :

(a) Conveyor Belt : It is a continuously moving belt or canvas, driven by a motor underneath and used to carry papers, documents, like goods like folders, files, etc. The moving belt may have one channel for carrying one set of papers or multiple channels for carrying several sets. A vertical guide is fixed along the length of the belt to keep the papers in a proper position through the process of delivery to the point of destination.

(b) Sandwich Belt Conveyors : Under this system, a sandwich belt is used to carry papers in between two canvas or rubber belts which run parallel. The sandwich belt can carry papers vertically and can be so laid out as to go around corners, over aisles or across railings. The tension is maintained by a system of pulleys and weights and can be controlled to drop the papers automatically at destination points.

(c) Roller Conveyors : Under this system, papers, etc., are put into a metal or plastic container which is then placed on rotating rollers placed side by side all along the route. The rollers are placed in a slightly sloping position so that the container moves along the roller due to gravity. When the container reaches the destination, it is picked up by the person concerned from the roller conveyor.

(d) Chain or Wire Conveyors : Under this system, papers are attached with clips which are fastened to chains or cables which in turn, are supported by split pipes or metal troughs. Overhead wire conveyors are generally used in departmental stores or warehouses.

(e) Vertical Lift Conveyors : When the office is spread over many floors, vertical lift conveyors may be used to move papers from one floor to another. Papers, etc., are placed in a tray[11] which moves up and down. Different trays of papers are received and emptied at the destination automatically or manually.

Chutes

These are wide channels or pipes (metallic or wooden) which run from a higher level to a lower level in a sloping manner. In western countries, they are used to drop mail or laundry from an upper floor to the receiving point on the ground floor. They may also be used to drop large bundles of papers, etc. from a higher to a lower level. The method is cheap to install and easy to operate; but it lacks the speed and sophistication of the conveyor belt system.

Lifts

When papers, folders, documents or registers etc., have to be transmitted continuously between two or more floors, a small lift may be installed. The lift may be operated electrically or hydraulically. Such lifts are used in libraries, hotels, hospitals, shopping complexes, malls and other organisations.

3. Mechanical Communication

Under this communication system, written messages are mechanically delivered to the persons concerned. Certain electronic devices have been invented with which written communication is possible without the actual delivery of such messages. These devices are :

1. Teleprinter or Telex : A teleprinter or telex works on electromagnetic principle. Messages can be sent from one place to another if at both ends teleprinters have been installed. "A teleprinter consists of two machines with a standard typewriter keyboard to be placed at the two ends for the transmission and reception of messages. Any message typed on one machine is automatically and simultaneously typed at the receiving end so that communication is instantaneous". Various branches of the organisation can be linked with the help of teleprinters for intercommunications. Teleprinters are easy to instal and operate and do not cost much.

2. Automatic Telex Service (or Teleprinter Exchange) : Under the automatic telex service, no clearance is required from the telephone exchange before the transmission of a message. Using a keyboard perforator and following the automatic teleprinter code, the message is punched on a tape, which is then fitted to the automatic transmitter and connected with the telex line, so that the message is carried automatically by the transmitter to the other end. This device works at a very high speed and facilitates quick transmission. But this service is available only in the four principle cities of India—Mumbai, Kolkata, Chennai and Delhi.

3. Teleprinters (Tele-Autograph) : This too, works on the principle of the teleprinter but transmits handwritten messages : The writing is electronically produced at the receiving end. To a message on a teleprinter, a switch is turned on and the message is written with a stylus on a metal plate. As the message is written, it is reproduced simultaneously at the receiving end. A telewriter can transmit messages only over short distances between main/head office and receiving room, or between two departments, or between the office and the warehouse or the factory. It offers an economical and high speed transmission and receipt of messages. Handwritten records

11. Neuner and Keeling; *op. cit.*

Fig.1.9. Fax Machine

Fig.1.10 Fax Machine with Advanced Features
Source : Google Image Search

are furnished and can be attached to inquiries, notices and instructions. It is possible to carry on a written conversation as well as messages can be sent and received.

4. Telefax (Fascimile Telegraphy) : Sketches, diagrams, drawings and formulae etc., cannot be transmitted on the teleprinter. Telefax, however, facilitates their transmission. The sketch or diagram is first drawn on a piece of paper, which is then wrapped round a cylinder in the machine. When the machine is switched on, it transmits fascimile of the diagram to the machine at the other end, where it is reproduced simultaneously. The machines at the ends are linked by an ordinary telegraph line. The telefax is extensively used now.

Advantages of Telefax : The advantages of the telefax are :

(a) Virtually any type or form of document, or drawing, whether typed, printed, or handwritten, may be transmitted. A black-on-white copy is received at the other end of the line.

(b) No skilled operators are required.

(c) Transmission can be over any distance.

(d) Transmission can be selective—any part of the document can be transmitted.

(e) The copies produced by the telefax receiving machine are used (and reproduced) instantaneously.

5. Television : In foreign countries, television is used in offices to transmit messages. The television equipment consists of a TV camera, a power unit and one or more master viewers. The television camera is focussed on the necessary records, statistical tables, important documents, memoranda, etc., which are to be seen or inspected. The image of these is received on the television screen placed at the receiving end. The television presents the message visually; in motion it projects a series of events. It shows the entire message and is feasible for conveying, completely and accurately, the entire image, which is very important in the case of blue prints, drawings, sketches or samples.

Closed circuit television systems are widely used in several countries including India by bank offices to verify specimen signatures and documents, by the filing department in the communication of documents or recorded matters to other departments; and by stockbroker firms in communicating the latest prices and quotations of securities to their main/head offices.

6. Videophone System : A Videophone enables the caller to see as-well-as hear the party at the other end. When the caller lifts the Videophone his image appears simultaneously on one half of his screen and on one half of that of the party he has called. When the other party answers, his image appears on the remaining halves of the two screens. Videophones are very popular in Japan and several other advanced countries.

4. Staff Location System

In large organisations, occasions arise when it is desired to find an important person quickly. Managers in a factory, departmental chiefs in a store, or doctors in a hospital may all be wanted urgently at a moment's notice.[12] Many systems of staff location are available, some of which are detailed below :

12. J.C. Deryer, *op. cit.*, p. 442.

1. Public Address System : It is the simplest and, in some circumstances, the most effective method of staff location. Under this system, a loudspeaker is used by which an appeal can be broadcast from a master station to all the departments or sections, requesting the attention of the person sought. Such systems are often used by the railways, departmental stores, hospital, airlines offices, etc. The main drawback of this system is that it is noisy and disturbs every worker.

2. Bells and Buzzers : In Indian offices, bells and buzzers are used very commonly. They may be used to call a messenger or a subordinate, who may then be given the message or assignment. The actual communication takes place later. This means some delay in the actual conveyance of message. Moreover, this system, too, is noisy.

3. Lighted Signals : Lighted signals are installed to attract the attention of a particular individual at a given movement. Under this system, each person on the call list has a code number (figure). Whenever a particular individual is required, his code number is lighted on the signal and a buzzer is operated. This system is also noisy and disturbs the workers in an office.

4. Wireless Call System : A lighted signal system requires :

(a) Coded signals;

(b) A vast number of signal stations to locate a particular person wherever he may be; and

(c) It is very noisy. The wireless call system has been introduced to overcome these disadvantages. This system consists of a central transmitting stations and the allocation of a portable receiver to each member of the staff to be called. Each receiver picks up only its own frequency. Thus, when a particular member of the staff is wanted, wireless signal is transmitted, which is received only by that member of the staff.[13]

However, the wireless call system is not common in our country and only the police and the army make use of this system.

5. Speaking Tubes : These consist of metallic, plastic or rubber tubes which connect different rooms in the office, and through which executives can talk to one another or their staff. It is very inexpensive to instal and operate this system : there are no running costs.

But this system suffers from some disadvantages. There are :

(i) Speaking tubes have a very limited range; beyond a distance, the voice disintegrates and becomes inaudible.

(ii) They are unhygienic and can spread communicable diseases. Moreover, a better and more effective method is provided by telephones.

Characteristics of a Good System of Internal Communication

Internal communication should be such which maximises efficiency at minimum cost and optimum speed. In order to achieve these objectives, the communication system must have certain characteristics which are briefly discussed below :

1. Simplicity : The system should be simple to operate and need not require elaborate set up or training of the users.

2. Economical : The communication system should also be cheap to install and run. However, this factor should be considered with reference to the organisational goals and policies.

13. *Ibid.*

3. Clarity : Clarity is a fundamental necessity in case of inter-communication. The system should allow clear communication. If the messages are not clear when they are delivered, forwarded or sent back the system will fail in its objective.

4. Attention : The communication system should attract the full attention of the receiver immediately on its receipt. If attention is not drawn, communication will be useless.

5. Use of Proper Channels : As far as possible, communication should pass through the well defined channels provided in the organisation. However, in some cases, the use of the informal organisation within the enterprise may be of help in effective communication.

EXTERNAL COMMUNICATION

External communication implies the transmission of information to people outside the organisation and its receipt from outsiders. Every modern organisation has to maintain a liaison with its suppliers, investors, dealers, customers, debtors, and creditors. Government agencies and other business houses. In fact, external communication may be regarded as the backbone of modern business. There are several methods of external communication—personal visits (face-to-face conversation) communication on the telephone, through the post, etc. These are discussed below :

1. Personal Visit

Personal visits for face-to-face conversation may be arranged only for special purposes. They take place when office executives visit their bankers, financial institutions, prospective buyers or sellers (to effect sales or purchases), Government offices or tax authorities, etc. The most important advantage of a personal visit is that it facilitates the making of decisions and the avoidance of misunderstanding; it helps to resolve disputes or conflicts, and so on. A job which may not be accomplished for months if written communication alone is relied upon is accomplished by a single personal visit. However, such visits involve considerable time and money.

2. Telephone

External communication is effected on the telephones as well. Although the telephone service is more costly than the telex or postal service, it provides the facility to face-to face conversation and has advantages which are comparable to those of personal visits. The following telephone services may be utilised for external communication.

(a) Local Calls : Local calls can be made within the local limits of the telephone exchange or a group of exchanges. Such calls are made to make immediate contact with branches, customers, etc.

(b) Trunk Calls : Two types of trunk telephone services are available, *viz.*, the S.T.D. (Subscribers Trunk Dialing) and I.S.D. (International Subscribers' Dialing) Services. Under the S.T.D., a telephone subscriber may dial any number directly (without reference to a local exchange) in another town or city connected under the S.T.D. services. It covers the whole of India. The I.S.D. service, similarly, provides connection to any other country's telephone number.

Control Over the Use of Telephone : It may be noted that the telephone is a more costly means of communication than the various other means of communication, such as correspondence through the post, the teleservice, etc. Its cost increases steeply for outstation and foreign calls. It is, therefore, necessary to exercise some control over the use of telephone. A telephone register should be maintained at each point and every call should be entered in this register. If outstation calls are not frequently made, it is advisable that the STD system may be disconnected to prevent its misuse by the office staff.

Phone Plus Facilities

With the introduction of modern state-of-the-art digital electronic exchanges, several special facilities can be provided to the subscribers from respective exchanges. These are known as 'Phone Plus Facilities' which are described below :

(a) **Call Waiting :** This service makes a subscriber approachable. Even if he is engaged on a telephone call, he comes to know that some one else is trying to call him. He may answer this call while putting the first caller on 'hold'. In fact, he can speak to both the callers alternatively.

(b) **Call Transfer :** This facility makes a subscriber never to miss a call. The incoming calls will be transferred to another phone number chosen by him. Thus, wherever he goes, call will follow him.

(c) **Abbreviated Dialling :** Also called as one touch dialling. This allows subscriber a short-cut approach to get his most sought after numbers by only dialling a short, pre-allotted code. If he dials, say a one digit short code, the memory dialler dials the complete number for him.

(d) **Hot Line :** This facility connects the subscriber to one, the most wanted telephone number straight away by just lifting the receiver and waiting for 5 seconds, whether in a local exchange or within the STD network.

(e) **Automatic Alarm/Wake-up Call/Reminder Service :** This facility enables the subscriber to wake up at any particular time desired by him. It also reminds him of an important appointment. Telephone will automatically ring at the pre-determined time.

3. Postal Services

External communication may be oral (by personal visits or the use of the telephone) or written. Written communication can be sent through the messenger service within the local area or through the postal service in local and other areas. A majority of written messages are sent through the post. A number of postal services are available, and the Office Manager should be fully aware of their comparative merits and costs. The rate of postage varies with the kind of service required. The following services may be utilised by business offices :

(a) **Certificate of Posting :** When an ordinary letter is posted, no receipt is generally issued by the post office. But under a certificate of posting, the post office, on payment of a prescribed fee certifies that a letter has been posted. This certificate is evidence of the posting of the letter in the event of a dispute, etc.

(b) **Registered Post :** Postal articles may also be sent by registered post. The post office issues a receipt in proof of registration and takes special care to send the article to the addressee. This article may be made. "Registered Acknowledgement Due", in which case the sender receives a signed acknowledgement of the receipt of the article from the receiver.

(c) **Recorded Delivery :** This is variation of the registered post system. Under this system, a record of the delivery of the article is kept by the post office, to obtain the signature of the receiver.

(d) Reply-Paid Service : The business reply-paid service provides a means by which postage on a reply can conveniently be paid by the addressee. Specially printed envelopes can be provided for instance, to a customer for this own use in sending in orders. Postage stamps are not used, but an account of the number of letters delivered is kept by the post office, and the addressee is charged accordingly.

(e) Postage Prepaid Service : When a large number of letters, etc., are to be posted by an office, it may do so without pasting postage stamps on them. Under this system, the total amount of the postage is paid to the post office in cash, and the post office marks the stamp "Postage Prepaid" on each article so posted.

(f) Value Payable Parcel (VPP) : Under the VPP scheme, the post office recovers the value of the postal article and remits it to the sender. This system enables business firms to send articles and realise their value from the receiver (or customer) through the post office.

(g) Insured Cover : Valuable articles—documents, bills, cheques, title deeds etc.—may be sent through post office under an insured cover. Such articles, however have to be registered. Under this scheme, the post office acts as insurer and is liable for any loss or damage to the article in the course of transit, up to the value for which it was insured.

(h) Telegraphic Services : One way of quickly handling messages over relatively long distances is by means of the telegraph. This service is fast reliable and extensively used. Telegrams capture attention and impel immediate action. They are used for practically in all kinds of business activities—for acknowledging orders, advising salesmen, ordering materials, calling for interviews, arranging meetings, sending money orders, etc. The ordinary method of sending a telegram is to fill in a form, stamp it and hand it over to the post office counter together with the requisite fee. Since telegrams are charged on the basis of the number of words used in them, a telegraphic message should be as brief as possible, and words like Shri, Mr., Kindly, Please, Thank you, etc., should be avoided. If the addressee has a telegraphic address, it should be used to effect a saving. Block letters should be used to avoid errors in the transmission of messages.

The following types of telegraphic services are available in this country :

Sending Telegrams has now become an outdated system of external communication. It has almost completely been replaced by modern and quicker methods such as S.M.S. and e-mail services.

COURIER SERVICES

With modern business requiring faster communications and failure of postal services to cope with the business requirements, we have witnessed phenomenal growth of courier services. The frequently levelled criticism at the post offices in terms of lack of speed and general inefficiency in delivering mail has offered huge growth opportunities to private courier service organisations. Though postal and courier charges differ substantially, yet the business affords it due to the speed and security in delivering the mail. Courier companies provide services ranging thus :

(i) Messenger Services : To deliver documents and small packages at local and regional levels.

(ii) Inter-State Services : Most courier services guarantee delivery within the country the next day (within 24 hours).

(iii) Overseas Desk-to-Desk Courier Services : These offer desk-to-desk document deliveries using air-courier services. Several international couriers with their own fleet of air crafts are operating in this field such as DHL Courier, Transworld Couriers, Express Air, United Parcel Services (UPS) etc.

Governing Factors : There are three factors which govern the choice of any particular method of external communication. These are :

(i) The *speed* with which the message is sought to be sent;

(ii) The desired *accuracy* of the message to be sent; and

(iii) The objective of maximum *economy*.

In some cases, special needs—for example, the need for secrecy or safety—may be the sole determining factors. In general, when speed is of primary importance, a telephone or telex message would be justified. When accuracy is important or a written record of the transmitted message is desired to be retained the communication should be sent telegraphically or by post. But when neither speed nor accuracy is important, a maximum economy in communication should be aimed at.

MODERN COMMUNICATION DEVICES

In the following pages, the latest and most modern communication devices of use in the offices are discussed. These devices have changed the face of modern office to a great extent. Technological advancements and changes are taking place at a very fast pace and any new innovation becomes old within a matter of few months. Some of these communication devices, however, are going to stay for long in modern offices.

PAGER

Paging started a bit late in India. In most countries, cellular services started long after paging. In India, paging and cellular services started almost at the same time. Cellular, more than a business tool, emerged as a status symbol but has gained much wider acceptibility over pager. Paging is a one-way wireless communication facility by which one can stay in touch with anyone—clients, office, family or friends, when one is on the move. If someone needs to contact a subscriber urgently, all he has to do is pick up the phone and dial the pager number of the subscriber to leave a message. The message is instantly transmitted to the subscriber on his pager wherever he is. Giving the subscriber instant access to the information he needs.

Fig.1.10. Pager

There are a variety of pagers to suit individual requirements. Numeric Pagers transmit messages in the form of numbers only. The number on the pager may be called back to receive the entire message. Alpha-numeric Pagers transmit the entire message in the form of alphabet and numbers.

Numeric Pager plus Voice Mail Service : It is an ideal combination of paging service and voice mail. With this service a subscriber can get unlimited messages in the voice of the caller at a nominal cost. The messages are sorted in voice mail box and can be retrieved as per convenience. The combination of 'Numeric Pager + Voice mail Service' is as efficient as an alphanumeric pager.

The use of Pagers have found a place in history in India. It has been completely replaced by cellular phone services.

E-MAIL

Electronic Mail (E-Mail) is more than just inter-personal messaging. Companies around the world are taking advantage of E-mail applications to enhance the way they do business. Now messages can be transmitted at a fraction of normal costs. One need not invest in expensive hardware/dedicated links—all one requires is a PC, a modem and a telephone line to make E-mail operational in the office.

The E-mail network is based on Tandem fault-tolerant hardware state-of-the-art packet switches, high speed leased links adequate dial-up access lines and back up I-NET links. This not only ensures high speed delivery but the linkelihood of transmission error remains near zero.

Uses of E-Mail

1. With application development tools like customised forms and scripts, one can electronically file reports and distribute information throughout the company and to vendors, suppliers and customers.
2. Using E-mail distribution lists, *marketing* department can send information such as sales leads, price charges, product announcements and competitive information simultaneously to sales people anywhere.
3. Remote *Accounting* departments can save time and reduce costs by using E-mail file transfer facility to send spreadsheets, graphics and other financial data to headquarters.
4. *Sales* branches widely scattered can expedite order processing and increase accuracy by using E-mail's customised electronic forms.
5. *Personnel* department by using E-Mail's electronic bulletin boards capability, can make time critical corporate announcements and post job openings.

This E-Mail equips an office with three flexible, cost effective services at the desktop-E-mail, Fax and Telex (All in one)—24 hours a day.

FAX-PRINTER-COPIER

Hewlett Packard, recently launched HP Officejet 300 Fax-Printer-Copier. Priced at around Rs. 45,000 it is a complete office solution. In addition to high quality printing, it transmits plain paper faxes, in just about 10 seconds. It can be programmed to speed dial upto 65 locations and can also broadcast a fax document upto 10 locations and receive fax transmissions. It has a 24-page fax memory, and will receive incoming faxes while printing or copying a document, and even when it runs out of ink or paper.

PHONE, FAX, TAM & COPIER WITH ALARM (FIVE-IN-ONE)

More than just a fax, Panasonic's PANAFAX UF-SI combines telephone answering machine (TAM) and copying functions in a single, compact unit. So one does not need an extra telephone line or a separate answering machine, and also is able to make convenient copies of bills etc., at the touch of a button. It also incorporates a timer alarm which emits electronic sound at preset time, warning of approaching deadlines or appointments.

Fig.1.12 Fax-Phone-Printer-capiers
Courtesy : Google Image Search

CELLULAR PHONES

The cellular phones (or Mobile Phone) is one of the most convenient developments of the late twentieth century. One can now make a phone call and be called almost wherever one likes, whenever one like. It is probably the most important telecommunication breakthrough in recent times. Today, one need never be out of touch with one's business, family or friends.

Cellular phone is free from the cord which normally connects a phone to the wall, so one can move about as one pleases. Cellular phones give all the benefits of an ordinary fixed phone, but with extra flexibility, mobility, security and whole range of new services. With Cellular phone, one can call anywhere and can be reached from any telephone in the world.

Cellular phones are not communication radios or walkies-talkies; instead they make use of both wireless and cable technology and combine radio transmission with the ordinary fixed telephone network. The cellular telephone network is divided into cells, each one controlled by a radio base station. This base station transmits and receive radio signals to a centrally located Mobile Switching Centre. This is designed on the most advanced and most popular digital system—The global system for Mobile Communication—GSM. Already GSM systems are operating worldwide.

SIM Card : When a person becomes a subscriber, GSM will give the subscriber an 'Subscriber Identity Module' (SIM) Card. It contains a microchip which also stores subscribers' phone numbers. Each SIM card has a unique security code called the PIN (Personal Identity Number), which is known only to the subscriber. So when a subscriber inserts his SIM Card into any GSM compatible mobile phone and enter his PIN, he has got his very own personal phone.

Services From Cellular Phones

Cellular phones provide the following services[14]

A. Standard Personal Services

1. Caller Identification : Cell phone flashes the caller's number on the display screen. This service comes absolutely free.

2. Call Divert : Subscriber can choose to divert his incoming calls to any number, whenever he does not wish to be disturbed.

3. Call Hold/Call Wait : This feature helps the subscriber to handle two calls simultaneously putting one caller on hold while he speaks with the other.

4. No Eavesdropping : If the subscriber wants to keep his call confidential then the digital signalling of the GSM system gives him protection against eavesdroppers.

B. Added Value Personal Services

1. Fax & Data Facility : This facility can be accessed on the mobile phone with a PC monitor and laptop.

2. STD/ISD : The subscriber can call any STD/ISD number at his convenience.

3. Short Message Service: It helps the subscriber to receive and send confidential messages in text of upto 160 characters. SMS service is now available in nine regional languages also, on certain service providers' network notably 'Idea' by and 'TATA INDICOM'-a Tata company.

---

14. By Essar Cellphone.

Fig.1.19. Different models of Mobile phones
Source : Nokia Advertising Materials

4. Voice Mail Service: If the subscriber choose to divert his incoming calls, to his voice mail box, his callers can record a message. He can retrieve them at his convenience.

5. Roaming: With the help of a Roaming SIM Card, cellular phone can now extend its reach to other towns/cities.

6. Stored Value SIM Card Service: Under this concept, a predetermined value is stored in the SIM card to cover future call charges.

7. E-mail: The mobile phone can be used to e-mail (office and any other account), chat etc.

8. Digital Photography, voice clips and text: Receiving and sending them down to others is now possible on cellphones, through Blue Tooth and GPRS technologies.

9. Multimedia services which are available on computers can now be availed on mobile phones.

Selecting a Cellular (Mobile) Phone: Nowadays, mobile phones do a lot more than just telephoning. Therefore, it is important to consider what functions one wants, while choosing a mobile phone. Also, apart from size and weight, ease of use, battery life, sound quality and visual appeal also count. Because portability is a key word here, the unit's battery life in terms of standby and talk times are important, as is the recharge time. If access to the internet is required, one should look for a WAP enabled mobile phone (*e.g.,* NOKIA E-series, 9300 etc.).

Modern mobile phones offers a wide range of features to choose from, with innovative, fun and highly personalised features to suit every palate. These include mobile chat, downloadable personal profiles like screen savers, picture messaging, a variety of ringing tones and voice dialing, infrared red ports, a symphony of add-on coloured covers, automatic volume control, stop watch, sound level meter, task journal and timed profiles and much, much more, modern cutting edge technologies offers endless features making it difficult to choose from.

Office in your pocket : Nokia has launched its latest and entirely new type of integrated communication system, NOKIA 9300 communicator. It is a fully featured GSM phone with enhanced communications and time management capabilities, combining digital voice and data services and personal organiser functions in a single compact, and easy-to-use unit. In addition to cellular phone, it enables users to send and receive faxes, E-mail, and short messages as well as access internet services and private and public databases. It is thus a mobile office which can fit in anyone's pocket. It is priced at Rs. 35,000.

Similar other latest innovations in Mobile Phone like i-phone, Google G1, vertu, Black Berry etc. have been discussed in the following pages.

INTERNET

The media which has changed the way people do business.

Internet : Internet is a network of computers worldwide which allow its users to share information. Apart from the e-mail service of the internet, with which most people are familiar, the World Wide Web (WWW) is the most-popular vehicle of business now available on the internet. It is a medium in which one can represent his business, products and services to the huge and quickly increasing base of internet users all over the world. The WWW may be loosely understood as the electronic YELLOW PAGES.

Millions of companies have turned to the internet as powerful yet inexpensive way to promote their companies, products and services. When an organisation links to the Internet, people can reach it anytime of day or night. Potential customers can get your products information with colour photographs, leave queries or place orders. Current customers can use the internet for product support to provide valuable feed back about new products.

Internet Electronic Mail gives a subscriber fast, easy yet inexpensive way to communicate with people, in over 150 countries around the globe, 24 hours a day, 365 days a year. The subscriber keeps in touch with customers, suppliers and corporate partners.

Internet Document Exchange lets a subscriber work with groups of people as a single unit.

WWW Services : Internet provides the following services :

1. Classified Services :

(a) Individual Listing : Suitable for small business and individuals, catering to foreign and NRI clients in India.

(b) Business Listing : Increased presence for business catering to foreign clients in India.

2. Corporate Services

(a) Individual Account : Suitable for small advertising needs of individual etc., (1-2 pages)

(b) Business Account : Suitable for medium advertising needs (3-10 pages) to showcase the products and services offered to overseas customers.

(c) Corporate Account : Suitable for companies desirous of establishing a corporate presence on the web. (10-15 pages).

Advantages of Internet : The estimated number of people surfing the INTERNET at any time is at 250-300 million and is expected to grow at the rate of 25-30% every year. Over Two million companies are also using web services.

Every Multinational Company and every company wroth the name is now on INTERNET and maximum of their purchase decisions are based on INTERNET Search. Apart from Global Communication, Internet provides the following advantages :

1. Increased Sales
2. New Customers
3. Global Presence
4. Business Round the Clock
5. Instant Customer Response
6. Low Advertising Cost
7. Instant Modification of Information.

INMARSAT (PORTABLE SATELLITE TELEPHONE)

INMARSAT is also termed as Portable Worldphone office. Priced at Rs. 3 lacs, this worldphone office provides access to the international dial up telephone + fax + Data Networks. The Inmarsat is available in a briefcase which contains antenna and RF in the lid and the phone unit in the base. The equipment is designed for quick and reliable operation under all conditions. Worldphone office is an ideal communication tool for business travellers and field workers. It incorporates the following features :

(i) User friendly backlit LCD display
(ii) Handsfree operation
(iii) Multilingual display support
(iv) Built in phone book
(v) SIM card for personal mobility management
(vi) Short message service (SMS)
(vii) Voice/Fax/mail
(viii) Call forwarding etc.

Fig.1.13. INMARSAT (Worldphone Office) by NERA

Inmarsat is designed for communication requirements of

(i) International business travellers.
(ii) Radio and TV Reporters.
(iii) Newspaper Reporters.
(iv) Relief and rescue organisations operating internationally.
(v) Expeditions.
(vi) Touring Vehicles.
(vii) Service vehicles, trucks operated by international carriers.
(viii) International couriers etc.

ELECTRONIC MEDIA IN COMMUNICATION

Managers have studied and are gradually adopting various electronic devices, that improve communication. Electronic equipment includes mainframe computers, minicomputers, personal computers, electronic mail systems, and electronic typewriters, as well as cellular telephones for making telephone calls from cars and beepers for keeping in contact with the office. The impact of computers on all phases of the management process will be discussed in connection with management information systems and will be mentioned only briefly here.[15] Let us first look at telecommunication in general and at the increasing use of teleconferencing in particular.

TELECOMMUNICATION

Although Telecommunication has come of age, a large number of companies are effectively utilising the new technology in a variety of ways. New ways are being innovated and put to use every day as shown by a few examples given below :

- Banks and companies are allowing its customers to transfer funds.
- Several Banks new allow Phone-Banking and Net-Banking facilities to the customers.
- Fascimile mail service allows delivery of documents across the globe within a very short span of time.
- Computerised Reservation System facilitates the bookings of :

15. Koontz etc. : *Principles of Managment.*

(a) Airline Tickets
(b) Railway Tickets
(c) Rooms Reservations at Hotels
(d) Movie Tickets
(e) Classified Advertisements
(f) Travel Arrangements etc.

- Path Labs etc. allow customers to see their medical reports online without visiting the lahoratories.
- Many companies now have detailed information regarding personnel — including performance appraisals and career development plans — in a data bank.

As one can see, there are huge possibilities to the applications of Telecommunication. But to make telecommunication systems effective, the technical experts must identify the needs of the managers and customers and to design systems that are useful.

Another use of electronic media is Teleconferencing.

ELECTRONIC CONFERENCING SYSTEMS

Traditional face-to-face conferencing systems had certain advantages like (i) Meeting people face to face, (ii) establishing support, (iii) observing body language, (iv) instant problem solving, and so on. However, this has become a luxuary, very few organisations continue to afford due to the drawback that business these days have branches located in diverse and geographical separate areas (in different cities or foreign countries) and a great deal of time and money is spent in travelling by participants who congregate to attend the traditional conferences. Large number of executives spend several days in attending a conference or convention.

Modern telecommunications have made possible an alternative to traditional conference. Participants need not meet face-to-face. A meeting can be held electronically by :

(i) Computer conferencing;
(ii) Teleconferencing; or
(iii) Video Conferencing.

Computer Conferencing

In a computer conference, the participants enter and access the computer information at their convenience or at a predetermined time. With computer conferencing, instant response is possible. In critical times, this may be very invaluable and entails huge savings of time and money. Computer conferencing provides the following distinct advantages.[16]

(i) Saves participants from physical presence at a designated meeting place, thus saving huge time and money in the process.
(ii) The system is confidential.
(iii) The information may be accessed instantaneously or saved and retrieved for future reference.
(iv) The information may be used by executives at their convenience.

16. Adapted from *Communication System and Procedures for the Modern office* By Nathan Krevolin : Prentice Hall : New Jersey

(v) Computer conferencing is easy to use and does not require

(a) elaborate set-up;

(b) huge expenditure;

(c) intensive training etc.

Teleconferencing

Teleconferencing[17] may be defined as, "bringing people together on telephone without having to spend money on travel." Teleconferencing has changed the way, companies do business. Teleconferencing makes use of speakerphone which permits controlled amplification of speaker's voice, which is connected with the participants (conferees) to connect with each other and communicate. This permits communications among individuals who may be in different geographically scattered locations and eliminates the need for face-to-face conferencing. The only drawback of Teleconferencing is lack of visual impact. The following reasons may be attributed to the ever growing use of teleconferencing:

(i) Easy to use (anyone can use a telephone)

(ii) Easy availability/access

(iii) Very inexpensive (costs negligible)

(iv) Easy to participate (From anywhere in the world)

(v) Big Time Saver (Takes less than a minute to set up a conference call)

(vi) Frequent conferencing possible.

Videoconferencing

Video-conferencing removes the drawback of lack of visual impact in Teleconferencing. It may be possible in two ways :

(a) By using Telephone + Electronic Blackboard

(b) By using Telephone + Television

(a) Electronic Blackboard. It is a rapid mathod of electronic visual communication and works as follows :

One participant writes or draws images on the Electronic Blackboard with a pen-similar to writing on a regular chalk board. The written matter or image is instantly transmitted to a video screen at another location. The Electronic Blackboard can be erased or wiped out and/or rewritten for transmission of additional information.

Drawback. Videoconferencing with the use of Electronic Blackboard requires the participants to visit the location where such equipment is available or require making an investment in the equipment by the company.

(b) Videoconferencing. It combines telephone/television communication system. It can transmit pictures, graphics, diagrams, illustrations, written text etc., instantly that can be viewed on a video/T.V. screen. A fax machine can be installed to obtain hard copies of the transmitted communication. It works as follows :

17. See also *Business Communication* By M.K. Sehgel and Vandana Khetarpal : Excel Books : First Ed. 2006.

The conference usually takes place in a room furnished by the company where cameras are also set up. The cameras are voice activated and focused on the participant whenever he or she speaks. The room also has video screens/T.V. screens for viewing the other participant's communication.

Videoconferencing networks can easily link distant locations by settelites.

A more popular and contamporary mode of videoconferencing is the use of *Computer* (P.C. or Laptop) with *Internet connection* and a *Webcam*, which provides the following advantages :

(i) Ease of use
(ii) Instant connectivity
(iii) No need of investment in equipment (Even Cybercafes can be used for videoconferencing).
(iv) Easy to operate and participate.
(v) Frequent conferencing possible.
(vi) Easy storage and retrieval of communication.

Nowadays even *Mobile phones* with *internet* and *speakerphone* facilities are being increasingly used for videoconferencing. This offers an additional advantage of communicating/conferencing while on the move.

LATEST INNOVATIONS IN OFFICE COMMUNICATIONS

1. Vennfer V. 1.0

A software based video conferencing system

Vennfer[18] is an advanced software based video conferencing solution based on a highly sophisticated software engine developed by a core team of international software experts of INTELLISYS[18].

It is a complete IP based video conferencing software solution that enables real-time audio, video, and data communication over LAN, WAN (leased lines, VSATs, VPNs) and broadband by using TCPIP multicasting technology thus conserving real time bandwidth in case of synchronous audio and video delivery at multipoint locations thus, providing a highly interactive communication medium.

Vennfer for Corporates

In a fast changing competitive world, where communication is being linked to the survival of corporates and the success of a 'Business Enterprise' is becoming directly proportional to how the work of communicating with thousands of employees, customers and partners at various levels is activated and achieved, with an ever shrinking budget.

With Vennfer you can reach employees, customers and partners in new ways, improve information exchange, encourage idea sharing, and facilitate collaboration *while reducing costs and increasing productivity and that means rapid return on the investments.*

With Vennfer you can empower your employees to be more productive, effective and efficient in every department of your real-time organisation and eliminate the cost associated with travelling.

18. © Intellisys Technologies Pvt. Ltd. (The material has been drawn from Google image search).

Vennfer is extremely suitable for corporates with multiple divisions and geographic locations with distributed workforce, partners, suppliers and customers to establish virtual conference rooms for your entire enterprise to conduct :

- top management meetings
- face-to-face meetings
- sales presentations
- brainstorming sessions
- HR-Corporate trainings

Fig.1.14. Multiple uses of Vennfer
(*Source* : Google Image Search)

- employment interviews
- corporate e-learning
- IT trainings and escalations
- Inter -departmental meetings
- staff meetings
- customer, partner and supplier meetings
- security and real-time surveillance

Not only does Vennfer ***drastically reduce the cost of live collaboration over standard hardware based videoconferencing systems*** but also brings down the operating cost to a fraction of the same with a lot more enhanced functionality.

Vennfer can be used for videoconferencing by any kind of organization including;

- Manufacturing organizations
- Financial organizations - Banks, Insurance, NBFCs, Mutual Funds
- Stock Exchanges/Brokers
- Healthcare - Hospitals
- Hospitality - Hotels
- IT - ITES / BPO / KPO / Software development houses
- MNCs
- Public Sector Organisations
- Government

Vennfer Product Features

Vennfer is specifically built for live, multi-media many to many collaboration. All participants, even those with disabilities, get the same superior quality, performance and dependability - with no lag time or garbled communication.

From two way live video, audio, PPT, browser, shared whiteboards to instant messaging and application sharing, all components are tightly integrated to provide the ultimate interactive environment for video conferencing and training. Whether you have few participants - or few hundred, Vennfer enables worldclass conferencing, communication and interaction platform. The various features of vennfer Video Conferencing solution are ;

(i) Multiple Video Delivery Screen : Vennfer is capable of deploying multiple reverse many to many videos at different client (starting from 6 locations it can go upto 37 locations) locations by using a very sophisticated software based multicasting technology at a conservative bandwidth across the LAN, WAN.

(ii) Programme Sharing : Any person in a meeting can share a programme (Power Point Presentation, Excel Sheet, whiteboards, application sharing) with the other participants. When you use the programme sharing feature, other participants can see the programme. When you allow control, other people can both see and use the programme. The total number of people who can successfully participate in your meeting depends on available network bandwidth and the speed of the participants' computer.

(iii) Audio Delivery : Vennfer is capable of deploying multiple audio based communication at different client locations by using a very sophisticated multicasting technology at a conservative bandwidth across the WAN.

(iv) Start Screen Control : Using Start Screen Control, "Vennfer" can call an unattended computer (host), and then access that computer's shared desktop. Once it is connected, it can work in the host's shared desktop and in any programme that the host computer has 'access to administrators' can give other users viewing capability of his computers' desktop via 'Start Screen Control' without giving them administrator privilege. The start screen is multicasted to all the users in the multicast group, thus consuming a single mode bandwidth.

(v) Switch User Mode : Switch User Mode enables the administrative control of "Vennfer" to be shifted to a user who had requested *for* the control, dynamically over a live session. Once the control is delegated, the user becomes the administrator with all the administrative powers and the former administrator becomes a user. The entire process of switching the users does not consume additional bandwidth and would not affect any other user.

(vi) SMS Shooter : This feature enables the administrator to send SMS alerts to his group members thereby giving them an intimation towards the timing of the meeting or pass on any urgent information. This ensures instant information delivery to the target group irrespective of their location. Some of the special features of SMS Shooter which makes it stand apart from a traditional SMS service are :

1. Text File Upload Feature
2. Dynamic Delivery Report
3. MS Excel Sending facility
4. Log File Viewer
5. SMS Merge Facility

(vii) Audio / Video Archival & Playback : This feature enables the administrator / participants to record all sessions (video & audio files) in the local hard disk of the user with the capability of playback on demand by the user.

(viii) Slide Generator : This feature helps to multicast different PPT slides as well as animations or other image files among the administrator and the client.

(ix) Browser Support : It helps you to access the internet and browse through different corporate web sites and share those webpages among the administrator and the clients in multi cast mode[19]

2. Vertu Ti

Vertu Launches Ascent Ti in India

Amidst music, dance and a fabulous light show, Vertu launched another mobile in the Indian market.: the Vertu Ascent Ti. The Ascent Ti is a quad-band 3G handset with a 3 megapixel camera with flash - the first in the Vertu series to have one. Vertu's motto "precision engineered for

19. Adopted from Material on Vennfer from Google Image Search.

strength and balance with a distinctly masculine edge" seems a fitting description of this very high-end phone.

Says Frank Nuovo, Vertu Principal Designer; "From the start the Vertu Ascent has been heavily influenced by the power, energy, and sheer precision of a beautiful car. With the Ascent Ti, this vision has been developed further using the high grade materials, design detail, technical superiority and unsurpassed performance associated with the luxury sports car industry. The result is a highly crafted handset of precision, balance and strength."

The Vertu Ascent Ti is handcrafted in England and looks as if it's been designed to a 'boys-and-their-toys' motif. And while the exteriors may embody some of the most brilliant automobiles ever designed, the software provides users with the same feel.

The Vertu is crafted out of Titanium, which explains the Ti' suffix (chemical symbol for Titanium). For those who came in late, Titanium is a non-corrosive element with the highest strength-to-weight ratio of any metal and an ability to withstand extreme temperatures.

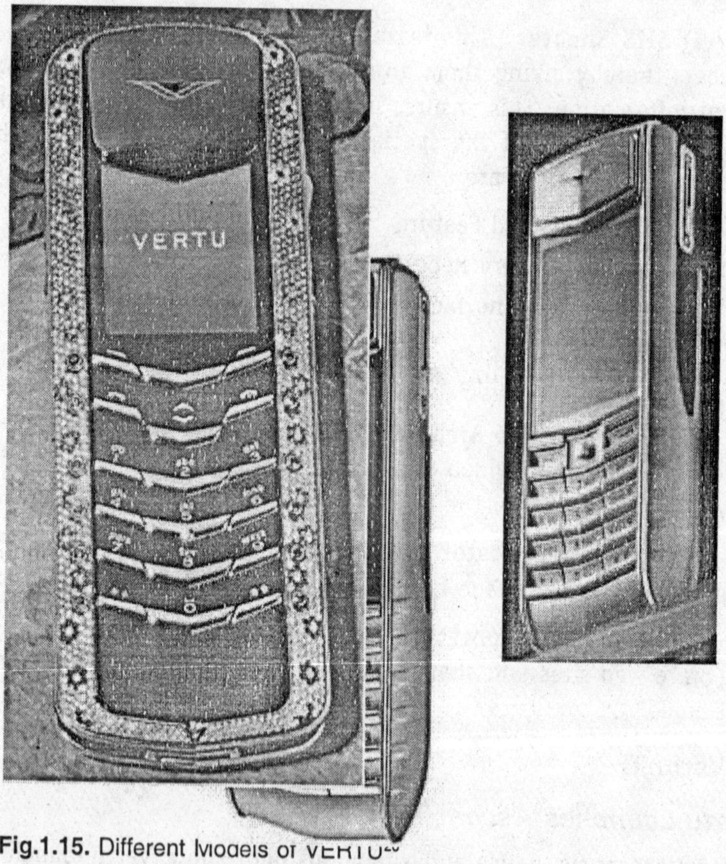

Fig.1.15. Different Models of VERTU[20]

The top rear of the instrument is covered in cowhide and it's available in three colors: black or red leather with a black ceramic pillow, or brown with a silver ceramic pillow. It also has a scratch-resistant sapphire crystal face made from the same material that's used for the camera lens.

20. Image drawn from Google Image Search

The Ascent Ti has 3 S40 interface - the latest version of course - and it's complemented with applications specific to these phones. For example, 'Vertu Fortress' technology allows the remote synchronization of contacts, calendar, notes etc. and backs up all stored data to a high security server maintained in an ex-military bunker at a secure location in the English countryside. Customers can access their private data via a personal account on vertu.com, If a customer loses an Ascent Ti phone, all data can be quickly reinstated to a new mobile phone.

The Vertu Ascent Ti is available in India at a not inconsiderable price of Rs 3,26,000 (MRP)[2] onwards.

3. Google G1 Mobile Phone

Google G1 Mobile phone Launched (Oct. 22, 2008)

T-Mobile showed off its new **G1** mobile phone at a press event in New York thus becoming the first carrier to offer a device run on Google's Android Open Source Mobile Platform.

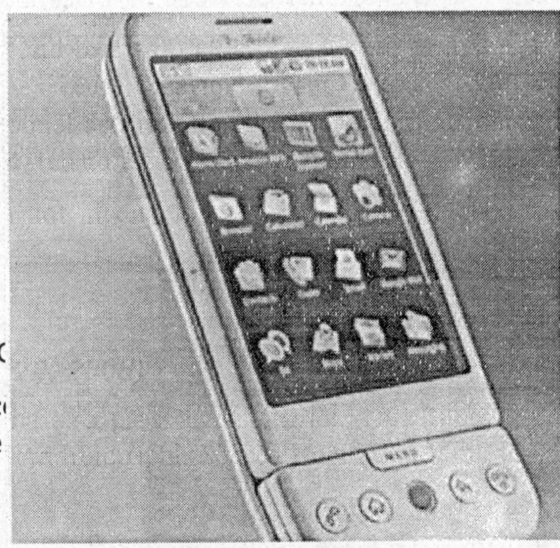

Fig.1.15. Google (

The device, which was developed by devic ... ires commonly seen on many of smartphones on the ... nd-drag capabilities, a pull-out QWERTY keyboard, ... ps, music and instant messaging.

But the big reason that the phone has generated buzz in recent weeks is because it will be the first ever to run on Android, a Linux-based open source mobile platform that Google first debuted last November.

One interesting item from the promotional video during the press conference appears to be a deeper integration of search into the mobile internet. It appears one can search from any page without launching a search application. There's also a dedicated search button on the physical

21. Text an Vertu provided by Shayne Rama (Nov. 24, 2007). Google Search

keyboard. The device is similar in size to the Phone, but heavier at 158 grams, and has a 3.2 inch touch-driven display with a resolution of 320 x 480 pixel.

Cole Brodman, the chief technology and innovation officer for T-Mobile USA. said that T-Mobile is hoping to give its customers a mobile Internet experience comparable to the Web experience they get on their home computers. The phone will run best on local Wi-Fi networks or on T-Mobile's GSM-based Universal Mobile Telecommunications System (UMTS) 3G network. T-Mobile officially launched its first US-based 3G network in the New York this past spring, and the carrier has live 3G coverage in 16 major markets, Brodman said. The company plans to have 3G coverage in 22 major markets by the end of this year.[22]

4. Black Berry

Black Berry is again a heavily featured Mobile Phone with **GPS, Wi-fi, XM Satellite Radio, On-line subscription Music** from e-music, **Push-to-talk** and **AT & T Mobile Music etc.**

Black Berry 8820 launches on AT&T

AT&T Inc. (NYSE) and Research in motion (RIM) have launched the first cellular and Wi-fi Black Berry IInd set — The Black Berry 8820.

The global Wi-Fi capabilities of the Black Berry 8820 from AT&T complement AT&T's industry-best domestic and intenational wide area wireless data coverage. AT&T enterprise customers can use the Black Berry 8820 with their corporate campus Wi-Fi networks for additional data coverage.

AT&T is the leading provider of Black Berry services worldwide and boasts the broadest domestic and international coverage area for wireless data services of any U.S. carrier. The Black Berry 8820 is powered by AT&T's nationwide (ii) EDGE network, the largest high speed national wireless data network in the U.S., with availability in more than 13,000 cities and towns and along some 40,000 miles of major highways. The quadband BlackBerry 8820 from AT&T keeps users who are abroad connected with **wireless e-mail, Internet access and other mobile applications through data services** in more countries - more than 135 - than any other U.S. carrier. Customers can also use the BlackBerry 8820 to make or receive wireless phone calls in more than 190 countries.[23]

"The new Black Berry 8820 builds on AT&T's leading domestic and international coverage footprint by giving customers the ability to link with their company's wireless campus network or access e-mail and browse the Web at Wi-Fi hot spots even in the few countries in which we do not have data roaming agreements." said Jeff Bradley, senior vice president-Marketing and Operations for AT&T's wireless unit. "That makes the Black Berry 8820 from AT&T an exceptional world phone for global use by business customers and individuals alike."

The Black Berry 8820 adds Wi-Fi capabilities to its industry-leading set of features, which includes extensive call management and premium phone features, built-in Global Positioning Satellite (GPS) - with support for such solutions as TeleNav GPS Navigator(TM) and TeleNav Track(TM) - AT&T's Push-to-Talk service, Bluetooth® 2.0. built-in media player and a microSD expandable memory slot for music, photo and video storage.

22. Text and Image posted by Remo labels: Aradraid, *Google Mobile*
23. Sources : http://www.wireless.att.com/blackberry 8820, & http://www.blackberry 8820.com.

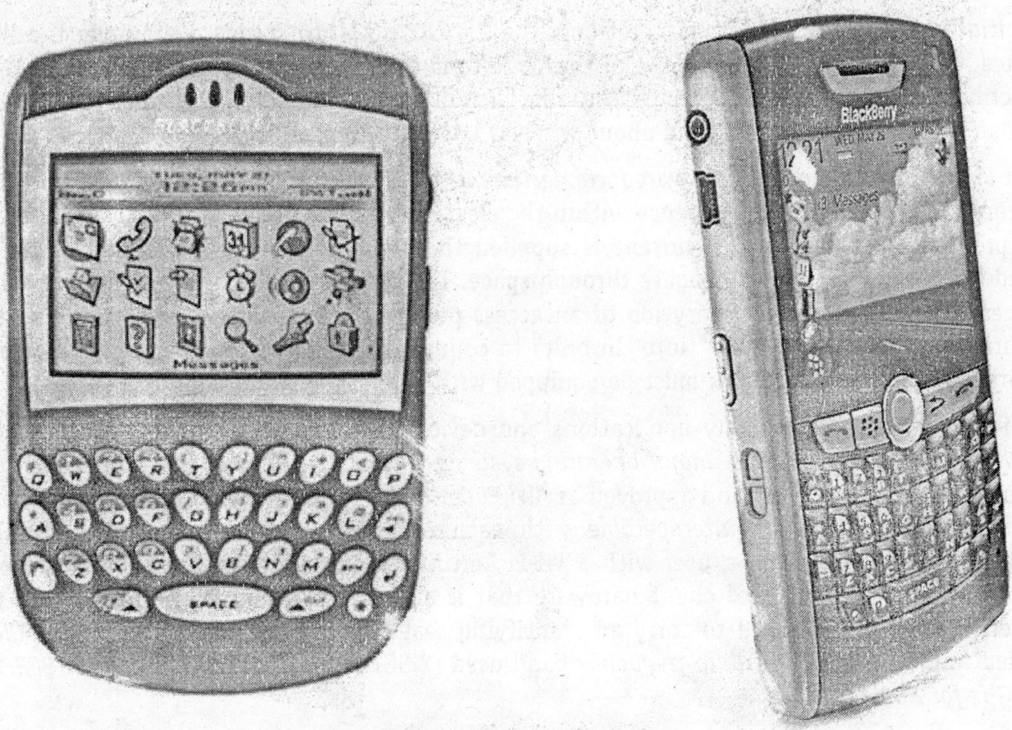

Fig.1.17 : Black Berry 8820
Source : Google Image Search

The Black Berry 8820 also supports AT&T Mobile Music, an integrated, on-the-go music experience that delivers "your music, your way" by providing simple access to a robust collection of music content, including access to online subscription music content from eMusic, XM Satellite Radio and more.

In addition, the Black Berry 8820 comes with a full QWERTY keyboard, an intuitive trackball navigation system and a large, bright landscape (320 × 240) display. Customers have a vivid and easy-to-use interface for the many popular capabilities of the Black Berry solution, including mobile access to **corporate and personal e-mail. text messages. Web-browing, organiser, multimedia and corporate data applications.**

5. Wi-Fi Technology

Wi-Fi is "The name of a popular wireless networking technology that uses radio waves to provide wireless high-speed Internet and network connections. The Wi-F-i Alliance, the organization that owns the Wi-Fi (registered trademark) term specifically defines Wi-Fi as any "wireless local area network (WLAN) products that are based on the Institute of Electrical and Electronics Engineers' **(IEEE)** 802.11 standards."[24]

24. *Sources* : 1. "How Wireless Networks Work" in the "Did you know...." section of Webopedia.
2. "Wireless LAN Standards Chart" in the Quick Reference Section of Webopedia.
3. Wi Fi Blu-ray com (Wireless Fidelity Debunked)

Initially, **Wi-Fi** was used in place of only the ***2.4GHz 802.11b*** standard, however the ***Wi-Fi*** **Alliance** has expanded the generic use of the Wi-Fi term to include any type of network or WLAN product based on any of the **802.11 standards,** including **802.11b. 802.11a,** dual-band, and so on, in an attempt to stop confusion about wireless LAN **inte-operability.**

Wi-Fi works with no physical wired connection between sender and receiver by using radio frequency (RE) technology, a frequency within the electromagnetic spectrum associated with radio wave propagation. When an RF current is supplied to an antenna, an electromagnetic field is created that then is able to propagate through space. The cornerstone of any wireless network is an access point **(AP)**. The primary job of an access point is to broadcast a wireless signal that computers can detect and "tune" into. In order to connect to an access point and join a wireless network, computers and devices must be equipped with wireless network adapters

Wi-Fi is supported by many applications and *devices* including *video game consoles,* home *networks. PDAs, mobile phones, major operating systems,* and other types of *consumer electronics.* Any products that are tested and approved as *"Wi-Fi Certified"* (a registered trademark) by the *Wi-Fi Alliance* are certified as *interoperable* with each other, even if they are from different manufacturers. For example, a user with a Wi-Fi Certified product can use any brand of *access point* with any other brand of client hardware that is also "Wi-Fi Certified". Products that pass this certification are required to carry an identifying seal on their packaging that states "Wi-Fi Certified" and indicates the *radio frequency* band used (2.5GHz for *802.11b, 802.11g,* or *802.11n.* and *5GHz for 802.11a).*

A common misconception is that the term Wi-Fi is short for *"wireless fidelity"* however this is not the case. Wi-Fi is simply a trademarked term meaning IEEE 802.11x.

6. Blu-ray Disc

Blu-ray Disc is yet another technological innovation in the field of Business communication. It is developed by **Blu-ray Disc Association** and its usage include :

1. Data Storage
2. High-Definition video
3. High-Definition Audio
4. Play-station 3 Gaming Technology.
5. Capacity : 25 GB (Single layer)
   50 GB (Double layer)

Media type High-density optical disc

Fig.1.25 Blu-ray Disc[25]

Blu-ray Disc (also known as *Blu-ray* or *BD*) is an *optical disc storag* media format. Its *main uses are high-definition video* and *data storage*. The disc has the same physical dimensions as a standard *DVD* or *CD*.

The name *Blu-ray Disc* is derived from the *blue laser* (violet colored) used to read and write this type of disc. Because of its shorter *wavelength* (405 nm). substantially more data can be stored on a Blu-ray Dise than on the *DVD* format, which uses a red (650 nm) laser A dual layer Blu-ray Disc can store 50 *GB*, almost six times the capacity of a double-dual layer DVD (or more than 10 times if single-layer).

Blu-ray Disc was developed by the *Blu-ray Disc Association*, a group representing consumer electronics, computer hardware, and motion picture production. As of September 20, 2008 more than 850 Blu-ray Disc titles have been released in the United States and more than 500 Blu-ray Disc titles have been released in Japan. There are over 1500 Blu-ray Disc titles released in the United States by the end of 2008.[25]

Origins

Philips and ***Sony*** started two projects applying the new diodes: ***UDO*** (Ultra Density Optical) and DVR Blue (together with ***Pioneer***), a format of rewritable discs which would eventually become Blu-ray Disc (more specifically, BD-RE). The core technologies of the formats are essentially similar.

7. CISCO Telepresence

Today's fast paced global business environment, requires continuous innovation and planning to respond rapidly to unexpected situations that affect business continuity. "Relationships and effective communications are critical to success, determining how competitive and responsive you can be, how quickly you can get to market. They can even play a role in your environmental responsibility".[26]

Cisco's invention in the area of business communication can help it. It delivers a unique 'in person" experience with remote participants — You can interact and collaborate with others like never before, moving faster and more effectively.

CISCO Telepresence interactions use industry-leading video, audio and environmentals to create real-time, live, in person communications.

According to Rebecca Jacoby, CIO, CISCO, **"Telepresence allows us to build relationships globally which accelerates productivity through innovation and a broader access to talent. This creates a competitive advantage that is even more enduring than the dramatic reduction in travel costs."**

It offers the following distinct advantages :

1. CISCO Telepresence connects people thousands of miles apart in dozens of locations, bringing them together with one simple connection.
2. It helps keep time-sensitive processes moving ahead presenting a cost effective and time-saving alternative to travel.

25. Sources : Google Image search (for photo and text)
26. Accelerating the Pace of Business : Cisco Telepresence.

3. Communication across language and cultural boundaries can be challenging and being 'in person' provides optimum benefits. Cisco Telepresence allows you to meet in person with customers, client, vendors and parties at the touch of a button, so that communication can be more effective and more available than ever before.
4. More than 60 per cent of communications is non-verbal and CISCO Telepresence delivers a subtleties of commnuication in tone, facial expressions and body language, leading to greater connection and understanding.
5. By reducing the need to travel by the employees, CISCO Telepresence[27] helps
   (i) boost productivity of employees;
   (ii) reduces carbon foot print;
   (iii) gives employees control over more of their valuable time; improving their quatity of life.
   (iv) with very high quarlity audio and high-definition video at low latency and a optimized meeting environment, CISCO telepresence help communicate and converse in real-time, catching every comment, gesture, expression and nuance of the conversation.
6. CISCO telepresence has been designed to take advantage of the tools used in offices every day, integrating with enterprise groupware and unified communications, so scheduling and starting meetings are extremely easy. There is no need for staff training, menus or manuals.
7. With dual-tone reliability and global connectivity CISCO telepresence provides for greater ROI than traditional video communications. You can be anywhere in the world at the touch of a button.

Fig. 13.19. CISCO Telepresence
Courtesy : CISCO Inc.

27. Inputs provided by CISCO INC. in a brouchure on "CISCO Telepresence".

8. Office 2020

The work place is getting a makeover. As New Age Corporates transform themselves, technology will be used to the hilt. The office[28] scenario 10 years hence will be like :

- Typewriters and cyclostyling machines will be History.
- Firms could recruit directly from social networking sites.
- Meetings could be conducted from the comfort of one's drawing room.
- Work stations could double up as personal assistants.
- Corporate offices could become redundant as many more employees choose to work out of their houses.
- Virtual 'Plug-and-Play' offices, where anyone can log in from anywhere and work will be in vogue.
- The four-day week is likely to become popular and leave more flexible.
- Business travel will become passe as Hot-desking and video-conferencing will become as normal as filing once was.
- Offices will have Intelligent furniture, like
  - — Chairs that will sense when a worker is stressed so that his workload may be reduced.
  - — Intelligent doors of tomorrow's office will have scanners to read identity cards and alert the PC to open the page last looked at by the worker.
  - — Microsoft has developed desks and whiteboards that allows ideas to be jotted down and exchanged during the meeting.
  - — An American Company has developed software that will take notes, like a personal assistant and provide a typed summary as well.
  - — Cubicles will be replaced with open community spaces.
  - — Wireless technology will allow employees to set up virtual offices anywhere they want.
  - — Lights with sensors that will dim depending on the number of people in the room.
  - — Carbon dioxide sensors that pump fresh air to keep energy levels high.
- Social networking sites will double up as recruitment centres.
- Companies will also create their own degree programmes at their own campuses to mould talent acording to their needs.
- Corporates will prefer freelancers and prefer contract employees to cut costs.
- Hierarchy and control of CEO will be diluted as there will be more transparency.
- In office 2020, employees will also be able to help write company policy that affects them and define best practices.
- In tomorrow's office, retirement at 60 will not be the rule, as majority of employers would want employees to work beyond that.
- The Gender divide will narrow as more women break the glass ceiling.
- Virtual office will make business travel a thing of the past.

C. K. Prahlad says

"Any company that can't imagine that future, won't be around to enjoy it."

---

28. Also see "office 2020 : A Sci-Fi odessey" By Sujata Dutta Sachdeva TNN, Posted on 28 Sep. 2008.

NEC ViVid Office 2020

The NEC Vivid office 2020 is the perfect solution for all working environments. It increases efficiency by providing printing, copying, faxing and scanning — all in full colour - while integrating seamlessly with the existing Communications systems.

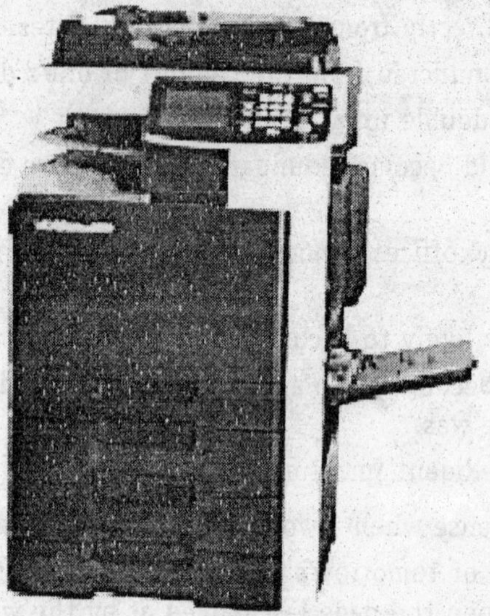

Fig. 13.20 NEC ViVid Office 2020

Source : Google Images Search.

Features of NEC ViVid Office 2020

(i) The NEC ViVid Office 2020 provides integrated communications features far beyond the usual printing, scanning and network e-mail. It brings integrated internet fax, facsimile, IP transmission, IP relay and auto archive/forwarding applications to the table as well.

The NEC ViVid Office 2020 is a must-see for those looking for the technology to make their businesses more effective and efficient by replacing monochrome devices or upgrading to new color devices.

(ii) *Make Color Copies Quickly :* The NEC ViVid Office 2020 can produce 20 colour-copies per minute and offers a fast first copy output that enables you to keep Lip with the pace of business.

(iii) THE NEC ViVid Office 2020 ATA GLANCE:

- 20-ppm Color/B &W Digital MFP
- Standard Printing: PCL & PS
- Standard Scanning:
- E-mail
- SMB, FTP, Scan to File, IP (available with Phase2)
- Available Duplex Print
- Available 70-Page ADFP

- Standard 250 Sheets
- Available By-pass Tray
- 3,350 Sheet Capacity
- Sort/Shift Finish option
- Fax Option w/Internet Fax/IP Fax
- Dual Line Fax Option

(iv) *Print from Anywhere on the Network*: Thanks to network integration, everyone in your office can connect to the NEC ViVid Office 2020 and print in color or black and white This extremely versatile printer comes standard with PCL5e/c PCL6 (XL) emulation networked printing and PostScript 3 emulation (Version 3015) for both PC and Mac operating systems.

It also offers duplex output up to 11" × 17" and extended features that include:

- Auto tray switching
- Account Track (50 accounts)
- Secure printing
- Separate scan
- User authentication (Synchronized w/Account Track)

(v) *Full-Featured Scanning*: The NEC ViVid Office 2020 offers standard network scanning in both color and black and while while utilising a wide variety of file formats, such as TIFF, PDF. or JPEG. Now you can import color documents, convert your paper document base to digital files and send all your information electronically.

(vi) *Centralise Faxing :* The NEC ViVid Office 2020 includes a high-speed fax option that enables you to combine all document faxing in one central location, thereby eliminating the need for multiple fax machines. And when you add a second dual port to the fax option with a multi-line option, you will double your fax communication capability. Other fax features include:

- 300 One Touch options
- Super G3 33.6 Kbps
- JBIG data compression
- PC fax
- Network fax
- Duplex TX
- Duplex RX
- F-code support
- Auto forward
- Stored Fax RX

(vii) *Secure Information :* The NFC ViVid Office 2020 includes user authentication, account tracking and other security enhancements to protect your information,

(viii) *Integrate ViVid Office 2020 with the Network :*[29] Fast, simple integration is a breeze with the NEC ViVid Office 2020. A total suite of solutions provide the device management, document control, network integration and administrative productivity tools you need. Standard network connectivity offers integration through your network to provide printing and scanning integration with full-color capabilities.

29. ***Source :*** "NEC ViVid Office 2020" NEC : Empowered by Innovation : Document Solutions : Google Images Search.

SUMMARY

Communication : Communication is an exchange of facts, ideas, opinions or emotions by two or more persons. Communication is a major function of an office. The selection of a communication system for the office should be based on :

(i) Speed; (ii) Distance; (iii) Accuracy; (iv) Secrecy; (v) Safety; (vi) Records; (vii) Impression; (viii) Cost; and (ix) Expansion.

The communication process is composed of :

(i) Perception; (ii) Encoding; (iii) Transmission; (iv) Receiving and Decoding; and (v) Responding.

Communication may be internal or external. It may be oral, written or mechanical.

Internal Communication : Internal communication may be inter-departmental or intra-departmental. It may also be :

(i) Oral; (ii) Written; (iii) Mechanical; or (iv) Through the use of staff location system.

A. Oral communication may take place through :

(i) Face-to-face conversation; or
(ii) Mechanical devices like the telephones, etc.

Telephone communication may be divided into the following categories :

(i) Direct exchange line; (ii) Direct exchange line with extensions; (iii) Private branch exchange system; (iv) Private automatic branch exchange system; (v) Private exchange system; (vi) Inter-communication system; (vii) Executive or loudspeaker system; (viii) Radio telephone; (ix) Telephone recording and answering sets; (x) Dictating machines; or (xi) Electric paging system;

B. Written Communication may take place through :

(i) Messenger service; (ii) Internal office mail service; or (iii) Mechanical devices like pneumatic tubes, conveyors, chutes, lifts, etc.

C. Mechanical communication devices include :

(i) Teleprinter or telex; (ii) Automatic telex service; (iii) Telewriter; (iv) Telefax; (v) Television; (vi) Television telephone system;

D. Staff location systems include :

(i) Public address system; (ii) Bells and buzzers; (iii) Lighted signal; (iv) Wireless call system; and (v) Speaking tubes.

External Communication: External communication may take place through:

(i) Personal visits; (ii) Telephones (local and trunk calls); (iii) Postal services, etc.

The postal services include : (a) Certificate of posting; (b) Registered post; (c) Recorded delivery; (d) Reply paid service; (e) Postage pre-paid service; (f) Value payable parcel (VPP); (g) Insured cover; and (h) Telegraphic services.

The following types of telegraphic services are available in this country :

(i) Cablegram; (ii) Ordinary and express telegrams; (iii) Phonograms; (iv) Reply-paid telegram; (v) Coded telegrams; (vi) Telegram "to follow"; (vii) Greetings telegrams; (viii) Multiple address telegrams; (ix) Press telegrams; (x) Courier services.

Speed, accuracy and economy are the governing factors in the choice of any particular method of external communication.

Modern Communication Devices :

1. Pagers
2. Voice Mail Service
3. E-Mail
4. Fax-Printer-Copier
5. Cellular Phone
6. Internet
7. Inmarsat
8. Teleconferencing
9. Videoconferencing
10. Telepresence (by CISCO) etc.

REFERENCES

1. Ernest Dale : *The Management and Organisational Behaviour.*
2. H.S. Levin : *Office Work and Automation.*
3. J.C. Denyer : *Office Management.*
4. Louis A. Allen : *The Management Profession.*
5. Neuner and Keeling : *Modern office Management.*
6. Newman and Summeer : *The Process of Management.*
7. Peterson and Plowman : *Business Organisation and Management.*
8. Redfield, Charles E. : *Communication in Management.*
9. Theo Haimann : *Professional Management.*

STUDY QUESTIONS

1. "Communication is a very important function of any business". Discuss the characteristics of a good system of internal communication. *(B.Com. (Pass), Delhi), (I.C.W.A., Inter.)*
2. (a) Write the use of Telex System.
   (b) What is the procedure for inward mailing?
   (c) Write the use of Xerox Machines. *(B.Com., Andhra Pradesh)*
3. Discuss the different methods of communication. Suggest measures to remove barriers to communication. *(B.Com., Bharthiar University)*
4. Write short note on :
   (i) P.A.X. & P.B.X. System. *(B.A. (V.S.) Delhi)*
   (ii) Importance of communication in a modern office. *(B.A. (V.S.) Delhi)*
5. Describe the services rendered by the Posts and Telegraph Office to the business community. *(I.C.W.A., Inter.)*
6. What are the common barriers to communication? How do you overcome them? *(B.Com. (Hons.) I, Paper VIIa 2009) (I.C.W.A., Inter.)*
7. What do you understand by "Communication". What factors you would keep in mind while choosing the various media of communication for a modern office. *(Co. Sectt., Prel.)*
8. Explain the significance of inter-communication facilities in a large business office. What are the different methods and mechanical devices being used in an organisation. *(Co. Sectt., Prel.)*

9. Write short notes on :
   (i) P.A.X. and P.B.X. System.
   (ii) Importance of Communication. *(C.o. Sectt. Prel.)*
   (iii) Teleprinter and Telex System. *(D.O.O.P., Punjab Univ.)*
10. What do you understand by inter-communication system? Make out a case for its introduction in a Modern Office. *(D.O.O.P., Punjab Univ.)*
11. Write note on 'principles of effective communication'. *(D.O.O.P., Punjab Univ.)*
12. "Inter-office communication is an important item in office organisation". What method of inter-communication are available in a modern office?
13. What are the different kinds of inter-communication in the office. *(B.Com., (Pass), Delhi)*
14. Explain the significance of Inter Communication facility in a modern office. What are the different methods and mechanical devices for oral and written communication. *(B.Com., (Pass), Delhi)*
15. Communication is a very important function of any business. "Discuss the characteristics of a good system of Internal communication". *(B.Com., Punjab)*
16. What are the various methods of duplication? Explain any two methods of duplication. *(B.Com., Delhi)*
17. Write notes on:
   (a) Handling Inward Mail *(B.Com., Delhi)*
   (b) Centralised Mailing System *(B.Com., (Pass) Delhi, 2000)*
   (c) Internal Communication in the office *(B.Com., (Pass) Delhi, 2001)*
   (d) Inward Mail Handling *(B.Com., (Pass) Delhi, 2001)*
18. What are the different modes of internal communication in the office? *(B.Com. (Pass) Delhi, 2002)*
19. "Communication is a very important function of any business". Discuss. Point out the characteristics of a good system of internal communication. *(B. Com.,(Pass) Delhi, 2003)*
20. Write short note on:
   Courier Services *(B.A. (Prog.) Delhi, April, 2008)*
21. What do you mean by communication? Discuss the Characteristics *(B.A. (V.S.) Prog./I-2009)*
22. Explain the semantic barriers to communication. *(B.A. (V.S.) Prog./I-2009)*
23. Write short notes in about 50-60 words each :
   (i) Guidelines for effective telephoning
   (ii) Teleconferencing
   (iii) Format of e-mails *(B.Com. (Hons) I Paper VII (a) Delhi 2005)*
24. Write are the barriers to effective communication? List and explain to briefly. *(B.Com. (Hons.) I Paper VII (a) Delhi 2005)*
25. Write short notes in about 50-60 words each :
   (i) Advantages of oral communication.
   (ii) Format of a Fax
   (iii) e-mail attachments *(B.Com (Hons)I Paper VII (a) Delhi 2005 Cat. B)*
26. What are the chief barriers to good communication? *(B.Com.(Hons.) I Paper VII (a) Delhi 2005 Cat. B)*
27. Write short notes of about 50-60 words each.
   (i) Upward Communication

(ii) Teleconferencing

(iii) Channels in Communication Process *(B.Com.(Hons.) I Paper VII (a) Delhi 2006 Cat. A)*

28. Describe the common barriers to effective communication *(B.Com. (Hons.) I Paper VIII (a) Delhi 2006 Cat. A)*

29. Write short notes of about 50 words each:

(a) You-centered communication

(b) Drawbacks of oral communication

(c) e-mail *(B.Com (Hons.) I Paper VII (a) Delhi 2006 Cat. B)*

30. (a) Discuss the causes of failure in communication and how they can be checked.

Or

(b) What is the importance of feedback in the communication process? Illustrate your answer with examples. *(B.Com.(Hons.) I Paper VII (a) Delhi 2006 Cat. B)*

31. Write a short note on strategies suitable for converying bad news. *(B.Com.(Hons.) I paper VII (a) Delhi 2006 Cat. B)*

32. Answer the following in about 200 words each :

(i) Describe the process of communication in an organisation.

Or

(ii) What are the channels of communication in an organisation and how do they effect the relationship between the employees and the (management). *(B. Com.(Hons.) I Paper VII (a) Delhi 2007 Cat. A)*

33. Write short notes of about 50 words each :

(i) Upward Communication

(ii) Drawbacks of Oral Communication *(B.Com. (Hons.) I Paper VII (a) Delhi 2007 Cat. B)*

34. (i) Comment on the importance of seven C's of good communication.

(ii) Distinguish between formal and informal channels of communication. *(B.Com. (Hons.) I Paper VII (a) Delhi 2008 Cat. B)*

35. Write short notes of 50-60 words each :

(i) Lateral Communication

(ii) Teleconferencing & Voice mail

(iii) Noise in Communication *(B.Com. (Hons.) I Paper VIII (a) Delhi 2008)*

36. Write short notes of 50-60 words each :

(i) Internal Communication

(ii) Tele-conferencing *(B.Com. (Hons.) I Paper VII (a) Delhi 2009)*

37. What are the chief barriers to good communication. *(B.Com. (Hons.) I Paper VII (a) Delhi 2009)*

Chapter 2

OFFICE CORRESPONDENCE AND MAIL SERVICE

CONTENTS

Chapter **2**

OFFICE CORRESPONDENCE AND MAIL SERVICE

> ***"Every office receives mail each day, and the method of dealing with it may have a great effect on the general efficiency of the office. The mail office should be organised and manned to ensure promptness, speed and accuracy."***

Correspondence and the handling of Mail are the two basic office routines of any organisation, which are closely related to other office services—typing and duplication, filing and indexing, forms management and communication, etc. Separate chapters, have been devoted to these related activities. In the present Chapter, we shall discuss the organisation of office correspondence and mailing service.

OFFICE CORRESPONDENCE

"Correspondence means communication in writing as between individuals and institutions on matters of common interest". It may also be defined as "written communication on subjects of mutual interest either within the organisation on with an outsider". Every business house has to keep in constant touch with its investors, suppliers, customers, branches and departments in different parts of the city, country or even the world. Moreover, much of the communication that takes place in any organisation is in writing. It may consist of a letter, a circular, a notice or a memorandum. It may be noted here that all this written communication forms the basis of office correspondence.

Office correspondence may be internal or external. Internal correspondence refers to correspondence between two individuals, departments or branches of the same office, or of any one of them with the head office of the organisation, and vice versa. External correspondence refers to the correspondence of the office with outside individuals, business firms, companies and other organisations. Office correspondence may be further classified as follows :

(i) **Routine Correspondence :** It includes correspondence on routine matters like inquiries, acknowledgements, replies, orders, letters, appointment letters, etc.

(ii) **Sales Correspondence :** It includes correspondence on matters relating to sales *e.g.*, sales letters, invoices, statements of accounts, collection letters, delivery letters, debit and credit notes, letters, etc.

(iii) **Personalised Correspondence :** It includes correspondence on matters involving personal or emotional matters, *e.g.*, "Thank you" letters, letters conveying congratulations and appreciation, introductory letters, letters requesting or granting favours, etc.

(iv) **Circulars :** Circulars and notices, etc., are identical letters which are sent to a large number of different individuals, departments of business firms. They are either cyclostyled, duplicated or printed and may be written on matters like change of address, change of phone number, the opening of a new branch, the introduction of a new product line, notices to shareholders regarding declaration of dividends, meetings, etc.

ORGANISING CORRESPONDENCE

Correspondence may be centralised by creating a separate correspondence section or department : or it may be decentralised—that is it may be carried on by each of the departments individually.

Centralised Correspondence

In a centralised correspondence section, a correspondence supervisor should be appointed to look after all the correspondnece. But even in such a case, separate secretaries of top executives may be appointed to handle their own specialised correspondence. For routine matters, these executives may requisition the help of the correspondence department.

Advantages : The advantages of a centralised system of correspondence are :

(i) Correspondence is specialised. As a result, there is greater proficiency and high standard of work.

(ii) Centralised correspondence facilitates effective follow-up and leads to better results by ensuring better continuity in correspondence.

(iii) The correspondence staff can be adequately and quite easily trained. The cost of training is fairly low.

(iv) Specialisation of the correspondence activity tends to increase the rate of output as well.

Disadvantages : The disadvantages of a centralised system of correspondence are :

(i) Delays may be caused because draft correspondence may be sent back and forth—from the correspondence department to a functional department and *vice versa.*

(ii) A centralised correspondence section may lack adequate technical and specialised knowledge of a particular functional department. This may result in inaccurate correspondence.

(iii) The work of functional departments may be interrupted because of frequent visits, inquiries, collection of information, etc., by employees of the centralised correspondence section.

Decentralised Correspondence

Under the decentralised correspondence system, each functional department makes its own arrangements for correspondence.

Advantages : The decentralised system of correspondence offers the following advantages :

(i) There is no interruption in the work under the decentralised correspondence system. As a result, there is a smooth flow of work, which increases efficiency.

(ii) Departmental correspondence takes care of the technical and specialised needs of different functional departments. The correspondence, therefore, is more accurate and unambiguous.

(iii) The sense of departmental loyalty on the part of the correspondence staff tends to result in better quality work.

(iv) Since correspondence is based on departmental information and facts, the correspondence staff possess better knowledge : the correspondence is, therefore, well drafted and more effective.

Disadvantages : The disadvantages of a decentralised system of correspondence are :

(i) Departmental correspondence staff may lack proficiency in the art of correspondence. This may create a poor impression about the organisation and adversely affect its reputation.

(ii) Under a decentralised system, the correspondence staff may not be adequately trained. The problems of absence and replacement may also upset departmental functioning.

(iii) There may be lack of co-ordination between different departments on policy matters, which will be reflected in the correspondence of different departments. This will have adverse effect on the reputation of the organisation.

Dealing with Correspondence

In practice, most offices in our country follow the decentralised system of correspondence. This is also true of Government and Semi-Government offices. In most offices, some clerks will act as correspondence clerks and prepare draft replies to the letters received in the department. The draft is prepared after collecting the relevant information and is then approved by the official concerned. In some cases, the reply is dictated by the executive concerned either to a stenotypist or to a dictating machine. The letter is then typed, checked and initialled by the clerk and signed by the executive when it is a routine letter; otherwise by the departmental manager. A letter requiring the attention of more than one department should be circulated rapidly to the various departments. Each department should mention in the margin or on the back of the letter or on an attached sheet, a note giving the particulars required of it. The department responsible for replying to a letter should incorporate these in its reply.

However, in Modern Offices, (of Corporates and MNCs) the executives or managers donot waste time and effort on such lengthy procedures. In many cases, every executive/manager is provided with a laptop which is used for making fast and quick communication via e-mail, internet etc.

Cost of Office Correspondence

"An efficient and economical communication service requires the correspondence of a good and effective quality should be produced promptly and at the most economical cost". It must be remembered that the cost of correspondence (letter-writing) is not limited only to the cost of paper and postages, but comprises the following costs as well :

(i) The time of the dictator and of the typist;

(ii) Stationery including carbon papers ;

(iii) The capital cost and the maintenance cost of typewriters /franking machine and other office equipment used for correspondence;

(iv) The cost of filing clerks, mailing clerks and messengers;

(v) The cost of stamping and wasted stationery;

(vi) The cost of office space;

(vii) Overhead expenditure, including rent, lighting, insurance, etc.[1]

Methods should be evolved to control and reduce these costs, including anything which reduces the time spent on form letters, which eliminates unnecessary letters and ensures standardisation of stationery, and encourages an investigation of the procedure followed for the purchase of stationery.

PRODUCTION OF CORRESPONDENCE

Correspondence has to pass through the following inter-related stages :

(i) Drafting or composing correspondence :

(ii) Approval of the drafted or composed correspondence.

(iii) Typing, cyclostyling, etc., of the approved correspondence.

Drafting or Composing Correspondence

The responsibility for drafting correspondence depends to a large extent on "the size of the office, the nature and volume of correspondence and the degree of mechanisation in the office". This responsibility may be shouldered by the following :

(i) **Under centralised correspondence :** By the correspondence section and the senior executives of the organisation.

(ii) **Under decentralised correspondence :** By the correspondence clerks in the operational departments.

(iii) **In small organisation :** By the owner or the office manager.

Principles of Drafting

Littlefield and Rachel lay down the following as the key principles to be followed in the composition of messages :

(i) *Determine the purpose of the message.* Usually, there is a central purpose of conveying certain information and an important secondary purpose of conveying a feeling of helpfulness and goodwill.

1. J.C. Denyer, *op. cit.*, p. 406.

(ii) *Plan the message.* Know the ideas that you want to put across, and arrange them in a logical sequence before you begin the communication.

(iii) *Use natural conversational language.* Aim at directness and simplicity.

(iv) *Be compact and clear.* Try to make one message do the job. Don't leave questions, raised in the letters addressed to you, unanswered.

(v) *Be brief but not too brief.* Give a thorough explanation, but be selective in using detail.

(vi) *Be courteous considerate,* friendly and helpful.

(vii) *Proof read carefully.* An excellent document can be ruined by a skeptical attitude generated by grammatical and typing errors. Spelling name improperly, typing numbers incorrectly and out of sequence, and failing to enclose necessary items are the most frequent problems. Proof reading should also involve checking for completeness.

Forms and Style of Office Correspondence

Not only the form and working of office correspondence, but its appearance is as important. The following points may be borne in mind in so far as the form and style of business letters are concerned.

(i) Paper : Paper should be of good quality and tastefully designed. It should not be overcrowded with matter or overdecorated.

(ii) Typing : The letter should be well typed and displayed. It is usual to type the letters in single spacing with double-spacing within the paragraphs. Adequate margins should be allowed and typing should not start from too near the heading nor carried too near the bottom of the page.

(iii) Typist : A capable typist should be employed to ensure that letters are appropriately paragraphed and punctuated, and that mis-spellings and grammatical errors are avoided. The typist should initial the letter so that reference may be made to him in case of need and responsibility may be fixed on him for any errors, etc., in typing.

(iv) Address : A correct address ensures a prompt delivery of a letter sent by post. An incorrect or incomplete address may result in delays and mistakes in delivery. It should be checked that the spellings in the various parts of the address are correct.

(v) Sender's Address : The sender's address should be given preferably in the lower left-hand corner on the address side or on the back of the envelope so as to ensure that, in the event of non-delivery, it does not go to the Dead Letter Office.

(vi) Post Category : The category of post by which the letter is to be sent—Book Post, Registered Post, VPP, etc.—should be clearly indicated on the letter as well as on the envelope.

(vii) Pin Codes : In case of foreign correspondence, the address should be written in roman characters. Correct pin codes should be given together with addresses on all inland and foreign letters.

The Letter-Writing Process

Leffingwell lists eight ways of answering a letter :

(i) The correspondent may dictate the entire letter to the dictating machine or to a stenographer.

(ii) He may dictate certain personal paragraphs and the numbers of form paragraphs to round out the letter.

(iii) He may answer it by form paragraphs or as a form letter. To add a personal touch, when desired, certain fill-in paragraphs or a personal opening sentence or postscript, may be written.

(iv) He may answer it with a printed letter/form.

(v) He may jot down an outline of the proper answer and let his secretary shape it up.

(vi) He may turn the letter over to an intelligent secretary without comment.

(vii) He may dictate a special letter which is to be sent to several widely separated recipients. Each letter may be separately typed, or its copy may be put on a photocopier.

(viii) When he wishes to show intimate personal interest, he may add a brief note in his own handwriting.

Six-Point Philosophy for all Business Letters

Realising the importance of effective business writing, particularly the importance of a business letter as a company representative, an image builder, the following six-point strategy[2] has been developed for writing all business letters :

1. Develop a human relations approach to writing : A business letter should be, like a handshake across a desk, have a personal touch. A letter is person-to-person communication. The aim should be to talk with, not communicate at.

2. Recognise the high value of a business letter : Cost and image—these are the two reasons a letter is valued so highly. First, the cost is high-Second, nothing can destroy the positive image a company has built faster than a faulty letter. Reputation and gained and lost business are at stake every time a letter is mailed.

3. Portray progressiveness and competency by using modern, up-to-date writing techniques and mechanics.

4. Develop a helpful attitude : Always ask yourself, "How would I feel if I got this letter"? Develop a friendly tone, not stiff, formal, old fashioned business writing. An apology when it is deserved can go a long way toward calming a complaining customer.

5. Organise the message to present clear facts and explanations, keeping your reader in mind : Present the message in such a way that the reader will understand, be convinced and feel satisfied.

6. Maintain only quality production : The impression the reader has should be a positive one.

The Use of Standard Paragraphs in Correspondence

In every office, practically a number of subjects require either an identical or generally a similar treatment; that is identical or generally similar answers. Standard paragraphs may be devised for use in such letters. But these paragraphs should be devised with some literary skill and care so that the "personal touch" is not lost and hackneyed phrases are not repeated, giving the impression that the dictator was disposing of the letters in a careless and uncommitted way.

---

2. Developed by Blue-Cross-Blue Shield of Texsas, U.S.A. (See Littlefiled and Rachel : *op. cit.*, p. 114).

Advantages : The use of well-devised standard paragraphs in business letters offer the following advantages :

(i) Better work can be done and better results achieved by the use of carefully selected words, sentences and paragraphs rather than by using words and phrases carelessly and thoughtlessly.

(ii) Time and labour in repeatedly constructing and dictating standard paragraphs can be saved.

(iii) The constant apprehension of the dictator that he may have used an improper, faulty or inadequate language in his dictation will disappear.

(iv) New correspondents can be easily trained to give dictation by using standard paragraphs.

(v) The typists and transcribers will produce a larger quantity of work.

Disadvantages : The disadvantages of standard paragraphs are :

(i) Standard paragraphs may be used indiscriminately. Thus the "personal touch" may be lost.

(ii) Badly drafted standard paragraphs leave a bad impression on the mind of the recipients of letters and adversely affect the reputation of the organisation.

Form Letters

Usually, offices have to send out identical letters to many different persons, firms etc. Instead of drafting such letters again and again "form letters" may be used. A form letter may be a standardised "form" or a printed postcard. According to Denyer[3] "a form letter is a standardised letter used by an enterprise to answer all correspondence of a similar and recurring nature, and which is used to give the same information to a number of correspondents". In form letters, only the date, name and address of the recipient are to be filled in to complete them. Form letters are used for debt collection, acknowledgement of orders or complaints, price enquiries, ordering of materials, requests for prices or delivery dates, etc.

Advantages : The use of form letters offers the following advantages :

(i) Considerable time, normally spent on separate drafting such letters, is saved.

(ii) Incoming routine letters can be speedily answered.

(iii) A form letter ensures a uniform practice in letter writing.

(iv) It reduces the cost of outgoing mail, for the task of filing in the necessary details can be left to junior clerks.

Disadvantages : The disadvantages of form letters are :

(i) They often lack the "personal touch". Their value, therefore may be discounted by the recipient.

(ii) Form letters may be tilted and official in style and may not have the desired impact on the recipient.

(iii) They may not be sympathetic to individual cases.

Since the advantages of form letters far outweigh their disadvantages, they have become a very important part of correspondence in most offices. It is, therefore, desirable that such letters should be most carefully drafted.

3. Denyer, *op. cit.*, p. 467, 468.

Blanket Letters : In case of Blanket letters, on a letterhead or on a sheet of paper are printed a few sentences or paragraphs covering the most frequently used statements in letters answering enquiries or sending out enclosures. The correspondent checks the appropriate item and mails the blanket letter instead of a specifically dictated letter.

Specimen of a Blanket Letter

INDO-EURO EXPORTS
NEW FRIENDS COLONY, NEW DELHI

Ref. No. Tel. No. ....

Dated ....

It is a pleasure to tell you that on the occasion of the Silver Jubilee celebrations of the firm, we are allowing a special Rebate of 5% on all your purchases made during the month of ......2009. The item ticked below indicates how we have handled this refund :

- The refund has been credited to your account as shown by the enclosed invoice.
- The refund is being sent to you by means of the enclosed cheque.
- The refund shall be adjusted in your future orders.
- Your instructions are awaited about the adjustment of the refund.

Advantages : The use of Blanket letters offer the following advantages :

1. Such letter can be used with catalogues, price lists, bulletins and other enclosures.
2. They make possible a respectable saving in time and money without offending the enquirer.
3. They make it possible to answer letters more quickly than through the usual routine of dictation and transcription.

Disadvantages : The disadvantages of Blanket letters are :

1. If considerable care is not given to the preparation of each statement used, such letter sounds like a cold way of handling correspondence.
2. They often lack, 'personal touch'. Their value may, therefore, be discounted by the recipient.

TYPING AND STENOGRAPHIC SERVICES

Typing : All written communication, including correspondence (letters, circulars, notices memoranda, reports, statements, etc.), prepared by the office should be typed or duplicated before they are despatched. Correspondence and other documents should be near and legible so that the written matter may be clearly read and understood by the recipients. Moreover, neatly typed or printed correspondence attracts attention and creates a favourable impression on the mind of the recipient of the efficiency of the office and thus enhances the prestige of the organisation. It goes without saying that typing/printing not only plays an important role but has become a "must" in modern office organisation.

Objectives of Typing : Typing may be done for the following purposes :

(i) To obtain a number (up to 4 or 6) of neat and legible copies of all written drafts, letters, etc., for purposes of despatch and record;

(ii) To copy out documents from statements, drafts;

(iii) To type documents from materials derived from a number of sources;

(iv) To type invoices or prepare receipts, tabulation and layout work;

(v) To prepare masters for duplication;

(vi) To transcribe a recorded speech or from a dictating machine;

(vii) To type documents about technical matters which require tabulation, careful layout and complicated figure work;

(viii) To type private and confidential matters.

Advantages : The typed material offers the following advantages over handwritten material :

(i) Typed material is easier to read than handwritten material. Its neatness enhances its appeal value.

(ii) More material can be accommodated on a page by typing than with handwriting. Typing is, therefore, economical.

(iii) Typing increases the efficiency of office operations.

Organisation of Typing (Departmental Typing Versus Typing Pool)

In a large organisation, typing work may be organised in two ways, *e.g.*, (i) It may be decentralised or departmentalised; or (ii) A centralised or typing pool may be set up.

For departmental typing, typists are appointed departmentally; whereas, in the case of "pool" typing, the typists are appointed and assigned to a "centralised typing pool". The following are the comparative advantages and drawbacks of both the systems :

Departmental Typing

Advantages

(i) The departmental typist knows his boss and his method of working. There is a "personal touch" between them.

(ii) The typists are available at short notice. This eliminates delays. Besides, work priorities can be properly known.

(iii) The departmental typist become familiar with the technical expressions and forms used in the department and can thus handle technical or specialised work more efficiently.

(iv) The departmental typist develops a sort of loyalty to his own department, a fact which improves morale and efficiency.

Disadvantages : The disadvantages of departmental typing are :

(i) There may be uneven workload for typists of different departments. As a result, there is idle time in some cases and frustration in others.

(ii) The departmental arrangement may become uneconomic by reason of the employment of a large number of typists.

(iii) Departmental typing does not afford much opportunity for the training of new typists.

The Typing Pool

Advantages : The advantages of the typing pool are :

(i) Since the typists are appointed and attached to the central typing pool and not to individual departments, the total number of typists is reduced, sometimes by as much as half. This is the economic advantage of the typing pool.

(ii) Expert supervision and even distribution of all typing work among typists becomes possible.

(iii) Typists can be trained to do a wider variety of work.[4]

(iv) Difficulties arising from the absence of some typists are reduced.

(v) Work can be allocated according to individual ability and experience, and working conditions can be suited to the needs of typists.

(vi) A wide range of computers, machines and equipment can be made available because they can be shared.

(vii) The performance of the typists in a typing pool can be easily judged. This generates a healthy competition among them and makes them more efficient.

(viii) The pool arrangement is ideal for the avoidance of unnecessary disturbance.

Disadvantages : The disadvantages of a typing pool are :

(i) Typists lose personal contact with their executives. As a result, there is loss in the continuity of understanding because the work of one executive is not always dealt with by the same typist.

(ii) The executive may not immediately have the assistance of a typist because he may not be immediately available. Delay may occur, which may prove costly.

(iii) Work priorities may be disturbed and urgent work may not be done on time.

(iv) When work of a technical or specialised nature is handled by different typists from time to time, the quality of that work is adversely affected.

(v) Under the typing pool system, a messenger service is required for the delivery and collection of typing matter.

The success or otherwise of the system depends to some extent on the complexity of the work. It has been found that the typing pool is a very efficient way of dealing with routine correspondence. It does not, however, provide a satisfactory substitute for private secretarial service, which is generally retained for the higher executives.[5] However, the best system is a typing pool under the supervision of an efficient in-charge, with individual typists attached to departmental executives to do their work only when called upon to do so. The benefits of the typing pool arrangement are enhanced under such an arrangement.

Stenographic Services : In addition to typists, stenographers are appointed in modern offices. Generally speaking, stenographers are attached to individual executives and are entrusted with the function of taking dictation from them and transcribing the dictation with the help of

4. G. Mills & O. Standingford, *op. cit.*, p. 23.

computers. They may also be required to note down (in shorthand) the proceedings of meetings of the Board of Directors or of any class of shareholders, etc. Stenographic work may be departmentalised or centralised in a "stenographic pool". The advantages and drawbacks of departmental and "stenographic pool" services are similar to those of departmental typing and "typing pool" respectively.

Dictating Letters

There is an art of dictation, which every office manager should cultivate.[6] It consists, broadly, of being sure in advance of the ideas to be expressed and being able to put those ideas in good language. Many writers of business letters make use of hackneyed phrases—the so-called 'business English'—"Reference you letter no...dated..." "we would advise you...", "your esteemed instructions received" and to finish by "assuring of our best attention at all times". Though it is very easy to memorise and use such expressions, their effect is rarely positive, for these phrases do not convey to the recipient the writer's desire to give real thought and personal attention to his affairs. "Constant practice and self-evaluation are necessary in order to be able to dictate letters which are pleasing to read and convey the message most effectively".

The following methods may be used in dictating letters :

1. Dictating to a Stenographer : The executive calls the stenographer and dictates to her. She makes use of a pencil and a pad and takes down the dictation in shorthand. In this way, a direct rapport is established between the executive and the stenographer and corrections in the dictation are carried out almost at the same time. The disadvantage of a direct dictation to a stenographer is that it necessitates the physical presence of the executive and the stenographer at the time and place of dictation and that this is a somewhat costly mode of getting out a letter or a report.

2. Dictating to Machine Writing Stenographer : In this case, instead of using pencil and pad, the stenographer uses a steno-type machine to take down the dictation. The dictated matter is later transcribed or typed in the usual manner. This kind of dictation has the same advantages and disadvantages as direct dictation to a stenographer.

3. Dictating to a Dictating Machine : In this case, the services of the stenographer are dispensed with. The executive dictates the letter to a dictating machine or a tape-recorder at his own convenient time and place, and sends the tape to the typist who replays it and types out the matter. This method offers the advantages of convenience, economy and mechanical accuracy. But this is not yet popular in India.

4. Dictating to a Typist : In this case, the executive dictates the letter directly to a typist who simultaneously types it out in draft or in final form. This is a costly method, for a considerable time of the executive is consumed in giving dictation to the typist.

The choice of the method for dictation depends upon a variety of factors :

(i) Cost;

(ii) The nature and volume of work;

5. *Ibid.*, p. 22.
6. G. Mills & O. Standingford, *op. cit.*, p. 16-17.

(iii) The availability and use of man and machine;
(iv) The convenience and accuracy desired; and
(v) The need for personal touch between the executive and the concerned staff.

Recommended Dictation Techniques

Littlefield and Rachel[7] have recommended the use of the following techniques for dictating letters :

1. Prepare for dictation before you begin : Plan message content; make notes or outlines where helpful. Arrange to have all matching correspondence and supporting documents on hand. Schedule most dictation for regular time periods each day, and avoid interruptions, if possible.

2. Learn to think in sentences and paragraphs : Dictating by word-or-phrase-at-a-time slows down the flow of thoughts.

3. Speak distinctly at a normal, even rate : Enunciate clearly avoid mumbling; avoid telescoping two or more words together.

4. Indicate paragraphs and unusual marks of punctuation : Indicate all punctuations, if possess this ability or are willing to develop it. It will contribute to clear thinking and accurate transcription.

5. Indicate corrections orally : Mark of indicator slip if using recording equipment.

6. Give full instructions regarding work requirements : Give time limits any special handling, number and distribution of copies and so on.

MAIL SERVICES

'Mail' may be described as the written communication that passes through the messenger service or the post office. Every business house maintains continuous contacts with its customers, suppliers, branches and departments, and Government agencies; and this is done by written communications of various types. Every business office, therefore, receives and sends a large volume of mail every day.

Business mail is of three distinct types :

(i) Incoming or inwards mail;
(ii) Outgoing or outwards mail; and
(iii) Inter-departmental mail.

These three types of mail may be in the form letters, documents, packets, parcels, telegrams, orders, remittances, etc. The method of dealing with the mail may have a great bearing on the general efficiency of an office.

Efficiency of Mailing Services

A mailing service is an integral part of office activity, and is the backbone of modern organisations. Prompt and efficient handling of mail in a planned and systematic way is essential for the overall furtherance of business interests. When the mail is large and there are several

7. *Op. cit.*, p. 118.

departments, it is essential to have a well-organised office, adequate staff and equipment, and the intelligent co-operation of every workers. An efficient mailing service offers the following advantages :

(i) It ensures continuous contacts with outsiders.
(ii) It creates a lasting impression on outsiders.
(iii) It improves inter-departmental relation and efficiency.
(iv) It supplements the efforts of the correspondence and records management departments, etc.
(v) In mail order houses, mailing is a costly affair. The efficiency of the mailing service may make this a less costly job.
(vi) The training of. juniors usually begins in the mailing department. Here, they learn, and get acquainted with mailing routines, the organisational set-up and the levels of authority and responsibility.

HANDLING AND DISPOSAL OF MAIL

To ensure a prompt and correct handling of mail, the mailing service should be planned and organised properly. A proper planning of mailing service involves the following :

(i) Providing facilities for the mail service;
(ii) Organising the mailing department (centralising the mail services);
(iii) Making arrangements with the post office;
(iv) Establishing mail routines (for inward and outward mail);
(v) Mechanising the mail service;

These aspects are being discussed below :

I. Facilities for Mail Service

The type and the extent of facilities to be provided for the handling of the mail service depend upon the volume of mail to be handled. For instance, the space and the number of mailroom staff depends upon the volume of the work and the extent to which mechanical equipment is used. A proper mail service facilities should be provided for at the time of formulating the layout plan for the office, so that the mailing service is integrated with the activities of the whole organisation and serves it in the best possible manner. Not only should the facilities be adequately provided (*viz.*, space, staff, equipment, etc.), they should be put to the most efficient use. The location of the mailroom is important. If it is situated somewhere near a post office, its efficiency tends to increase.

II. Organisation of the Mailing Department

A proper organisation of the mailing department is essential, for it ensures an efficient and economical performance of the mailing service. An unorganised mailing service results in mistakes and delays, increases the cost and adversely affects the working of different departments by interrupting and holding up their work. The necessary organisation should cover the following four phases of work :

(i) Opening, sorting and distribution of inward mail;

(ii) Collection of information for replies;

(iii) Dictation, typing and signing of replies;

(iv) Making up and despatching the outward mail.

The selection of a suitable system of organisation for the mailing department depends upon the size and nature of the business and the volume of mail handled by it. The mail may be handled by one particular person, or by individual departments, or by a centralised mailing department.

Centralised Mailing Service

If the 'mailing service' is centralised, a separate mailing department will have to be created. This department is headed by a supervisor and the work is performed by well-trained personnel. The mailing service is generally centralised in big offices, where the volume of mail is very substantial. In a small office, where few letters are sent out and received, a single person may handle the mail. In some offices, the inward mail is centralised but the outward mail is handled by individual departments. The primary object of the centralisation of the mailing service is to promote efficiency through specialisation. A centralised mailing service offers the following advantages :

(i) The responsibility of handling mail (inward, outward and inter-departmental) is entrusted to the mailing department. All the other departments are relieved of this work. The duplication of effort is avoided.

(ii) Specialisation of the mailing activity ensures accuracy and speed.

(iii) Mailing operations can be systematised. Proper systems and routines can be evolved and combined with mailing operations, which would make for savings in time and money.

(iv) *Trained* and *well-qualified* staff can be employed, which would step up the efficiency of the mailing operations.

(v) A well-trained and expert supervisor may be appointed to head the mailing department. *Better supervision* and *co-ordination* would ensure a smooth and speedy performance of mailing operations.

(vi) The *mechanisation* of the central mailing department is possible. Various time-saving devices (machines)—letter openers, folding and sealing machines, franking machines, etc.—can be put to the best possible use.

(vii) Centralisation ensures a better *control over the use of postage stamps* and their proper accounting. Overstamping, under-stamping or non-stamping are avoided.

(viii) Centralisation saves time :

(a) By a prompt distribution of inward mail;

(b) By a prompt recording of inward and outward mail;

(c) By a prompt and careful opening and scrutiny of the envelopes and their enclosures of the inward mail and careful folding, inserting into envelopes and despatch of outward mail;

(d) By making time schedule arrangements for the collection and despatch of the outward mail of various departments;

(e) By routing unopened mail of a confidential nature to the proper addressee;

(f) By making special delivery and other arrangements with the post office;

(g) By training junior employees in office routine procedures and systems.

III. Arrangements with the Post Office

Small business houses often prefer to have their inward mail dropped into their letter boxes twice or thrice daily by the postman on his round; and they drop their outward mail in the nearest post box or at the nearest post office. But big business houses usually make special arrangements with the postal authorities. These are :

(a) Post Boxes : Post boxes are available on rent at certain major post offices. Any individual or firm may rent such a box from a post office, from which he or his messenger may collect his letters and parcels. Every post box is allocated a number, and any postal article bearing that number is placed into that post box. Only fully paid unregistered mail (*e.g.*, letters, inland letters, post-cards, aerogrammes, newspapers, books and postal packets, etc.) and dropped into the post boxes. The renter of a post box or his messenger may clear the post box at any time during the business hours of the post office on production of a delivery ticket (bearing the same number as that allotted to the post box) supplied by the postal authorities.

Advantages : Post boxes offer the following advantages :

(i) Regular and early delivery of correspondence;

(ii) Correspondents may write only the post box number instead of the detailed address of the addressee;

(iii) The renter or his messenger may clear the post box as and when he desires to do so.

(b) Post Bags : Under this arrangement, a bag and a lock and duplicate key are supplied by the renter to the post office (the other key being retained by him). All postal articles addressed to his firm are placed by the postal authorities in that bag, which is delivered to the renter or his messenger at the counter of the post office on the production of a delivery ticket supplied by the postal authorities during the hours prescribed for making such deliveries. This system offers the following advantages :

(i) It provides a safeguard against tampering with the letters between the post office and the firm's office.

(ii) This arrangement is particularly suitable in mail order business, when a large volume of inward mail is received.

(iii) The renter may use such bags to despatch unregistered outward mail to the post office.

IV. Establishing Mail Routines

The establishment of efficient procedures and routines for the handling of incoming and outgoing mail is an important aspect of planning an efficient mailing service, for they make a favourable impact on outsiders and reflect the general efficiency of an organisation. The routines to be followed for incoming and outgoing mail are discussed separately.

Handling Incoming Mail

Once it has been decided whether incoming or inward mail is to be centralised or departmentalised, it is essential to lay down an efficient procedure for its handling. The following routine is suggested for this purpose :

1. Receiving the Mail : Mail or 'dak' is ordinarily delivered by the post office through its postman twice or thrice a day. If a numbered post box or post bag has been rented, a messenger is sent to the post office at specified times to collect the mail. Some incoming letters may also be received through messengers or peons of other offices or departments. A suitable arrangement would have to be made to receive all such mail. In small offices, mail is received by the chief executive or his secretary or receptionist. But in big offices having a separate mailing department, a clerk is entrusted with the responsibility of receiving the incoming mail. Whosoever receives the incoming mail signs and acknowledges the receipts for registered mail, parcels or letters delivered by the peons of other offices etc.

2. Sorting the Mail : After the mail has been received in the mailing department, it should be sorted out before it is opened. It is easier to sort out sealed envelopes than different sized pieces of paper. Sorting may first of all be done of private letters of the employees and of business letters.

Business letters should be sorted out into three groups :

(a) Registered and unregistered letters or mail;

(b) Sealed and unsealed envelopes; and

(c) Confidential and urgent letters and other official letters.

Sorted mail makes the delivery of letters convenient and quick. For instance, correspondence addressed to the heads of departments should be delivered to their secretaries. Sealed envelopes should be opened before the unsealed ones because the latter usually consist of invoices, price lists and other less important matter. Envelopes marked *confidential, private* or *personal* or otherwise addressed to the executive should be delivered unopened to the concerned person or department. It is necessary that a supervisor or some executive should be present to supervise the sorting and opening of the mail, especially when cash, cheques, postal orders or other documents are received in the mail. The mail should be sorted by appropriate sorting devices; and if letter trays or wire baskets are used, they should be in containers ready for delivery to the different departments. Pigeon-holes may be preferable when there are a large number of departments.

3. Opening the Mail : Letters may be opened by hand or by letter opening machines. A paper knife is mostly used in offices to slit open envelopes, etc. If the number of letters is very large, a letter opening machine may be used with advantage. This machine has a revolving knife edge which slices a very thin piece of the side of an envelope and ensures its safe opening. It is advisable to shake the contents to the other side of the envelope before feeding it to the letter opening machine.

The morning mail is generally the heaviest. Special arrangements should, therefore, be made to ensure that, when the office opens for business, the mail, or a bulk of it has been sorted, opened and distributed, ready for the attention of the staff concerned. The following guidelines may be followed in this connection.[8]

8. Leffingwell, *op. cit.*

(a) The sorting and opening of the mail should start at least half an hour to one hour before the opening time of the office.

(b) The Office Manager should see to it that the work in the office starts immediately after the opening of the mail, otherwise the time and money spent on an early opening of the mail would be wasted.

(c) The mail opening staff should be fully conversant with the method of sorting and opening the mail. If a mailing manual has been prepared, it should be used.

(d) After an envelope has been opened, it is necessary to carefully remove the contents from it. Empty envelopes should be checked before they are thrown away. This enclosures and sometimes the empty envelopes of the letters as well, should then be fastened by a pin or clip or stapled.

4. Scrutiny of Contents : After the removal of the contents from the opened envelopes, their contents should be scrutinised to find out for whom, and for which departments, they are meant. The sorting of letters on a departmental basis is done at this stage. Before sending the mail to the concerned departments, the enclosures to the letters should be checked, compared and verified with the covering letter to find out whether they are in order or not. Sometimes, the enclosures are cheques, bank drafts, postal orders or valuable documents. If any discrepancy or omission is found while scrutinising them, the matter should be immediately brought to the notice of the mailroom supervisor. Letters in which certain previous references are given may be sent to the filing department, where the letters and the relevant files may be sent to the concerned department.

5. Stamping the Mail : All letters, etc., received in the office should be stamped with the date of their receipt. Where the time of receipt is also important, it should be noted on the communication. In some offices, the mail is serially numbered. The stamping of the date may be done with rubber stamps. The time and the serial number may be written by hand or with the help of *dating,* numbering and time-recording machines. Wherever necessary, the empty envelope should be pinned with the letter as evidence of the date and time of its receipt, which are indicated by the post mark. Sometimes, a specially designed rubber stamp, is used to provide for the noting of instructions for treatment as well as for the date and reference number. A design of such a stamp is given below :

INDO-EURO EXPORTS

No. .... Date ....

Received ....

Ackd ....

Replied ....

Filed ....

6. Recording the Mail : Many offices, particularly banks, municipal corporations, Government offices and professional firms, keep a record of each letter received by entering its particulars in a Letter Received Book or Inward Mail Register. The particulars usually entered are :

(a) The Serial number;

(b) The date of receipt;

(c) From whom received;

(d) Subject;

(e) Enclosures; and

(f) Initials of the person to whom the letter was handed over for attention.

Subsequently, the date and nature of the reply and the date on which the letter was filed are entered by the filing clerk. A specimen of an Inward Mail Register is given below :

Inward Mail Register

S.No.	*Date*	*Sender's Name and Address*	*Subject*	*Contents*	*Department Referred*	*Date Reply*
1.	2009 Sept. 29	Black and Burn Co. Ltd., East Park Rd. Calcutta	Order	Letter	Sales	Oct. 5
2.	"	Fantasy Ltd., Connaught Place, New Delhi	Payment	Letter	Account and Cheque	Oct. 2

The advantages of an Inward Mail Register are :

(a) It is an analysed record of the nature and number of communications received and answered.

(b) Delay or default in attending a particular letter may be found out and action taken.

(c) It fixes responsibility for a lost document.

(d) In case of lost or mislaid correspondence, the matter is more easily remedied since the address and subject of the correspondence are available from the Register.

Although the maintenance of the Inward Mail Register offers certain advantages, its use has been abandoned by most commercial firms. When the volume of correspondence is large, the maintenance of such a register; causes delay in distributing the mail; is cumbersome and time-consuming; and is expensive. In most offices, however, it is maintained for the purpose of recording the particulars of all registered and insured letters which have been received. When valuable documents—share certificates, transfer deeds, etc.—are received by post, proper records should necessarily be keet of them to ensure their proper disposal.

7. Distributing the Mail : The last stage in handling the inward mail is its distribution to the concerned executives and/or departments. Where the recording of the inward mail is practised, the initials of the receiving clerks or executives of different departments should be obtained on the mail register in acknowledgement of their receipt.

8. Follow-up : Letters received should be properly attended to and answered, or the necessary action should be taken thereon. They are then filed properly. Follow-up action by departmental heads or individual executives should be taken if and when it is called for. Any lapse should be attended to, and a serious view taken of it if it is repeated.

Inward Mail Routine : Although inward mail handling is an elaborate and complex affair, however, it should be carried out as quickly as possible by any successful organisation. The following is an illustrative list of steps involved in the inward mail routine of a big business office :

1. All letters are taken care of 30 minutes before the office opens.
2. Envelopes marked PRIVATE, PERSONAL or CONFIDENTIAL are sorted out and kept unopened in a separate tray to be forwarded to the respective persons or departments.
3. Other envelopes are opened by a letter opening machine.
4. Contents of letters opened are checked and passed on to the supervisor.
5. Cheques are stamped with the crossing stamp and are entered in a book.
6. All letters are stamped with the date and time and entered in Inwards Mail Register.
7. The junior staff takes the mail to different departments 15 minutes after opening of the office.
8. The supervisor is referred to, if the department named is not identifiable.

Handling Outgoing Mail

Every organisation sends out mail each day, and a good office system ensures that it is done in the most economical and efficient manner. Although it is a comparatively minor aspect of office management, it is one with which every Office Manager should be familiar. For reasons of efficiency and economy, the outgoing mail service should be centralised. In order that he may perform his job efficiently, the mailroom supervisor, who looks after the outgoing mail, should have a thorough knowledge of postal rules and regulations, clearing timings of post offices, banks, etc., and the postage rates for different types of articles. The following routine is suggested for the handling of outgoing mail :

1. Production : The production of outward letters involves drafting or dictation and the typing of letters. All outward mail should be produced before despatch.

2. Signature and Reference : Every outward letter or mail should be signed, and the authority to sign office mail should be clearly defined. Ordinary routine letters, circulars or form letters may be signed by a junior executive or a correspondence clerk; but important letters should be signed by departmental heads or the executive/director concerned. Whosoever signs the letter should verify and check its contents. The verification may also be done by a correspondence clerk or typist, who should initial the letter; and then it may be signed by the executive concerned. Signatures are placed in full on the originals; but the copies are initialled. After the signature, the outgoing letters have to be marked with a reference number (code number) or symbol or file number for future reference. This is known as referencing. Every organisation follows its own method of coding and referencing. For instance, a letter from the accounts department of an organisation sent to a customer may have the reference as Accts/1053/09, where *Accts* stands for Accounts, 1053 is the serial number of the letter and 95 indicates the year 2009

3. Collection of Outward Mail : In some offices, different departments send letters duly typed, signed, addressed and placed in envelopes to the mailing department, which despatches them. However, in many offices, the mailing department's messenger visits different departments at scheduled times and collects the mail from the trays marked outgoing mail and deposits it in the mailing department. In large offices, mail may be collected 3 to 4 times a day to ensure an even flow of work in the mailing department throughout the day. This improves the efficiency of the despatch section.

4. Entering mail in Outward Mail Register : Before letters are posted, a record of them should be entered in the Outward Mail Register or Despatch Register. The particulars usually entered in this register include :

(a) The serial number;
(b) The date;
(c) The contents of the letters;
(d) The address of the receiver;
(e) The name of the department sending the letters; and
(f) The value of the stamps used.

It may be noted that only those letters which are sent through the post office are recorded in the Despatch Register. The letters which are sent through the office messenger are recorded in the peon book. A despatch serial number is given to each letter, which is also recorded on the letter.

5. Folding Letters : The letters are now folded and inserted in their envelopes. Before folding the letters, the address of the addressee should be noted down on the envelope in which the folded letter is inserted. While folding the letters, the following considerations should be borne in mind :

(a) If window envelopes are used, the folding should be done in such a way that the address becomes fully visible through the window.
(b) Inland letters and aerogrammes should be folded as per instructions on their cover.
(c) Letters and enclosures should be folded together.
(d) Letters should be folded the minimum number of times, according to the size of the envelope.
(e) Envelopes of a suitable size should be used.
(f) Folding and inserting machines may be used for quick operations.
(g) Inland letter forms, circulars, invoices, etc., are sometimes cut in such a manner that they look like envelopes when folded as per instructions.

6. Preparing the Envelope : After folding, the letter is inserted in the envelope, which should be properly and correctly addressed. A complete and correct address ensures a quick and prompt delivery of the letter to the addressee. Pin codes should be given Addresses may be written by hand or typewritten, or written with the help of addressing machines. A great saving in time can be affected and it can be ensured that letters do not go to wrong addresses by a proper use of window envelopes. The sender's address should also be written on the envelope in the left hand corner on the address side or on the reverse of the envelope in order to enable the post office, in case of nondelivery, to return it un-opened and without delay.

7. Sealing and Stamping : After preparing the envelope, the step is to seal it with an adhesive, gum or cellotape. In large organisations, huge volume of outward mail may be sealed with the help of sealing machines. The different categories of mail—Book Post, Registered cost, V.P.P. or Insured Articles—should be sealed in accordance with postal rules. The next step is to 6 mail which is to be net by post. This stamping should be done carefully, for overstamping causes loss and understanding creates a bad impression about the organisation. Letters, etc., to be sent by messenger, should not be stamped. The use of franking machines may be made where a large number of letters are despatched frequently. For the purpose of stamping or franking, the latest copy of the Postage and Telegraph Guide, containing postage and other rules, should be made available to the mailing department.

8. Posting : Ordinarily, all stamped unregistered mail is put in the post box. Letters addressed to local correspondents are generally sent through messengers. Letters marked U.P.C. (Under Postal Certificate), Registered, Recorded Delivery, or V.P.P., are delivered at the counter of the post office. The office may also make special arrangements of the despatch of urgent letters to the General Post Office or an RMS post office even after normal office hours.

V. Mechanising Mail Services

The mailing department staff has to engage in many repetitive and monotonous activities in the course of the performance of their functions. In large organisations, the handling and disposal of mail calls for speed and accuracy of the mailing service. Many mechanical aids have been devised for use in mailing department. The use of these machines in the mailing department :

(i) Eliminate wastage;

(ii) Increase the speed of operations;

(iii) Ensure accuracy;

(iv) Avoid misuse of postage;

(v) Simplify the postage accounting system;

(vi) Speed up the delivery of letters; and

(vii) Ensure the overall efficiency of the organisation.

Some of the devices which may be profitably used in the mailing department are :

1. Letter Opening Machines : These are used for opening envelopes of different sizes at great speed. Each can open 50 to 200 envelopes per minute, depending on whether it is manually or electrically operated.

2. Time-Recording Machines : These machines are used to record the time and date of receipt or despatch of mail. They are electronic clocks which automatically print the time and date when envelopes are inserted in them.

3. Addressing Machines : These are used to print addresses on letters, etc., which are sent to regular correspondents.

4. Folding Machines : These are used to fold a large number of letters, etc., of identical size at a speed of up to 10,000 per hour.

5. Sealing Machines : These are used to automatically moisten and seal the flaps of envelopes at a speed of upto to 5,000 envelopes per hours.

6. Inserting Machines : These are used to insert folded letters into envelopes at a great speed.

7. Tape Moistening Machines : These are used to seal bulky packets and parcels, etc. They take a roll of strongly gummed tough paper tape and moisten it before affixing it.

8. Franking Machines : These are used for automatically printing, in bright red ink on letters, post cards and labels, passed through them, a franking design comprising of the postage charge, the date of posting and, if desired, an advertising slogan. These machines save time and eliminate the possibility of errors in stamping and misuse of stamps.

9. Sealing cum Stamping Machine : It is an electrically operated machine which not only seals the envelopes but also franks, stacks, and counts them at a great speed.

10. Mailing Scales : These are weighing machines which weigh letters, envelopes and packets to ascertain the correct postage to be affixed on them.

11. Bundling Equipment : The purpose of this equipment is to tie and bundle packages and bundles. Since this equipment is capable of performing at much faster rate than are humans, the utilisation of such equipment allows considerable saving in time in preparing the outgoing mail.

12. Other Equipment : Apart from these, various other equipment—paper knife, paper clips, staplers, etc.—may be required in the mailing department.

It should be noted here that the mechanisation of the mailing service cannot be suggested for a small office, where a few letters are received or despatched every day.

VI. Supervising the Mailing Service

A constant supervision of the mailing service is essential for its efficient performance. Where the mailing service is centralised, an efficient and experienced supervisor, who possess a thorough knowledge of the routines of the mailing operations and the current rules of the Posts and Telegraphs Department, should be employed, who should supervise, guide and allocate the work among the different employees of the mailing department. He should be responsible for getting the work done most efficiently and economically. The mailing routines should be periodically reviewed by him, and improvements or changes should be made in them according to the changed circumstances.

SUMMARY

Office Correspondence : Correspondence means communication in writing between individuals and institutions on matters of common interest. Office correspondence may be internal or external. It may be further classified into :

(i) Routine Correspondence; (ii) Sales Correspondence; (iii) Personalised Correspondence; and (iv) Circulars.

Organising Correspondence : Correspondence may be centralised by creating a separate correspondence section; or it may be decentralised—that is, it may be carried on by each of the departments individually. Centralisation offers the advantages of :

(i) Specialisation; (ii) Effective follow-up; (iii) Training of staff; and (iv) Increased output.

Its disadvantages include :

(i) Delay; (ii) Lack of adequate technical and specialised knowledge; and (iii) Interruptions in the work of departments.

Decentralisation offers the advantages of :

(i) No interruption; (ii) Better quality of work because of departmental loyalty of staff; and (iii) Better knowledge on the part of the departmental staff.

Its disadvantages are :

(i) Lack of proficiency in the art of correspondence; (ii) Inadequate training of staff; and (iii) Lack of co-ordination between different departments on policy matters.

Production of Correspondence : The first stage in the production of correspondence is its drafting or composing. The principles of drafting include :

(i) Determining the purpose of the message; (ii) Planning the message; (iii) Use of natural conversational language; (iv) Comprehensiveness and clarity; (v) Brevity; and (vi) Courteous, considerate, friendly and helpful attitude.

The second stage is the approval of the drafted or composed correspondence. The third stage is the typing, printing, etc., of the approved correspondence.

Standard Paragraphs in Correspondence : Standard paragraphs may be used in reply to letters which require identical or generally a similar treatment. Well designed standard paragraphs offer the advantages of :

(i) Better results; (ii) Saving in time and labour; (iii) Avoidance of faulty or improper language; (iv) Easy training of new correspondents; and (v) Increased work output.

The disadvantages are :

(i) Loss of the personal touch; and (ii) Risk that a bad impression may be created by the use of badly drafted standard paragraphs.

Form Letters : A form letter may be a standardised form or a printed postcard. In form letters, only the date, name and address of the recipient are to be filled in. The advantages of using form letters are :

(i) Saving in time; (ii) Increased output; (iii) Uniformity; and (iv) Reduction in the cost of the outgoing mail.

Their disadvantages are :

(i) Lack of personal touch; (ii) Lack of desired impact on the recipient; and (iii) May not be sympathetic to individual cases.

Typing and Stenographic Service : All written communications, including the correspondence prepared by the office, should be typed or photocopied before they are despatched. Typing offers the advantages of :

(i) Neat and legible copies; (ii) Ease in reading; (iii) Economy; and (iv) Increased efficiency in office operations.

Organisation of Typing : The typing service may be departmentalised, or a centralised or typing pool may be set up. The typing pool offers the advantages of :

(i) Economy; (ii) Expert supervision and even distribution of all typing work; (iii) Allocation of work according to individual ability and experiences; and (iv) Facility of sharing of a large variety of machines and equipment.

Its disadvantages are :

(i) Lack of personal touch with the executive; (ii) Occurrence of delay; (iii) Disturbance of work priorities, etc.

Stenographic Services : Stenographic work may also be departmentalised or centralised in a stenographic pool. The advantages and drawbacks of the stenographic pool are similar to those of the typing pool. Letters may be dictated to :

(i) A stenographer; (ii) A steno-type machine; (iii) A dictating machine; or (iv) A typist.

Mail Services : The term mail refers to written communication which passes through the messenger service or the post office. Business mail may be :

(i) Incoming mail; (ii) Outgoing mail; and (iii) Inter-departmental mail.

Handling and Disposal of Mail : It involves the following :

(i) Providing facilities for the mail service; (ii) Organising the mailing department; (iii) Arrangements with the post office for post boxes, and/or post bags; (iv) Establishing mail routines (i) Handling the incoming mail.

The routine involves :

(a) The receipt of the Mail; (b) The outline involves the sorting the mail; (c) The opening of the mail; (d) The scrutiny of contents; (e) The stamping of the mail; (f) The recording of the mail; (g) The distribution of the mail; and (h) Follow-up.

Handling Outgoing Mail : The routine involves :

(i) Production; (ii) Signature and reference; (iii) Collection of outward mail; (iv) Entering mail in the outward mail register; (v) Folding letters; (vi) Preparing the envelope; (vii) Sealing and stamping; and (viii) Posting.

Mechanising Mail Services : This is done by using :

(a) Letter-opening machines; (b) Time-recording machines; (c) Addressing machines; (d) Folding machines; (e) Sealing machines; (f) Inserting machines; (g) Tape-moistening machines; (h) Franking machines; (i) Mailing scales; and (j) Other equipment.

REFERENCES

1. Carl Heyel : *Handbook of Office Administration.*
2. Chappell and Read : *Textbook of Business Communication.*
3. Dartnell : *Office Manager's Handbook.*
4. G. Mills and O. Standingford : *Office Organisation and Methods.*
5. J.C. Denyer : *Office Management.*
6. Leffingwell and Robinson : *Text Book of Office Management.*
7. Littlefield and Rachel, etc. : *Management of Office Operations.*
8. Neuner and Keeling : *Modern Office Management.*

STUDY QUESTIONS

1. Outline the procedure for handling incoming and outgoing mails. Do you think that the centralisation of the mailing department will improve efficiency in the handling of mail? *(B.Com. (Pass), Delhi)*
2. Describe briefly an efficient method of handling incoming and outgoing mail in a big business house of Bombay having several departments and engaged in inland and foreign trade. *(I.C.W.A., Inter.)*
3. Assume you are in the staff of a management consultancy firm and your firm is retained by a company with ten administrative departments to evolve a system for the receipt of inward mail, distribution to various departments and despatch of outward mail Lay down a procedure. *(Co. Sectt., Prel.)*
4. What are the advantages and disadvantages of handling all mail-incoming, outgoing and inter-departmental-within one centralised department of a company? *(Co. Sectt., Prel.)*
5. What arrangements would you make for dealing efficiently with large and varied outward mail? Mention the equipment you would use to speed up the work and also what steps you would take to ensure that enclosures are not omitted. *(Co. Sectt.,)*
6. Suggest a routine to be followed for an effective and efficient despatch of outgoing correspondence. Do you prefer centralisation of despatch work? Name the various mechanical devices commonly used in despatch section of an office. *(Co. Sectt. Prel.)*
7. For what reasons is the handling of outgoing mail a much more complex service than the handling of incoming mail? Describe briefly the kinds of mechanical equipment that are available for expediting work in the mail room. *(D.O.O.P., Punjab University)*
8. Describe the procedure for maintaining incoming and outgoing mail of an office. *(D.O.O.P., Punjab University)*
9. A Company having several departments faces the problem of dealing with the large volume of their inward and outward mails. The secretary of the company requests you to submit a report laying down a procedure that will enable the company to deal with them effectively. *(I.C.W.A., Inter.)*
10. "A business letter should be brief, effective, and should convey the right message". Explain this statement. *(B.A. (Com.) I Delhi)*
11. "A good letter is one which is clear and brief". Comment. Or Give your arguments in favour of centralised correspondence system in office. *(B.A. (V.S.) I-Delhi)*
12. What are advantages and disadvantages of centralised mailing service in an office. *(B.Com., II V.S. Delhi)*
13. Write short note on : "Inward Mail". *(B.Com. II (N.S), Delhi)*
14. Outline an efficient method of handling incoming and outgoing mail in a big business house of Bombay having several departments and engaged in inland and Foreign trade. *(B.Com., Punjab)*
15. Write notes on: Incoming and outgoing mail handling *(B.Com., (Pass) Delhi, 2002)*
16. What do you understand by centralisation of office services. *(B.A.(Prog.) Delhi April, 2005)*
17. What is the procedure for handling incoming mail ? *(B.A. (Prog.) Delhi 2007)*
18. Write note on "Outward Mail System *(B.A. (V.S.) Prog.-I 2009)*
19. Write short notes in about 50-60 words each :
   (i) Indianisms in written correspondence. *(B. Com (Hons) I Paper VII (a) Delhi 2005 A)*
   (ii) Sender and Receiver functions
   (iii) Inward Mail *(B.Com.(Hons.) I paper VII (a) Delhi 2007A)*

Chapter 3

MANAGEMENT REPORTING

(Office Reports & Precis Writing)

CONTENTS

Chapter **3**

MANAGEMENT REPORTING
(OFFICE REPORTS & PRECIS WRITING)

> ***"Organisational distance, specialisation and limitations of human Comprehension force management to rely heavily upon reports in communicating information both upward and downward".***
> **— C.L. LITTLEFIELD**

With the growth in the size of modern business organisations and with the ever-widening activities of the State, there has been a growing need for communication within a group. Business decisions are not taken by the old "rule-of-the-thumb" approach, but are now based on a scientific analysis of the information made available to business executives. The regular flow of such information and communication—reports and statistical data—to different executives is essential for a sound basis for policy decision, planning and the successful attainment of business objectives. Apart from the executives, such information and communication has to be provided to several other interested parties in the business—the shareholders, investors, etc. An oral communication of such information is neither desirable nor feasible in all cases; it should be supplied in writing and should be some proper form—in the form of a report.

What is a Report? A report is a summary of information.[1] It is a communication from someone who has information to someone who wants to use that information. A report is defined as a document in which given problem is examined for the purpose of conveying information, reporting findings, putting forward ideas, and sometimes making recommendations as the basis of action. It is a statement of facts related to the business operations which are necessary for an evaluation of progress and for decisions. A report is a presentation of facts and findings about an activity or an event. It may also be described as "a statement prepared to present facts relating to planning, co-ordinating performance and the general state of the business in an organisation".

George R. Terry has defined a report as, "a written statement based on a collection of facts, events, and opinions and usually expresses a summarised and interpretative value of this

1. Littlefield, *op. cit.*

information. It may deal with past accomplishments, present conditions, or probable future developments. According to Johnson[2] : "A good business report is a communication that contains factual information organised and presented in clear, correct and coherent language". Reports are used by members of the management to plan, organise and control business operations. A system of reporting is vital to any management information system, but especially to a responsible, decentralised management. It follows, therefore, that each manager should report on those operations of the firm for which he has accepted the responsibility and authority.

Purposes of Reports : An office report serve the following purposes :

(i) It serves as a means of communicating information to those who need and use it. For instance :

(a) It presents factual information to the management in order to facilitate planning and co-ordinating;

(b) It provides the required information to shareholders, creditors, investors, customers and the general public;

(c) It presents alternative propositions or courses of action to the management.

(ii) It provides a valuable record of documents for the business which can be made use of in the future :

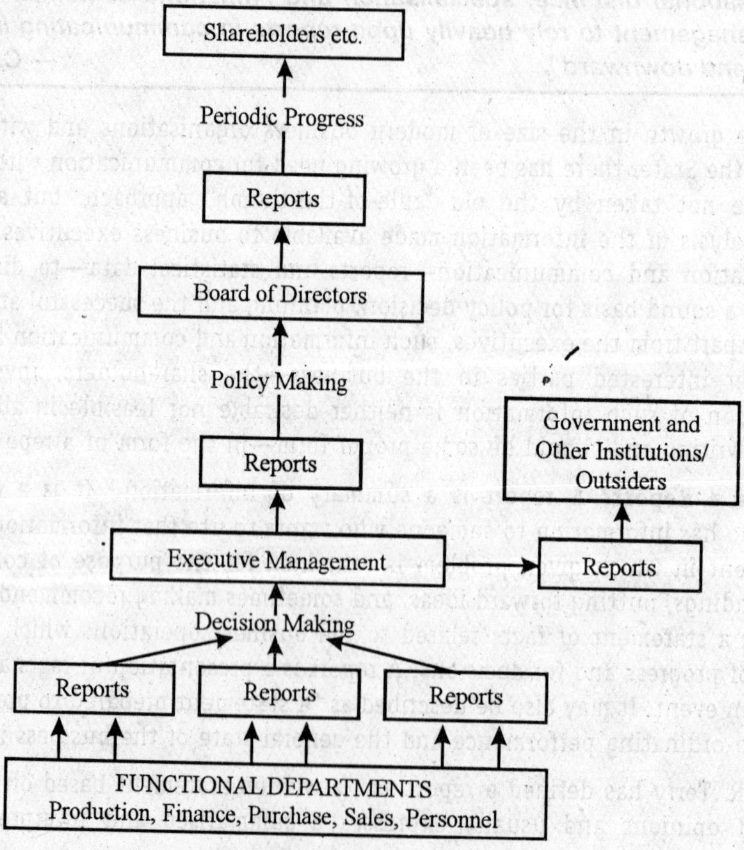

Fig.3.1 Reports : Purposes and Importance

2. Johnson & Savage, *Adn istrative Office Management*.

(iii) It provides the facts and results (and recommendations) of an investigation or survey or inquiry conducted on behalf of the shareholders, management or the Government :

(iv) It offers a basis for the measurement of executive/departmental performance.

In order to be effective, an office report should :

(i) Serve some purposes;

(ii) Be well drafted, simple in language and unambiguous;

(iii) Be brief but comprehensive; and

(iv) Be based on or supported by reliable factual information or statistical data;

Types of Reports

Reports can be classified into private, public, company, departmental, restricted, non-restricted, technical, non-technical, periodic, routine and special, statutory and non-statutory[3]. However, for purposes of office usage, they may be classified into the following categories :

1. Routine Report : It is prepared from time to time to record the present facts & figures. If it is prepared at regular intervals, it is also known as a periodic report. Generally speaking, it contains a mere statement of facts, in a detail and summarised form, without any opinion or recommendation, and seeks merely to convey some information to the management on the progress of some matter. Examples of routine reports include; material handling reports, production report, sales report, costs report, auditor's report, director's report, etc.

2. Special Report : A special report may be prepared by an individual or a body or a committee entrusted with some special inquiry, and is presented to the superior body calling for it. It usually contains the advice or the recommendations of the reporter on a certain matter of special, non-routine nature. Examples of such reports include market research report, turnover report, product development report, plant location report, etc.

3. Statutory Report : In some cases, a report is a statutory requirement, and has to be prepared in accordance with the requirements of the law. For instance, under the Companies Act, 1956, a joint stock company should prepare and file the following reports with the Register of Companies :

(a) Directors Reports to the annual general meeting;

(b) Annual Returns;

(c) Statutory Report;

(d) Auditor's Report.

4. Technical Report : The difference between a technical report and those described above is only a matter of contents. Technical reports are prepared by technologists and their contents are generally in the form of statistics and figures. Examples of technical reports are project reports, engineering reports, plant maintenance reports, etc.

A report may be formal report or an informal report.

(a) *Formal Report :* A formal report is one which is typically analytical in nature; that is, it is presented to the reader in a rather formal format and consists of several fairly standardised

3. Terry, *op. cit.*, p. 125.

parts. Formal reports are either statutory reports or non-statutory reports. Reports submitted by officials or executives of companies, co-operative societies, local bodies, etc., are usually formal reports.

(b) *Informal Reports :* An informal report is like informal communication. It does not follow any prescribed or official form or procedure. It may involve verbal reporting in person or over the telephone or may take the form of a letter. According to Quible,[4] informal reports may be of the following types :

(i) Short report—containing a discussion of facts as well as conclusions and recommendations;

(ii) Progress report—providing information about the progress of a specific plan or programme;

(iii) Staff report—report presenting facts and offering conclusions and recommendations on staff matters;

(iv) Justification report—justifying a particular course of action or recommendation.

REPORT WRITING

The writing of a report is an art which can be studied and cultivated. The information and recommendations placed before the management of a business are of little value unless they assist in the formation of judgments and lead to decisions. A report which does not stimulate thought and lead eventually to action may be of passing interest to the reader; it serves no useful purpose.[5] It does not justify the cost incurred on its preparation. Report writing requires considerable training in :

(i) The collection of relevant data;

(ii) The arrangement of the data in a logical manner; and

(iii) The arriving at a conclusion;

A good report should contain all the relevant facts; it should marshal these facts in a logical order, discuss them in a simple language, and arrive at some conclusion. It is necessary that a report, to be effective, should have the following characteristics :

(i) It should present accurate data. Inaccurate data lead to wrong analysis, conclusions and recommendations.

(ii) It should be presented in a simple and unambiguous language.

(iii) The report should be clear and analytical.

(iv) It should be brief but comprehensive.

(v) It should be well-planned and well-organised. The subject matter, conclusions and recommendations should be separately given.

(vi) It should be properly addressed to the reader, and dated and signed by the reporter.

4. Zene K. Quible, *op. cit.*
5. Mills & Standingford, *op. cit.*

Planning and Organising Reports

As stated above, a good report should be well-planned and well-organised. Tyler G. Hicks has suggested a four-step approach to planning and organising of reports[6] :

Planning and Organising a Report
Step 1 : Prepare Material (i) Collect information, facts, illustrations. (ii) Check to see that you have all the information needed. (iii) Decide on the purpose of the report : who will read it? Why does he want it? What does he require? How will he use it?
Step 2 : Plan Report (i) Classify material. (ii) Make an outline. (iii) Make a through list of major and minor subject headings.
Step 3 : Writing Report (i) State the subject, purpose, and plan in the introduction of the report. (ii) Describe the equipment, procedures and results in the body of the report. (iii) Summarise the conclusions and recommendations. Give emphasis where emphasis is due. (iv) Condense the report in one or two paragraphs in the abstract. (v) Prepare a table of contents, a list of illustrations and tables, appendices and bibliography.
Step 4 : Criticise Report (i) Examine the report as a whole, the plan and the proportion of parts. (ii) Check the agreement of the title, the table of contents, the introduction and the abstract. (iii) Check the proportion of paragraphs and sentences. (iv) Examine the details of text transitions from topic to topic, part to part, sentence structure and wording.

Form of the Report

Report should be so written as to be easily read and understood and to facilitate reference, without difficulty, to any of its parts. There is no one way in which a report may be written; its layout should differ according to its purpose and the person for whom it is intended. For instance, an informal report may be set out in the form of a letter in which the plan of writing followed in business letters may be adopted. But a formal report generally has the following :

(i) Heading : The report should give a main heading which should indicate, as concisely as possible, its contents.

(ii) Address : The report should be addressed to some defining reader or body of readers, *e.g.*, to the Managing Director or to the Board of Directors.

(iii) Table of Contents : This should consist of heading and sub-heading describing the various sections (chapters or topics) of the report, and indicating the number of the page on which they are to be found.

6. Adapted from Tyler G. Hicks, *Successful Technical Writing*, McGraw-Hill, p. 155.

(iv) Introduction : It should state the terms of reference which the reporter was given and define the problem to be solved and all other relevant facts.

(v) Findings or Facts : In this part, the findings of the reporter are presented. These findings should be based on the facts and the data collected by him. The statistical data, charts and diagrams it contains may be referred to in an Appendix.

(vi) Conclusions and Suggestions : This section should show how the conclusions were arrived at. The reporter may also offer his suggestions or commendations. In a lengthy report, this part may be separated from the body.

(vii) Summary : In lengthy reports, a summary of the entire report is usually given.

(viii) Appendices : They may consist of statistical tables or graphs, specimens of forms, minority reports, etc.

(ix) Signature and Date : The report should be signed by the person responsible for it, and dated. If the report prepared by the committee is signed by an individual member, he should sign "for and on behalf of the committee." The names of all members of the committee should be given.

Report in a Letter Form

A report may be in a letter form. In such a case, the use of 'Dear Sir's or (gentlemen) is made in the start and the complimentary close is made with the words 'Yours faithfully or Yours truly'. A letter form of report might be arranged as follows :

Addressee	Address
Dear Sir(s)	Dated

Subject heading

1. Introduction/Terms of Reference
2. Findings/Results of Investigation
3. Observations
4. Recommendation, if called for

Yours faithfully

(Signature)

Official Designation

In the arrangement, paragraphs may be numbered unless the report is very short. This facilitates reference. Such headings may also be used to advantage in a long report.

Report in a Memorandum Form

"Memorandum" 'may be defined as an internal letter, as contrasted with letters going outside the organisation, as shorter and less formal than an average report. A report may be in a 'memorandum' form which dispenses with both opening, salutation and complimentary close. Some companies call memorandums as inter-office-letters or inter-organisation reports.

The memorandum is generally written under pressure of time. The memorandum writer has to analyse a situation quickly and to write it concisely. In this process, he must :

1. Decide on the object or main theme of the memorandum.
2. Subordinate every fact or idea to this main object and show how these facts are related logically to the main theme.
3. Reject any superfluous or irrelevant material for the receiver's understanding of the main theme.

Purpose of memorandum : Memorandums serve the following three purposes :

1. It serve as a reminder and maintains a permanent record of meetings, conferences, discussions, policies, procedures, etc.
2. It conveys information and policy decisions both upwards and downward within the organisation.
3. It maintains a flow of information across the levels or ranks of an organisation.

Guiding Rules for Reports

The drafting or preparation of a report is not an easy task. A high standard of report writing connotes a high standard of written English. However, by practice, one can achieve a fluency in writing and speaking. Continual criticism is also necessary to achieve this objective. In addition, the following guiding rules for drafting reports should be noted :

(i) *Make only reports which have definite aim :* The purpose of the report should be known to the person preparing it. And the writer should tell the reader what he wants to know.

(ii) *Write always in first person :* However, when a report is submitted by a committee it should be written in the third person.

(iii) *Be positive and use positive statements :* Avoid negative statements.

(iv) *Write in the narrative form,* stating the facts, findings and recommendations in a logical manner.

(v) *Keep to the subject.* Facts not related to the subject should be strictly excluded. Avoid ambiguity.

(vi) *Strive for simplicity.* Use simple words and sentences : Avoid technical terms or business phraseology which may not be understood by the reader.

(vii) *Carefully observe the rules of punctuation.* Otherwise, sense of the report may be lost.

(viii) *Separate facts from opinion :* A mere expression of opinion without supporting factual data is not a report.

(ix) *Give a Title to the report :* So that it can be seen at a glance what the report is about.

(x) *The report should be introduced by quoting the terms of reference.* It should be made clear why the report is required and as to what it should contain.

(xi) Make specific recommendations.

(xii) *Give the correct and complete data or* factual information supporting the report.

(xiii) *Keep the report brief*, but complete and comprehensive.

(xiv) *Always read over everything you have written.* Do not regard it as finished until you are satisfied that it expresses exactly what you wanted to convey.

Reports of Meetings : The reports of meetings are usually not addressed to any person in particular and may not have any particular title. Reports of committee meetings are written in an impersonal way and in the third person, using the past tense. On the other hand, reports of company meetings are prepared in the form of minutes of meetings. The Companies Act, 1956, requires the drafting of minutes of all the meetings of the shareholders and of the Board of Directors or of the committees of the Board of Directors, etc.

Reports vs. Minutes : A clear distinction should be made between the minutes and the report of a meeting. The report should contain a detailed description of the proceedings at the meeting, including the motions, resolutions, amendments, opinions, suggestions, discussion and comments thereon. It is written in the narrative form, on the other hand, the minutes of a meeting relate to the decisions reached at it and do not contain in detail the discussions that took place. Minutes serve the purpose of evidence in law courts. Reports do not have the same legal significance unless they are incorporated or identified in the minutes in some way.

Evaluating the Report

The reports prepared within the organisation should be evaluated continuously since business data, economic conditions and organisation situations are changing continuously. In the absence of such continuous evaluation, some reports may be duplicated and some other may be prepared for areas for which reports are not needed. In evaluating such report, questions such as the following should be answered :

1. Is the report necessary at all?
2. Can it be eliminated or combined with other reports?
3. Can it be condensed?
4. Is it comprehensive?
5. Are all data relevant to the purpose and use of the report?
6. Is the frequency of its issue reasonable? Can it be altered?
7. Is the report useful to the management in decision making?

If it is observed that a report is useless, it should be abandoned. If it can be combined with other reports, such combination must be adopted forthwith. Routine reports which do not serve any useful purpose may also be discontinued to achieve economy in office operations.

Specimens of Reports

1. Routine Report

Auditor's Report

Ray & Ray
Chartered Accountants
77 East Park Road
Delhi - 110006
Date : 10th July., 2009

The Directors,
The East India Hotels Limited
Oberai Maidens
Delhi - 110007

Dear Sirs,

We have audited the attached Balance Sheet of The East India Hotels Ltd., Delhi, as on 31st March 2009 and also the annexed Profit and Loss Account of the Company for the year ended on that date and report that :

(i) We have obtained all the information and explanation which, to the best of our knowledge and belief, were necessary for the purpose of audit.

(ii) In our opinion, proper books of account, as required by law have been kept by the company so far as appears from our examination of the books.

(iii) The Balance Sheet and Profit and Loss Account dealt with by the report are in agreement with the books of account.

(iv) In our opinion and to the best of our information and according to the explanations given to us, the accounts give the information required by the Companies Act, 1956, in the manner required and give true and fair view :

(a) In the case of the Balance Sheet, of the state of affairs of the Company as on 31st March 2009 and

(b) In the case of the Profit and Loss Account, of the profit for the year ended on that date.

For Ray & Ray
Chartered Accountants
Sd/-
Partner

2. Special Report

Problem : The Managing Director of Modern Chemicals Ltd. seeks your advice as a Cost Accountant on the purchase of two fork lift trucks for the movement of materials which is presently done by manual labour hired on a purely temporary basis. You observe that :

(i) All the materials are stored in 45-gallon drums;

(ii) Some of the materials are in liquid form and can be circulated through pipes; and

(iii) Losses in material handling are quite substantial. Write an appropriate Report.

(I.C.W.A., Inter.)

REPORT

The Managing Director,
Modern Chemicals Ltd.,
New Delhi

Sub : Purchase of Fork Lift Trucks for Material Handling

Dear Sir,

I have gone through the details of the present method of material handling and have observed that :

(i) All the materials are stored in 45 gallon drums which are considerably bulky and require very careful handling, particularly when handled by manual labour;

(ii) Some of the materials are in liquid form and can be circulated through pipe lines; and

(iii) Losses in material handling are quite substantial. The reasons for those losses is that the materials are presently handled by manual labour employed on a purely temporary basis. There is no permanent material handling staff at the storehouse and in the production plants.

Regarding your proposal to buy fork lift trucks, I give below my opinions and recommendations :

(i) Since some of the materials are in liquid form and can be circulated through pipelines, it would be better to instal pipelines for these material. The installation of pipelines is advantageous in the following respects :

(a) They are not very costly to install;

(b) Not much maintenance cost will be incurred on the pipe-lines;

(c) They are easy to operate;

(d) Material losses can be reduced to the minimum;

(e) Large amounts can be saved on the labour costs normally incurred on material handling.

(ii) Non-liquid materials may be handled by any of the following material handling devices.

(iii) Trucks, fork lifts, cranes, trolley conveyors. Belt conveyors and automatic conveyors, pullies, overhead chain conveyors, monorail, wheel barrows, vibrators, etc. The use of a particular type of material handling device depends on the purposes and costs involved.

(iv) Fork lift trucks are a mechanised form of material handling equipment. They are very costly and require heavy maintenance costs as compared to other material handling equipment. Moreover, they have to be operated by skilled workers. In the circumstances, permanent operators will have to be employed. However, the use of fork lift trucks is advantageous in the sense that a large quantity of materials can be handled in a very short period of time.

I hope you will consider these facts while taking your decision on the purchase of fork lift trucks.

Yours faithfully,
Sd/-
Cost Accountant

New Delhi
15th Oct. 2009

PRECIS WRITING

The word precis has been derived from the French word *pressee* which is connected with the English word *precise*. A *precis* means a summary of a given passage; so precis writing is the same thing as summarising. A precis is a gist of a lengthy passage expressed in as few words as possible; but at the same time. It incorporates all the main ideas and points in the original passage. It does not contain any comments, recommendations, etc., nor does it have any place for examples.

Precis writing is very useful for official purposes, when a summary of the letters, correspondence, minutes or documents has to be prepared for an official who has no time to read the originals. A precis of these documents enables him to grasp the main ideas with little effort.

A precis is always shorter than the original. It expresses only the main theme and is short of all unimportant details. Although no strict rule can be laid down for the length of a precis, it should be borne in mind that it should not contain more than one-third of the number of words contained in the original. In condensing three pages of print into one, it is clear that much must be omitted. The art of precis writing lies in making the right omissions, and in skilfully combining what is left.

Specimens of Summarising

(i) He was hard up for money and was being pressed by his creditors.	He was in financial difficulties.
(ii) He got up and made a speech on the spur of the moment.	He spoke off hand.
(iii) The secretary received a letter which did not bear the name of the writer.	The secretary received an anonymous letters.
(iv) The manager acted in a manner that rendered him liable	The manager acted illegally. to prosecution.
(v) The reply was completely off the point and useless.	The reply was irrelevant.
(vi) This is a parcel which is incapable of being sent by post.	This is an unmailable parcel.

Method of Precis Writing

Precis writing not only pre-supposes mastery of the language but also a penetrating mind, concentration of thought and intensive brain work. There is no short cut to precis writing. The following method or procedure may be followed for precis writing :

Step 1. Reading :

(a) Read the passage carefully, several times, if necessary, to get a general idea of its meaning. The more you read it, the clearer will be its subject and what is laid about the subject.

(b) Go through the passage again, underline the different points it contains, and number them in the margin so that no point is left out which is to be included in the precis.

(c) Examine the passage sentence by sentence to determine which sentences and words are essential and which are not. Strike out what is not essential. Get rid of repetitions, examples and illustrations.

(d) Arrange the essential points in the best possible way to make an outline of the summary. Generally speaking, the order of the original is retained.

Step 2. Writing :

(a) Supply a short title which will express the subject.

(b) Attempt to write a summary of the points. The first draft may be the rough draft, and the precis may have to be rewritten.

(c) If the summary is too long, as probably it will be; rewrite it to bring it to the required length of one-third the original.

(d) Use your own words as a rule. A precis which is made of words and phrases borrowed from the original will, in most cases, not be clear to anyone who has not read the original. However, you must retain the most important words of the original.

Step 3. Revision :

(a) After making the final draft, carefully revise it before writing the fair copy. While revising, see to it that :

  (i) The precis contains all the important points of the original;

  (ii) It is only the gist of the original;

  (iii) It should be a connected whole, although divided into paragraphs or sections which should not appear as separate notes; and

  (iv) It should be complete in itself;

(b) See that there are no mistakes in spellings, punctuation, grammar or idioms used;

(c) Write out the precis in a fair copy under the heading or title selected by you.

EXAMPLES OF PRECIS WRITING

Passage 1:

Air safety experts in India rue the fact that increasingly commercial interests seem to override safety concerns. "The increase in the number of incidents and accidents during takeoff or touchdown of flights is due to the lack of proper training and safety oversight," says Capt Mohan Ranganathan, an air safety expert alluding to the need for transparency. "The Alliance Air crash in Patna in 2000 killed 55. But the DGCA website for accident/incident data shows nil accident/incident data shows nil air crashes for airlines," he adds.

In India, air accidents/incidents are investigated by the DGCA, the civil aviation regulatory authority. For long, aviation observers have demanded an independent investigation authority, like the US's National Transport and Safety Board (NTSB), for instance. The Indian Pilots Guild, a union of Air India pilots, endorses this.

"The Commission of Railway Safety, which looks into rail accidents for the sake of impartiality, comes under the ministry of civil aviation. Aviation should have an independent body," says an Indian Pilots guild spokesperson. What it has is the National Air Safety Board, that was formed by the DGCA in January 2008 and is not independent. The board is supposed to meet at least four times a year. "It has hardly met in the last one year." said a source.

Capt R S Otaal, General Secretary of Indian Commercial Pilots Association, says a majority of the cases was due to crew fatigue. "The number of incidents has been on the rise after scientifically-backed rest rules for pilots were put in abeyance last year," he says. It's also an open secret in the aviation community that rest rules for pilots are often violated and commercial interests override bad weather in deciding whether a flight should land or not.

Multi-let flights, like a Mumbai-Nagpur-Raipur-Kolkata one for instance, are a case in point. "Last year; on one of these sflights, the commander tried to land, but did a go around as the aircraft was rocking badly. He managed to land in the second attempt. What he should have done was diverted the flight. But then, he would have had to go back to Nagpur and continue with two other flights. Such decisions are sure-fire recipes for disaster;" says a senior airline commander.

"The International Civil Aviation Organisation the FAA and the European Union are concerned about the lack of qualified manpower and lack of proper safety oversight in India. The Government will not be in a position to prevent a major accident, which is round the corner; unless we have a transparent and honest system," says Capt Ranganathan, the air safety expert.*

Solution :

Title : ***Carriers flying into Trouble***

Precis : There is a growing demand for transparency in accident investigations and Air Safety Experts feel that commercial interests seem to override safety concerns in an increasing number of cases. In India, DGCA investigates Air accidents/incidents as also looks into rail accidents. DGCA formed National Air Safety Board in 2008. It is not an independent body. Moreover, it is supposed to meet atleast 4 times a year, but had not met in the last one year. A Spokesman of Indian commercial Pilots Association blames crew fatigue as a major cause of accidents/incidents. He says rest rules are often violated and commercial interests overside safety norms. Other reasons are lack of qualified manpower and lack of safety oversight in India. A major accident at any time could not be averted unless we have a transparent and honest system.

Passage 2 :

At the time of elections political leaders dole out to the hungry million dainty dishes galore which they taste in dreams only but rarely in reality. As we all love to see delightful dreams and fear the dreadful ones, democracy which at regular intervals gives us the opportunity of dreaming exciting dreams and escape nightmares, deserves three cheers, though E. M. Foster was contented with two 'cheers for democracy'. And three cheers for elections which save democracy from being devoured by dietatorship, the most dreadful.

Now every election is a battle of wits. The maxim 'that in war what matters is the man behind the gun', may be proved wrong, but not the belief that in the election wrangles what matters is the campaign. The cleverer the compaigner, the more successful will be the campaign and the more hopeful its outcome. So election campaigns in democracies 'the world over' are well organised and planned as the projects to land man on the moon was. And the manifestoes of political parties, which can be justly called elections promises, are the corner stones of their organising, planning and conducting election campaigns.

Some of course, will disagree with our terming manifestoes synonymous with promises and say that the manifesto of their party is an epitome of their programme for the betterment of the

*Passage by Manju V. TNN : Times of India, Delhi 25-05-2009.

people, they are committed to implement after their glorious victory. They may be right as they are bonafide patriots. But being democrats they should suffer our sceptical idiosyncrasy, particularly when it does not undermine their infallibility. So they should not feel indigent about our innocent audacity to make manifestoes synonymous with promises. Moreover, they should regard it as layman's licence as it does not imply to dilute the significance of their claims, doubt their credentials and ridicule their selfless devotion to democracy. They should rather indulge in this casual freedom, as the word manifesto, is meaningless for us, laymen, who understand better what the word promise means. We, as well as, the men behind manifestoes, know that promise is the mother of the hope that constantly keeps struggling for its release from the stifling folds of fears, the offsprings of frustration, Privation and uncertain future.

Politicians may have not they understand human nature better than students of psychology. They know that whatever they might do, they cannot please all. So they aim at pleasing many and displeasing a few, as in an election what matters is the support of many. Nevertheless the nature of election promises varies with the nature of election promises varies with the nature of problems which pester people. At what pitch certain notes are to be played is decided by politicians in the light of people's expectations, sentiments and interests.

In our country, of course, what counts is emotional appeal — mass appeal. The promises, though varying with the status of the political parties in the fray, were saturated with emotions. All India parties had a stance different from those of regional of State parties and independents. They seemed to be vying with one another. Some indeed made fantastic promises to the electorates, probably with a view to displaying their ingenuity at being poetically visionary. So far the ruling party had been harping on the eradication of poverty, solving unemployment problem and a government that works. The first promise is too tall to be practical and the facts prove this beyond doubt. Poverty is so deep-rooted in India that only drastically revolutionary steps can eradicate it, perhaps, in a democratic state, no political party, can afford to take such steps. So the promise of eradicating poverty was just to keep the people in a mood of expectancy and drug them into complacency. So is the case with the promise of solving unemployment problem, for providing employment setting up of industries taking up new projects making education job-oriented and many other steps are needed.

Election promises are determined by the circumstances at the time of elections. Politicians promised to give clean administration, meaningful education and peaceful solution to many problems. It will be a break with the old practical tradition if the parties start working in a manner that they honour the wishes of the people. Today a common man thinks that politics is nothing else but fraud; sanctity of political promises, they think, lies not in observing them but in breaking them. This feeling has demoralising effect on the people, and corrosive effect on politics.

Nevertheless a little ill must be suffered for a great gain, as election promises may fool some for one term some for all terms but not all for all terms. And as this truth dawns on the political carecrists, their election promises will cease to the hyperbolic and high-sense will dominate their campaigns. If election promises today are a prelude to the flippant politician's lies in the time to come, there is little need for running down the most noble concept of government which leaves ample room for the exposure of promise maker's sincerity through his performance in the year following his return to Legislative.

It is the biter who is ultimately bitten, thanks to the power invested in voters who cannot resist being lured by *rosy* election promises.

Solution:

Title : Futility of Election Promises

Precis : At the time of elections, political leaders make promises which are subsequently forgotten or never fulfilled. Electorate are cheated with promises made by political leaders and parties. The manifesto of parties are an epitome of their programme for the betterment of the people promising like eradication of poverty, unemployment, corruption, provision of free education, free eatables like wheat, rice etc., guaranteed employment to the poor, creating further reservations, setting up new industries/projects for creating employment, making education job-oriented and many other steps.

The promises generally are too tall to be practical and the facts prove these beyond doubt. Today a common man thinks that politics is nothing but fraud. Sanctity of political promises lies not is observing them but in breaking them. Election promises are looked upon as Devil reading scriptures. However, electorate vests in them the power to bite such politicians making a mockery/ fraud of promises.

Passage 3

Woman and girls are half the world's population, do two-thirds of the world's work hours, receive a tenth of the world's income and own less than a hundredth of the world's property. It was to attack this world-wide "apartheid of sex" that the U.N. launched the Decade for women back in 1975.

Two out of three of the world's illiterates are women. Faced with high costs of schooling and limited job opportunity for the educated, many parents tend to invest only in boys. The importance of girls' work in the home and the high incidence of teenage pregnancy are also cited as barriers to female enrollment. But some countries are trying harder him other — Nepal had given cash rewards to schools which had more girls in their classroom and Kenya is more scholarships and lower fees to women students.

Women are inching forwards in politics — a move seen by the U.N. as essential for every kind of progress. Women's movements have emerged in almost every nation. One result is that most of the countries are reporting a steady rise in the percentage of women exercising their right to vote. There is also a slight but world-wide increase in the number of women being elected to public office.

New figures from the International Labour Organisation nail another myth that mean are the farmers and the food growers. In the developing world today women are responsible for 50 per cent of total food production. A recent survey in Tanzania, for example shows that women work an average of 2600 hours a year in agriculrure as opposed to only 1800 a year for men. In Africa as a whole, 60 per cent of all agricultural work, 50 per cent of animal husbandry, and 100 per cent of food processing is done by women.

Women are continuing to get a raw deal from the health services. Three quarters of the health problems of the developing world could be prevented by botter nutrition, water, sanitation, education and immunisation, all of which are usually the responsibility of women. But eighty per cent of medical and health budgets are devoted to dector and hospitals promoting curative medicine to a small proportion of the population. In the rural areas only about fifteen per cent of the population have access to modern health care centries during pregnancy and child birth, more than half of the world's women have no tained help. Only a third have access to family planning.

Overall, a woman's double burden of bearing and bringing up of children as well as working outside the home remains the heaviest millstone around the neck of female emancipation. For millions of women in the Third World —who cook and clean, sew and wash, plant and weed, care for the old and bring up the young, a sixteen hour day is not uncommon. For these women, there is neither the time nor the energy nor the opportunity to invest in training, careers, or self-development.

In the industrialised world, pay differentials have narrowed considerably but, on average, a woman is still paid one half to three-quarters of the money that a man can earn for doing the same job.

Throughout the developing world, a major problem is that women's work is often invisible-a man laying a water pipe in a city is part of the statistics of development. A women carrying a days supply of water from a well to a village is not. Her work, though vital to the task of meeting the daily needs of the family, goes unrecorded and unrewarded. It is wrongly believed that only a male child can keep the dynasty alive. Women through their sincerity add lustre to the family's name. At in-Laws' house they have to be content with subordinate position. The apartheid of sexes is a blot on our civilization and an instance of man's arrongance. For preserving democracy this inequality will have to be finished.

Solution :

***Title* : Place of Women**

Precis : UN launched the 'Decade of the Women', back in 1975 to attack the 'Apartheid of Sex' which puts women in the back seat, as a second rate citizen of the world. Women, who are half of the world's population works two thirds of world's hours, receive 10% of world's income, and less than 1% of world property, are more than 66% illiterate. There are stray incidents of empowering the women through education, participation in active politics, to elect them in public offices, to improve their lot in better provision of health services and access to education, employment and family planning.

Overall, the scenario is a grim reality of discriminating women against men, in cases, for example, pay differentials, access to health services, and opportunities for training, careers or self-development. The Apartheid of sexes is a blot on our civilisation and an instance of an arrogance. The conditions for women should be bettered. Democracy will be at risk if women are not given their right place.

SUMMARY

Office Reports : A report is a summary of information. It is a statement of facts related to business operations which are necessary for the evaluation of progress and for decisions. An office report serves the following purposes :

(i) Provides a means of communication;

(ii) Provides a valuable record of business documents for future use;
(iii) Provides facts and results of an investigation; and
(iv) Offers a basis for the measurement of performance.

Types of Reports : Reports may be :

(i) Routine reports (like production report, sales report, costs report, auditor's report, etc.)
(ii) Special reports (like market research report, turnover report, plant location report etc.)
(iii) Statutory report (like annual report, statutory report, auditor's report, etc.) or
(iv) Technical report (like project reports, engineering reports etc.) A report may be formal report or an informal report.

Report writing : Report writing is an art and requires considerable training in :

(i) The collection of relevant data; (ii) The arrangement of the data in a logical manner; and (iii) At conclusions.

Characteristics of a Report : A report should be :

(i) Accurate; (ii) Simple and unambiguous; (iii) Clear and analytical; (iv) Brief but comprehensive; (v) Well planned and well organised; and (vi) Properly addressed, dated and signed by the reporter.

Planning and Organising Reports : The steps in planning and organising reports include :

(i) Preparing materials (ii) Planning reports; (iii) Writing reports and (iv) Crticising reports.

Form of the Report : A formal report :

(i) Contains heading; (ii) Contains Positive statements; (iii) Is written in narrative form; (iv) Keeps to the subject; (v) Strives for simplicity; (vi) Gives correct and complete data; (vii) Is brief; and (viii) Is read over after everything has been written.

Reports vs. minutes : A report contains a detailed description of the proceedings at a meeting, including motions, resolutions, amendments, opinions, suggestion, discussions, and comments thereon. On the other hand. The minutes of a meeting related to the decisions reached at it and not contain in detail the discussions that took place.

Precis writing : A Precis means a summary of a given passage. Precis writing is the same thing as summarising. A Precis of letters, correspondence, minutes or document is very useful because a busy executive has no time to read the originals. It enables him to grasp the main ideas with little effort.

Methods of Precis writing : It involves :

(i) Reading the passage carefully;
(ii) Underlining the different points it contain;
(iii) Avoiding non-essential matter in the passage;
(iv) Arranging the passage in the best possible way and writing the summary;
(v) Giving the summary a title; and
(vi) Revising the final draft before writing the fair copy.

REFERENCES

1. Betty J. : *Developments in Office Management.*
2. Brown L. : *Effective Business Report Writing.*
3. G. Mills and O. Standingford : *Office Organisation and Methods.*
4. Graham Greaves and Hoffman : *Report Writing.*

5. Johnson and Savage : *Administrative Office Management.*
6. Littlefield and Peterson : *Modern Office Management.*
7. O. Standingford : *Simplifying Office Work.*
8. Tyler G. Hicks : *Successful Technical Writing.*
9. Zene K. Quible : *Introduction to Administrative Office Management.*

STUDY QUESTIONS

1. What are the important principles which should be borne in mind while drafting business reports? *(B.Com. (Pass), Delhi)*
2. Distinguish between "Routine" and "Special" reports. Discuss briefly the principles that should be borne in mind in preparing special reports. *(B.Com. (Pass), Delhi)*
3. State the difference between "minutes" and "reports". Also set out the stage in which you proceed for drafting a report. *(I.C.W.A., Inter.)*
4. You have recently joined ABO Co. Ltd., as secretary. Write a report to the managing director on the defects in the routine work of the company's office. *(B.Com., Bombay)*
5. Draft report as secretary of your company for submission to the Board on the recent trend of sales of your company, suggesting steps for improvements. *(B.Com., Mumbai)*
6. Draft a brief report for submission to the chairman of your company on a proposal for the mechanisation of the office, referring to the advantages thereof from the point of view of the company, its employees and the outside public. *(B.Com., Kolkata)*
7. What are the functions of a "report"? State some general principles which may help a writer to produce a clear and accurate report. *(I.C.W.A., Inter.)*
8. The chief executive of a fast-moving consumer goods industry is worried that the realisations from dealers are getting delayed of late due to binding delays in the office and asks you, as the Office Manager, to investigate and submit a report with your recommendations. Draft such a report. You may make any suitable assumptions. *(I.C.W.A., Inter.)*
9. Draft a report for submission to the Directors of your company on the agitation of the workmen for higher percentage of Bonus and threatened strike by workmen. *(D.O.O.P., Punjab Univ.)*
10. Discuss the principles which should govern the drafting of a business report. *(D.O.O.P., Punjab Univ.)*
11. Write short notes on :
    (i) Difference between report and memorandum.
    (ii) Difference between statutory and non-statutory report.
    (iii) Difference between formal and informal report. *(D.O.O.P., Punjab Univ.)*
12. In the capacity of a company secretary, write a report on the existing communication system in your organisation. Include any suggestions for improving it. *(D.O.O.P., Punjab Univ.)*
13. How do minutes differ from reports? *(I.C.W.A., Inter.)*
14. What forms a good report? What are its different types? Describe briefly special reports. *(I.C.W.A., Inter.)*
15. What is an office report? State the principles of report preparation. *(B.Com. (Pass), Delhi)*
16. What is an office report? State the main points to be considered in drafting an office report. *(B.Com. (Pass), Delhi)*

17. You are asked by the director of your company on desirability of acquiring new premises for the office. Draft a suitable report in this regard. *(B.Com., (Pass) Delhi)*

18. Write short note on :

(i) Office Report *(B.Com. (Pass), Delhi,2000) (B.Com. (Punjab))*

19. Describe the format of a Project Report.

(B.Com. (Hons) I Paper VII (A) Delhi 2006A) (B.Com. (Hons.) I Paper VII (A) Delhi 2009)

20. Write short notes in about 50-60 words each:

(i) Features of a long report.

(ii) Different methods of Visual Presentation *(B.Com. (Hons.) I Paper VII (A) Delhi 2005A)*

21. Distinguish between Minutes and Reports. *(B.Com.(Hons.) I Paper VII (a) Delhi 2008)*

PRECIS WRITING

22. These are sections from the General Annual Report of a company. Summarise the sections under suitable headings :

(i) Director's Responsibility Statement

Your Directors wish to inform that the Audited Accounts containing Financial Statements for the financial year ended 31st March, 2004 are in full conformity with the requirements of the Companies Act, 1956. They believe that the Financial Statements reflect fairly, the form and substance of transactions carried out during the year and reasonably present your Company's financial condition and results of operations.

Your Directors further confirm that :

(i) In the presentation of the annual accounts, applicable accounting standards have been followed.

(ii) The accounting policies have been consistently applied and reasonable, prudent judgement and estimates are made so as to give a true and fair view of the state of affairs of your Comapny as at 31st March, 2004 and of the profit for the financial year ended 31st March, 2004;

(iii) Proper and sufficient care has been taken for the maintenance of adequate accounting records in accordance with the provisions of the Companies Act, 1956 for safeguarding the assets of your Company and for preventing and detecting frauds and other irregularities;

(iv) The annual accounts of your Comapny have been prepared on a going concern basis.

(ii) Appreciation

Your directors place on record their deep appreciation of the assistance and guidance provided by the Hon'ble Ministers Secretaries and other officals of the Ministry of Mines, the Central and the State Government Your Directors thank the financial institutions and banks associated with your campany for their support as well.

Your Company's employees are instrumental in your Company scaling new heights, year after year. Your Directors place on record their deep appreciation of the commitment and contribution of your Company's employees.

Your involvement as shareholders is greatly valued.

For and on behalf of the Board

Mumbai

Kumar Mangalam Birla

24th April, 2004

Chairman

(B. Com.(Hons. I Paper VII(a Delhi 2005 A)

23. Summarise the following passage and give it a suitable title.

Motivation is an internal force and we cannot measure the motivation of others directly. Instead, we typically infer whether or not other individuals are motivated by watching their behaviour. For example, we might conclude that an engineering friend who works late every evening, goes to the office on weekends, and incessantly reads the latest engineering journals is highly motivated to do well, Conversely, we might suspect that an engineering friend who is usually the first one out the door at quitting time, rarely puts in extra hours, and generally spends little time reading up on new developments in the field is not very motivated to excel. In the end, how successful these two engineers actually are with their respective projects is likely to depend not only on their motivation, as reflected in respective efforts, but also on their ability to handle the engineering subject matter Furthermore, working conditions can affect their performance. Numerous interruptions, extra assignments, or cramped office space may negatively influence performance. On the other hand, a quiet place to work, the help of assistants, and ample support resources, such as equipment, may have a positive effect on project performance. Thus actual performance is likely to be function of ability, motivation and working conditions. As a result, it is important that managers hire individuals who have the ability to do what is required. Then the management challenge is providing working conditions that nurture and support individual motivation to work toward organisational goals.

Management scholars have developed a number of theories that help us understand what motivates people at work. Our inner needs such as those of food, companionship or growth and cognitions such as knowledge and thoughts about efforts that we put and rewards we might receive, lead to various behaviours. Assuming that the behaviours are appropriate to the situation, they may result in rewards. The rewards then help reinforce our behaviours, fulfil our needs and influence our cognitions about the linkages between our behaviour and possible future rewards — (331 words) *(B.Com. (Hons.) I Paper VII(a) Delhi 2005 B)*

24. Make a precis of the following passage and suggest a suitable title:

Industrial Relations & Human Resource Management

The Company has always recognised manpower as its asset and that people are driving force for the growth and expansion of any company. The Company has always laid special emphasis on the training and development of its people during the year. Industrial relations during the year were cordial and peaceful.

The Company has taken a number of new initiatives like Balanced Scorecard for performance management and strategy deployment, Customer Relationship Management (CRM) to plan, build, retain and enhance profitable customer relationship and Supply Chain Management (SCM) to improve efficiencies and reduce costs.

As on March 31, 2002, the Company had 3,543 employees consisting of "I.T., counsellors, 371 coordinators and 3,172 facilitators.

Outlook

As India progressively moves to a free market environment, international producers will have increased access to the Indian market either through the establishment of manufacturing bases in India or from overseas. Indian manufacturers therefore would urgently need to re-engineer themselves, wherever possible, to compete in this environment in terms of costs, quality and product innovation. The initiatives of Abhishek Industries Limited over the past several years to modernise its facilities, focus on high-end products, substantially reduce its costs and to enhance its customer orientation will enable the company to face the global challenges ahead, both within India and in overseas markets.

Cautionary Statement

Statements in the Management Discussion and Analysis describing the Company's objectives, projections, estimates and expectations may be 'forward looking statements' within the meaning of applicable laws and regulations. Actual results may differ materially from those expressed or implied, important factors that couki make a difference to the Company's operations include economic conditions affecting demand/supply and price conditions in the domestic and overseas markets in which the Company operates, changes in Government regulations, tax laws and other incidential factors. *(B.Com.(Hons.) I Paper VII (a) Delhi 2006 A)*

25. Summarise the following passage in about one-third of its length and give it a uitable title:

Despite the pick-up in excise duty collections, which rose from overall 8.6 per cent to 15.7 per cent in the last month of the April-November period, the under-performance under this head become a continuing problem for successive finance ministers. To some extent, the modest level of excise collections (less than one-third of the Centre's gross tax revenue this year, and not much more than revenue om corporation tax) is explained by classification issues. Of the total customs revenue target for this year of Rs. 52,178 crores, roughly 45 per cent is to come from countervailing duty (CVD), which is essentially levied in lieu of excise duty. However, while this would boost the share of excise in the total, it does not explain the slow rate of increase in excise collections from one year to the next, especially when industrial growth is buoyant, Over the last three years, the average annual increase in collections has been less than 12 per cent, which is significantly slower than the overall rate of tax growth for the centre. It is hard to explain why this should be the case, when manufacturing is not a laggard sector of the economy. One explanation could be the plethora of rax rates and excise exemptions that still remain in the books, and the corruption this spawns as manufacturers try to take advantage of classification confusion, or multiple rates, or simply bribe officials in order to be able to pay lower duties. A study conducted by the National Institute of Public Finance and Policy estimates that the tax loss due to small-scale industry exemptions is around Rs. 12,500 crores. Similar exemptions are available for investors in backward states (the loss on this account is estimated at Rs. 2,000 crores) and on various commodities (Rs. 4,000 crores is lost under this head under the excise and customs heads). Anyone in doubt has merely to visit Baddi in Himachal Pradesh (which has become a tax haven), or look at the investment headed for Uttranchal, .another favored state. Another issue fo which the Finance Minister needs to devote some attention has to do with the modernisation of the tax-collection machinery. While the income tax machinery has been streamlined and modernised considerably, with the introduction of computerised records and the creation of a Tax Information Network (TIN), this does not apply to the excise department. If an individual spends Rs. 15 lakhs on buying a car and his income tax returns show an income of just Rs. 3 lakhs, the TIN will help the taxman catch him/her, or at least that is what it is supposed to do when fully operational. In the case of the excise department, however, there is no such IT-based system to catch under-reporting or lack of reporting. Indeed, everyone knows that modvat credits have been a racket for some time, precisely because the system is not foolproof. Straightforward analysis based on the Centre for Monitoring Indian Economy's Prowess database makes the problem clear. The top 50 excise-paying firms in the country accounted for around 70 per cent of the total excise paid by all the linns in the database. Yet, in terms of value addition, these firms accounted for only about half of total. In other words, the excise department appears to be doing a good job when it comes to the larger firms, but a whole lot of medium-scale ami smaller firms are not getting adequately taxed. Part of this could be due to the fact that the firms are exempt from taxes by virtue of their size. But the data certainly suggests that there is a substantial amount of excise evasion going on. A Finance Minister who is known to be keen on achieving his deficit reduction targets must improve excise-collection figures (627 words).

(B.Com.(Hons.) I (Paper VII (a) Delhi 2006B)

26. Make a precis of the following passage and suggest a suitable title.

Improvement Initiatives:

Your Company during the year under review undertook several initiatives to enhance its global competitiveness. The ASPIRF. programme encompasse: improvement initiatives like Six-Sigma, Total Productive Maintenance (TPM). Small Group Activities, Suggestion Management involving cross-section of employees. A new initiative 'ASPIRE Unlimited' programme based on the i'heon of Constraints (TOC) propounded by Dr. Eliyahu Goldratt is the latest challenge undertaken by your company to achieve excellence in quality. The key to success of this initiative is to devise business strategies aimed at increasing turnover and profitability through focusing markets as the 'constraint'. Various initiatives such as Buffer Management in the Supply Chain, Critical Chain Project Management and in Mining, under this programme have been undertaken. Your Company continues to focus its efforts and investments in Research and Development, Quality, Safety and Environment. As a result of the above initiatives, your C ompany has been able to achieve various operational improvements including the reduction of operating costs and increased branding presence through customer value management.

Safety :

In line with our Corporate Vision to improve the safety and quality of life of employees, your Company has initiated a safety excellence journey under the guidance of DuPont Safety Resources, world-class leader in safety. DuPont has helped to improve the safety performance of many industries across the globe The safety programme, which began at the Steel Works, has been rolled across all locations including mines. These initiatives have shown perceptible change in the behaviour of employees at and outside the place of work. Gains achieved are irreversible. The company aspires to become world-class in safety.

Human Resources :

Given the Company's ambitious growth plans in India and overseas, development of human resources assumes an even more important dimension. To prepare the Company's human resources for future responsibilities in terms of professional skills as well as business skills, several initiatives have been undertaken, such as rotation policy, leadership development programme, sponsored diploma programme and e-leaming.

(B.Com.(Hons.) I Paper VII (a) Delhi 2007B)

27. Summarise the following sections from the Annual report of a Company:

Chairman's Message:

"In order to pursue its global vision and to achieve size and scale of operations, it is imperative for the Company to expand its global footprint,"

Dear Shareholders,

During 2005, the global generies pharmaceutical industry underwent dynamic changes in the business environment. On the one hand, the developed markets led by the US were subjected to severe price erosion, while on the other hand, emerging tkets witnessed further increase in generic penetration, providing newer M-tunities to companies such as Ranbaxy. The industry experienced consolidation amongst key generic players, a trend which is expacted to gain momentum in the future.

Performance:

The Company's global performance during the year was impacted primarily by the adverse pricing pressures in our key market, the U.S.. However, despite this, we gained in market share for our products in the US, reflecting our commitment to fortify our existing presence in this market.

It is important to note that the Company's performance in other global markets such as BRICS (Brazil, Russia, India, China, South Africa) and Asia, has been buoyant. This has helped the Company maintain its global sales at the same level as last year, at US $ "1,178 million. I would like to mention here, that globally the outlook for 2006 is promising for generics in general, as a greater number oi branded products lose patent protection and face genericisation.

During 2005, the Company demonstrated its commitment to bring value to its' shareholders by implementing several projects company-wide, which are expected to yield results in the coming years. In this regard, the Company's foray into new markets, such as Canada and Italy, and the increase of its stake in its Japanese Joint Venture from 10% to 50%, will help improve the Company's performance in the long term. Several beneficial projects, related to capacity augmentation, modernisation and automation, at its manufacturing locations in India and overseas, have also been implemented.

Research and Development

A major recognition of Ranbaxy's contribution to the world of science was the inauguaration of its new Research and Development Centre by the Hon'ble President of India, Dr. A.P.J. Abdul Kalam. During his address, the President appreciated the progress made by Ranbaxy and recognised the value brought by its research community to the world of science. He expressed his desire to see Ranbaxy as the first Indian Company to launch its own molecule in the global pharma space. He also expressed his confidence in Ranbaxy's ability as a Pharma leader to bring glory to the nation, by placing India as a 'shining star' on the global firmament. Our commitment to fight the diseases of the developing world, is reflected through the progress our scientists have made on our anti-malarial molecule, RBx 11160, which is being developed jointly with Medicines for Malaria Venture (MMV), Geneva. During the year, this molecule successfully completed Proof of Concept Phase II(a) studies and the activities for Phase II (*b*) studies are underway, with trials in India, Thailand and Africa scheduled to commerce by mid-2006. *(B.Com. (Hons.) I Paper VII (a) 2007 Delhi Cat. B)*

28. Make a precis of the following passage and suggest a suitable title :

Old business and hiring structures are both being replaced by a global sourcing model that places emphasis on doing the work where it makes more sense, sourcing resources from where they are the cheapest and of the best quality and delivering where there is the best client interface. This had led to the formation of a global workforce that collaborates seamlessly to create profit for the host country and the country where the organisation is headquartered.

Globalisation of IT has led to extensive movement of professionals from one country to another. Technology also has the potential to change culture and economic structures. Changes in behaviour, technology, demographic resources and global competition are forcing businesses to strategically adopt to new ways to fill talent scarcity gaps. It is interesting to note how different companies around the world are sourcing talent to fill their needs.

Companies are recruiting talent to immigrate back to their homelands from all over the world. And money is not the prime motivator for global movement as people are willing to make the move for less. It's the improving quality of life around the world that compels talent to consider such a move.

Another trend is the split between recruitment and deployment. Thus an IT company can be headquartered in Mumbai, recruit programmers from the Philippines and deploy them in the UK.

Organisations are also investing in developing robust internal growth opportunities. Companies are more open to hiring fresh graduates and investing in their training—both for technical skills as well as domain knowledge. Some other changes that are happening in the hiring process are newer locations globally that are now becoming the hiring base especially at the entry level. More number of expats are coming in at senior positions to be based in India and senior executives are relocating with their families to India—whereas till sometime back, it would not be so. *(B.Com. (Hons.). I Paper VII (a) Delhi 2008)*

29. Make a precis of the following passage in 100 words, and suggest a suitable title :

"CRISES CHANGE people's mindset and their behaviour. The deeper and longer the crisis, the deeper and more permanent are the changes.

Businessmen are now asking, "When will things get back to normal ?" If by normal they mean the way things were back in *early 2008*, then the answer is, "Not for a long time."

That sounds pessimistic but actually isn't. On New Years' Eve 2007, youngsters thronged restaurants and shopping centres. *Jobs were easy, credit cards rampant,* and *mall builders* optimistic. In numbers, those days may come back. The jobs, the sales, the salaries, even the credit will eventually climb back to that 'normal'. But what won't come back is that euphoric feeling.

In America, people say that the *Great Depression* changed the way a whole generation thought about money, about financial risk and about savings. In India, things will never get as bad as that.

Indians who joined the workforce before 1990 or so have a different way of thinking about money. They grew up in an atmosphere in which intelligent college students used to get easily depressed just thinking about the future. And they don't take opportunities for granted.

I think a good majority of the later generation has negative savings and a negative net worth. They have casually predicated years—even decades—of their future on being able to maintain a growing income flow. And that is exactly where the economic crisis has hit like a psychological tsunami.

I don't know whether the crisis will get much worse. But if all it does, if it readjusts a whole generation's attitude to savings, it would almost be worth it. The future is not a straight line upwards. Instead it is a cycle that will have its ups and downs.

This realisation alone could save India's vaunted household savings rate from being flushed down the drain of the new consumerism. *(B.Com.(Hons.) I Paper VII (a) Delhi 2009)*

Chapter **4**

OFFICE FORMS — DESIGN, MANAGEMENT AND CONTROL

CONTENTS

Chapter **4**

OFFICE FORMS — DESIGN, MANAGEMENT AND CONTROL

> ***"In many offices, if indeed not in most, practically no scientific analysis and study has ever been made of the forms in use, and the result is an unnecessary waste of time, paper, effort and money."***
> **— LEFFINGWELL AND ROBINSON**

OFFICE FORMS

According to Leffingwell, "forms are printed sheets of paper or cardboard used to collect and transmit information."[1] They are the basic tools of all office work, and they assist in the fundamental functions of receiving, recording, arranging and giving information in the office. Every office activity centres round one or the other printed form. What is more, by reason of their close affinity with office systems, forms have a bearing on the efficiency of office organisation. That is why Frank M. Knox has plainly stated that "nothing happens in an office except to, or by means of, pieces *of* paper." Denver[2] defines an office form as "a printed piece of paper or card on which entries are usually made against marked headings." It excludes plain envelopes which are stationery, but includes all printed matter of any kind. Without printed office forms, all information would be given in an arbitrary way, and little systematised attention would be paid to data. By using forms, every essential information required for an efficient conduct of the business is recorded, arranged and transmitted in a systematic way. Moreover, the use of forms leads to a considerable saving in time and energy, for they reduce the amount of manual or machine writing. This becomes possible because, on all the forms, constant and fixed data is printed and blank space is left for valuable information to be inserted. The person using the form need not write the fixed data again and again; he has only to fill up the blank space on the form. Apart

1. Leffingwell and Robinson: *Textbook of Office Management*, p. 21
2. J.C. Denyer: *Office Management*, p. 411.

from saving time, the use of forms reduces the cost of office operations. Since office work constitutes various routine operations, the use of forms reduces the monotony of repeatedly writing various items already printed on the forms.

To sum up, "An office form[3] is a printed piece of paper which provides space for entering records, information or instructions which are to be conveyed to other individuals, departments or enterprises." Examples of forms are purchase orders, requisitions, debit-notes, pay-in-slips, invoices, account sales, etc.

Purposes of Forms: The purposes of forms may be summarised as follows:

1. They make clear *what information* must be gathered and communicated.
2. They provide a *specific location* for each item of information needed, thus speeding data entry, processing, and reference.
3. They *eliminate* the need for recopying standard or *repetitive information.*
4. They facilitate use of *multiple copies,* often greatly simplifying procedures as a result.
5. They *identify records* and facilitate filing and future reference.

Advantages of Using Forms

1. Simplify Systems and Routines: Office forms make clear what information should be gathered. Thus forms simplify office systems and routines. No office system can afford to function smoothly without them.

2. Reduce Cost of Office Operations: Office forms eliminate the need for recopying repetitive or standard information and thus save time and energy. The result is a reduction in the cost of office operations.

3. Facilitates Operations: Forms make for uniformity in appearance and format. They facilitate identification of records and simplify filing and sorting operations.

4. Preservation of Records: Forms help to preserve records of business for filing and future reference. Since forms preserve records, they also help the organisation in achieving better planning procedures.

5. Fixation of Responsibility: Individual responsibility can be fixed by providing a column in the forms for the initials of the person who has filled in or checked the form at any stage of the work.

6. Facilitate Data Processing: Forms provide a specific location for each item of the information that is needed; they facilitate the work of data processing and reference.

7. Other Services: If forms are used as records and are properly preserved, better services can be provided to vendors, dealers, customers, shareholders, creditors, etc. Good forms project a good image of the organisation among the public, and enhance the goodwill of the organisation.

---

3. According to Littlefield and Rachel etc., 'A form is a piece of paper with fixed data and blank spaces for variable data." Thus information that is constant or known in advance can be made a standard part of the form. It is then necessary lo fill in only the information that varies with each transaction: this information is labelled specifically and occupies a standard position on the form, thus reducing uncertainty and saving time.
4. Littlefield and Rachel etc., Management *of Office Operations,* p. 159.

Types of Forms

Office forms may be broadly classified on the basis of the operations or office functions for which they are used, e.g., accounting forms, stores control forms, application forms, sales forms, purchase forms, correspondence forms, etc.

Office forms may also be classified as:

(i) *Single copy forms,* which are complete in themselves and often become the source documents;

(ii) *Multiple copies forms,* which are made in duplicate or triplicate (or more copies may be obtained) and which may be used to transmit information or serve the function of providing additional records;

(iii) *Internal office forms,* which are received or used by the employees of the business, *e.g.*, accounting forms, application forms, memorandum forms and requisitions; and

(iv) *External contact forms,* which are sent to customers, creditors and others, *e.g.*, order forms, invoices, cheques, purchase orders, etc.

Some types of forms may be used by the office more frequently than the others. They may also be in different designs, shapes, sizes and colours.

FORMS CONTROL[5]

As already stated, forms are an important element of an office system. They are the basic tools of all office activity. Generally speaking, all office forms are handled at least three times; someone has to put the information on the form; someone has to read and understand it after the information has been written down; and, many a times, someone has to copy the information or part of it on still another form; then, after everybody has seen it, the forms are filed, bound into book form, or destroyed.[6] In view of these facts, it is obvious that careful attention should be paid to the design, proper use and effective control of forms for that would ensure appreciable savings to any office.

However, if too much emphasis is laid on the use of forms, the result would be that the number and types of forms may increase more than is actually necessary, and office work would multiply. Instead of improving efficiency, the usage of forms may adversely affect it and step up the cost of office operations. There is, therefore, a need for a proper management and control of the use of forms, so that only the relevant forms are introduced and are designed to ensure economy and efficiency in office operations. The addition or elimination of only one form may mean the addition or elimination of one or more clerks to handle that form. It has been estimated that, for every rupee worth of printed paper, Rs. 20 to Rs. 25 of clerical labour is required to use the form and deal with it. Hence, the necessity of forms management and control.

5. According to Littlefield, "Forms control is a means of exercising management control over the costs of producing and processing forms," *op. cit,* p. 166.
6. Leffingwell, *op. cit.*, p. 211.

Objectives of Forms Control

By means of forms control,[7] the office management seeks to achieve the following objectives:

(i) To retain and use only those forms that are really necessary;

(ii) To ensure that the necessary forms are designed most efficiently, and render the best possible service at the lowest cost;

(iii) To produce forms by the most appropriate and economical method;

(iv) To provide copies of forms only to those who have a justifiable reason for having them;

(v) To study whether the introduction of new forms, or the revision of old forms, is essential;

(vi) To review periodically all the forms in use so as to determine their utility in current situations;

(vii) To evaluate form design primarily on the basis of the time required to use the forms.

B.H. Walley[8] lists the following five reasons for forms control:

(i) To have a record of all the forms in use in the company;

(ii) To combine and eliminate as many forms as possible;

(iii) To reduce the size of the forms in use and to see to it that they are used more frequently;

(iv) To prevent the indiscriminate use of new forms;

(v) To co-operate with the reprographic services department in choosing the best method of document reproduction.

Steps in Forms Control

Forms control implies a proper designing, printing, economical use and supply of forms so that office work may be efficiently and effectively performed. The following steps may be suggested for a proper forms control:

1. Establishing Centralised Administration: The first step in forms control is to set up a centralised authority for it. In large organisations, a Forms Control Department may be established, and an executive may head this department. Alternatively, a committee of individuals possessing adequate knowledge of forms and their control may be set up or a Forms Supervisor may be appointed as a centralised authority for forms control. Whatever the alternative employed, it is essential to have a central authority of forms control with responsibility for performance.

2. Preparation of Forms Register: The centralised forms control authority should collect at least two copies of each and every office form in use and paste them into a Forms Book or Forms Register. A separate list or index of all the forms included in the Forms Book Register should also be made.

3. Listing of Office Routines: Since the designing and use of forms are closely linked with office procedures and routines, it is necessary for the forms control section to obtain a list of these routines. The relevant forms may then be classified, marked and numbered according to the procedure or department using them.

7. Denyer, *op. cit.*, p. 411.
8. *Op. cit.*, pp. 16-168.

4. Investigation and Analysis: All forms should be analysed periodically to determine whether any of them can be eliminated, combined with others, or improved. Such a step may sometimes call for a reorganisation of some office routines. For instance, a single copy form may be converted into a multiple-copies form so that its copy or copies are passed from one office worker to another, with a slight change in the routine. Some forms may be re-organised. This may mean that forms not required are eliminated, and the basic information relevant to different forms is printed on each of them.

5. Printing and Reproduction: After adopting the forms, the forms supervisor should decide on the method of reproduction to be followed. The printing of the forms may be done outside the organisation; but their reproduction may be done in office, with the help of the stencil or other duplication/reproduction process. After consulting the heads of various departments, the forms supervisor should decide on:

(a) The quantity of forms required;
(b) The quality of paper to be used;
(c) The design and size of the form.

Finally, with the approval of the Office Manager, an order for the printing of forms should be placed.

6. Standardisation of Forms: Lastly, if the situation warrants, it is better to have standardisation. A standardisation of forms ensures that the size, colour and quality of the paper used and printing style for all the forms is uniform and standardised. It reduces the cost of forms and confusion about its use.

Determining Quantity of Forms

It is important to determine the exact and economical quantity of forms to be produced or ordered at one time. This is required to ensure.

(a) An even flow (supply) of forms without interruption;
(b) Avoidance of unnecessary capital which is blocked in forms which are procured when they are not immediately required; and
(c) Economy through bulk procurement of forms, keeping in view that there is no unnecessary wastage of forms and that they do not become outdated. To decide about the quantity of forms to be ordered, the following factors should be carefully considered:
   (i) Past experience of the rate of consumption;
   (ii) Capital investment to be made for bulk order;
   (iii) Lead time for obtaining supplies;
   (iv) Expected saving in the cost of ordering quantities;
   (v) Possibility of changes in a form;
   (vi) Cost of storage and interest on the capital invested in forms.

If it is decided to arrange for 10 weeks supply of forms and the lead time for getting supplies is 2 weeks it would be appropriate to order a quantity that would last for 12 weeks. A cost benefit analysis should be made, and it should be ensured that the benefit derived from bulk orders is not less than the total additional cost of storage and loss of interest on the capital invested. For this purpose the following formula may be used to determine the most economic quantity to be ordered:

$$EOQ = \sqrt{\frac{2AO}{C}}$$

where,

EOQ = Economic Order Quantity (also called the standard quantity to be ordered)

A = Average consumption over a period (say, a week, a month, etc.)

O = Ordering costs per order

C = Carrying cost of forms expressed as a percentage of the invoice price of forms.

FORM DESINING

The designing of forms is an important function of office management. Since forms are the basic tools of office systems and routines, it is necessary that they should be well designed and complete in all respects. The guiding principle of form design is that the efficiency of the office staff should be maximized so that the cost of office operations may be reduced. It should be remembered that the cost of labour in processing the forms is generally 20 to 25 times more than the cost of paper and the printing of forms.

J.C. Denyer lists the following disadvantages of a badly designed form over a well designed form:

1. Forms are basic tools of office work, *i.e.*, for recording and communicating information. A badly designed form impedes this function most seriously and jeopardises the working of the entire organisation.
2. Badly designed forms inherits mistakes in clerical work. Sometimes a single error may cost the company many times more than the cost of printing and forms put together.
3. A badly designed form is bound to increase the manual labour required to process it and impair efficiency.
4. A badly designed form may also have an adverse impact on the goodwill and reputation which the organisation enjoys.
5. A badly designed form may have a psychological effect on people using it. It may lead to frustration among people using it.
6. Office forms are related to systems of the organisation. A well designed system may be ruined by badly designed forms.

Forms Design[9] properly done, is the purposeful creation of that effective form which is an adequate information processing tool. Three things identify the effective form:

1. It is an integral part of the information processing system in which it is used. The system will not function properly unless this form is used with each transaction in the right way at the right time.
2. It facilitates the recording, analysis and transmission of clearly defined data items. It includes all of the information required to complete a particular transaction; it does not

9. Carl Heyel: *The Encylopaedia of Management*, 2nd Ed., p. 268.

contain excess or extraneous data. Another form is not required to supplement or facilitate its use.

3. It can be used with the minimum of special knowledge or training. The nature, meaning and significance of the data to be entered are clearly indicated in the form itself.

A proper forms designing may eliminate a few forms by combining one or more forms or improving upon them. This would result in savings in the cost of the eliminated forms and in wage bills. To some extent, these objectives may be achieved merely by a simplification of the forms. There are certain other principles of forms design which should receive the serious attention of the forms supervisor.

Principles of Forms Design

In designing forms, the following principles should be observed:

1. Principle of Purpose: The purpose for which a form is required should be ascertained before it is introduced. The general purpose of a form is to make clerical work easier than would be possible if a blank sheet is used. When a plain sheet of paper can serve the purpose, there is no need to introduce a form. The form designer should obtain answers to the following questions, before introducing a new form:

(i) What is the purpose of the form?

(ii) If the form has more than one purpose, which is the most important?

(iii) Is the purpose justifiable?

(iv) Will the purpose of the form be fully accomplished by its use?

(v) Is there another form, for the same, or a similar purpose, now in use elsewhere in the office?

A form should be used:

(a) To record something;

(b) When recording is done repetitively;

(c) When it is necessary to record all relevant information at one place;

(d) When it is desirable to fix the responsibility for the work done on individuals by providing spaces for their initials on the form.

2. Principle of Standardisation: According to this principle, the size of the form, the quality of paper, the method of reproduction, etc., should be standardised so that the maximum economy in cost of forms may be achieved.

3. Paper and Paper Sizes: Standard paper sizes should always be used where possible and the forms should fit in available filing equipment. The size of the form should be the smallest that will accommodate the information required. Paper quality should be in keeping with the forms' intended use. Different coloured paper should be used with discretion. Non-standard sizes, carbon interleaved paper, carbon less copy paper and gummed pads should only be used if there is a confirmed economic use for them. Adhering to standard paper sizes will ensure less wastage in cutting and ease in printing. The internationally acceptable paper sizes are designated as per the following code numbers:

Designated Code No.	Size of Paper (Mm)[9a]
A0	841 × 1189
A1	549 × 841
A2	420 × 549
A3	297 × 420
A4	210 × 297
A5	148 × 210
A6	105 × 148
A7	74 × 105
A8	53 × 74
A9	37 × 53
A10	27 × 37

4. Principle of Centralised Control: The process of designing, use, replacement, elimination, etc., of forms should be centrally controlled. Duplication of forms and retention of outdated or replaced forms and wastage in the use of forms can be avoided by having a centralised control of forms under one executive (who may be the forms supervisor or even the office manager himself) who would be responsible for their design, printing, etc.

Form Designing Process:[10]

The form design may be achieved systematically in a series of stages. These are:

(i) List the items to appear on the form and check that each serves a purpose;

(ii) Determine the order in which the items should appear to suit the convenience of the person filling up the form;

(iii) Determine the order in which the items should appear to suit the convenience of the person reading and using the form;

(iv) Compromise, if necessary, between (ii) and (iii);

(v) Determine the space necessary for each item;

(vi) Prepare rough layouts leading to the final draft.

Factors Affecting Form Design

In designing the forms, it is necessary to consider the following factors:

1. Purpose: Forms should suit the purpose for which they are designed. The general purpose of every form is to make clerical operations easy, but the specific purpose of every form should be ascertained, keeping in view the kind, source and mode of receiving the information required and the alternative means of obtaining it.

2. Ease in Use: Forms should be so designed that they are easy to use. A form which is to be used on typewriter or on a book keeping, billing or adding machine should be so designed that there is a minimum number of starting places for the typist, because each new starting position on the form requires an extra operation in setting the machine. Moreover, on all such forms,

9a. B.H. Walley: *Handbook of Office Management.*

10. Mills and Standingford, *op. cit,* p. 389.

there should be accurate spacing between the typed lines (10 lines to 4 cms.) So as to avoid the necessity of adjusting the typewriter after every line. Also, horizontal and vertical lines should be omitted on such forms because they are quite unnecessary.[11]

3. Simplicity: Forms should be simply designed so that everyone may easily learn their use. Information should be placed on the form where it will best serve the purpose. However, simplicity should not be at the cost of the purpose for which a form is meant. Simplicity implies clear column headings, adequate numbering and simplicity of the language in which instructions are given. The information *on* the form may be logically arranged in the following order:

(a) All identification matter (such as name, address, serial number, etc.) should be somewhere near the top right-hand side of the form. When forms are to be bound at the top, the identification matter should be at the bottom.

(b) Adequate space should be provided on the body of the form for the entries to be made on it.

(c) Special instructions, such as shipping instructions, on an order form should be placed at the appropriate place, in bold type, to catch the eyes of the user.

4. Title and Numbering: Every form should have a name and number. A name is more easily remembered than a number. The usual practice is to give both on a form. To avoid confusion, all such names should be standardised and printed on the form. The name should be short yet clearly descriptive, arid the numbering system, should be clearly thought out. A serial number should be assigned to each type of form to facilitate record-keeping by the store-keeper.

5. Proper Size: No form should be longer or bigger than is necessary to ensure that what is to be written on it is entered in a readable form. The size of the form may be determined by considering the following factors:

(a) Columns should be wide enough to allow for the entries to be made;

(b) Columns should be long enough to allow for the average number of entries to be made;

(c) The nature of the description required to be entered at the top and the space needed for it.

It is advisable to fix standard size of the form so that wastage may be avoided while cutting the standard size paper available in the market.

6. Proper Type Face or Printing: If the forms are to be printed, a clear type face should be chosen so that they may be read with ease in natural or artificial light. The type to be used usually depends upon the purpose for which a form is needed. However, an effort should be made to give a neat look to it. It is not advisable to use more than one type face, or at the most two type faces on any one printed sheet.

7. Use of Proper Paper: The quality of paper which is used should be appropriate to the purpose, having regard to the extent to which it will be handled and the method of making entries on it. The principal considerations are:

(a) *Physical Handlin* : If a form is handled many times or is to be retained for reference over

11. Leffingwell, *op. cit.*, p. 216.

a long period, a good quality of paper is necessary. If on the other hand, it is to be used once or twice only, it would be appropriate to use a less expensive paper.

(b) *Appearance:* The quality of the paper has a considerable effect on the appearance of forms. For example, invoices are sometimes on high quality paper to create a good impression on customers,

(c) *Methods:* The paper should be suited to the clerical processes through which it will pass. "If entries are to be made in ink, a non-absorbent paper should be used; if in pencil, almost any quality would be suitable. If several carbon copies of a form are required, a thin paper would be required. Photo copying processes may call for the use of translucent paper."[12]

According to Littlefield, "Paper for a form should be dictated by use, including:

(1) Appearance;

(2) Amount of handling,

(3) Number of copies to be produced in one writing,

(4) Length of time to be retained, and

(5) Specific use of form.

8. Provision for Punching, Sorting, Perforation etc.: Forms should alow for the operations of punching, scoring and perforating. If forms are to be punched for filing, standard spaces for holes should be provided. Scoring refers to the drawing of a line to indicate the place at which a form is to be folded for purposes of filing, storing, etc. Perforating refers to row of small holes, as over a sheet of postage stamps, or to a series of short dashes which cut partially through the paper. Most printers are equipped with perforating machinery; but the exact place for perforation should be indicated by the form designer.

9. Other Elements in Forms Design: Apart from all these factors, the following points[13] should be borne in mind when designing forms:

(a) Company titles should not be used on internal forms.

(b) A place for the signature should be provided at the bottom right hand side of the form.

(c) Instructions on filing in the form should, as far as possible, be placed at the top of form.

(d) In designing a form, a ballot-box type design should be encouraged so that only the requisite data are recorded. When possible, the use of abbreviations should be encouraged.

(e) The thickness of ruled lines should determine.

- The boundary betwen data items.
- The areas which need special attention.
- The boundary between parts of a form.
- Lines where signatures are needed or data required.

12. Mills and Standingford, op. at., p. 391.
13. See Walley, *op. cit., p.* 172.

(f) Wherever possible, the form should be designed to accommodate the minimum data. For example, a tick or a cross should indicate the answer to a question. This is better than making it necessary for a person to say "yes" or "no".

(g) The forms designer should be aware of the filing arrangements in effect in the office so that adequate margins should be allowed on forms for punching or perforating etc.

(h) Wherever data are recorded sequentially, the boxes or columns should follow the sequence,

(i) If the form is to be mailed, provision should be made for the use of window envelopes.

(j) When forms are used as source of documents for the Electronic Data Processing (EDP), the layout should be arranged with a view to easy card/tape punching.

Methods of Form Designing

The design of record and report form is very important from the standpoint of indicating the data required, use of the paper surface, and indicating the sequence in which information should be entered. The different methods (plans) of form designing as given below should be carefully considered:

1. Boxing: Under this plan, the entire surface of the form is "boxed" in with most of the printing to show the data to be inserted entered in upper left hand corner, or at the top of each 'boxed' area. If this plan of design is followed skilfully, it makes better use of the form surface than any other plan; and provides as well, a good appearing record and report form; and are easily used by the clerical force.

2. Lines: This plan of designing forms provides for the use of lines chiefly as a basis both for printing the information required and the entering of the data. In other words, the instructions and data are entered on the same line level. This is the most common plan of preparing forms. Its effectiveness depends chiefly on the order in which data is provided for, and the extent to which the printed information describes the data required.

3. Headings: In designing forms, headings are used commonly to call attention to the information areas in which data is to be entered. Usually, the headings occupy considerable space, and sometimes result in wasting paper surface. If used carefully, this plan helps make a good looking form and facilitate entering and reading report data.

4. Columnar Design: Often it is helpful to adopt the columnar idea so that information may be entered in columns. This type of design is particularly applicable to the tabulation of figures where this is a form of information to be transmitted or recorded.

5. Spacing: Spacing is important for both appearance and use. Typing requires spacing in multiples of one-sixth inch. Handwriting requires one-fourth to one-third inch between lines.

As a general rule, neither of these methods of form design will be used exclusively method of design depends chiefly on the use to be made of the form and the type of information to be recorded on it. Skilful application of these methods in the form design should rest improved design, economy in paper, and greater simplicity in clerical operations, regardless of the method chosen.

SPECIMENS OF FORM DESIGN

Form 1: Purchase Order

INDO EURO EXPORTS

NEW FRIENDS COLONY,
NEW DELHI - 110065
(Purchase Order)

No.......

Tel. : 27651701
22514865
Fax : 23114445

Dated.............

Dear Sir,

Your quotation No.........dated .... has been accepted. Please supply the following items mentioned herein and the term and conditions mentioned overleaf.

S.No.	*Description*	*Unit*	*Qty.*	*Rate Per Unit*	*Amount*	*Delivery Required*		*Remarks*
						Date	*Place*	

Terms of Delivery ____________

Packing/Shipping Instructions

Terms of Payment ____________

Bank Through ____________

Copy to 1. ____________

2. ____________

3. ____________

For **Indo-Euro Exports**

Purchase Officer

Form 2: Invoice

INDO-EURO EXPORTS No. 157/09

NEW FRIENDS COLONY,
NEW DELHI - 110 065

(Invoice)

No.......

Tel. : 27651701
22514865
Fax : 23114445

Dated.............

Sold to M/s ____________ Invoice No. ____________

Customer No. ____________

____

Shipped to ____________

____

____

S. No.	*Qty.*	*Description*	*Stock Code*	*Unit*	*Rate per unit*	*Gross Amount*	*Discount if any*		*Net Amount*
							Rate %	*Amount*	

Total Due Rs.

Please make the payment:

Before ____________ For **INDO-EURO EXPORTS**

Through ____________

E. & O. E Sales Manager

Designing Forms for External Use

These are the forms which are set by one organisation or commercial undertaking to another and often include purchase orders, letter heads, delivery notes, invoices, statements of accounts, etc. Forms in general use in different organisations should conform, as far as practicable, with normal practice in size and design, so that they may be used, handled and filed with ease in the recipient offices. Such conformity saves time and minimises errors in the reading of the forms, for items of informaion are found in the expected position. The British Standards Insitute has drawn up standard sizes and recommended layouts for letter heads, orders, delivery notes, invoices and statements of accounts. It has recommended that :

(i) On all letter heads, reference should consist of "Your Ref. and date," and "Our Ref. and date";

(ii) On orders, the suppliers' reference, the customers' reference and the date of order should be given in sequence;

(iii) On all forms, the bottom is reserved for printed terms and conditions or instructions, etc., or for a reference to conditions printed on the back, and so on.

Designing EDP Forms: With the increase in the use of computers in modern offices, EDP forms have added a new dimension in forms designing while the features of both the EDP and non-EDP forms are common, certain additional points should be taken care of while designing EDP forms. These are:

(i) Computer forms are printed on continuous stationery which consists of long uncut rolls of paper which are perforated between each page.

(ii) Whereas non-EDP forms are roller-fed on typewriters, EDP forms are printed by holes on their edges.

(iii) Line and space requirements and the size of EDP forms are also different than for typed or handwritten forms.

(iv) Where forms are required in multiple copies for use by different departments/persons, specialised form sets for use in computers should be used.

(v) For designing of EDP forms, advice of software designers/programmers should be taken.

MICR & OCR Forms: A significant development in forms design has been the development and widespread utilisation of MICR (Magnetic Ink Character Recognition) and OCR (Optical Character Recognition).

MICR process is used extensively in banks to sort and process cheques. It employs a magnetised ink that can be sensed or read by specialised machines. The MICR numbers printed on cheques are those needed to clear cheques promptly — the cheque number, the branch code number, the routing/transit number and so on. The characters are read by automatic equipment and transmitted to a computer for processing-updating account balances and printing a customer's bank statement.

OCR is a system that permits alphabetic and numeric data to be read by electronic means. OCR differs from MICR in that no particular kind of ink must be used since the machine that reads the characters does so in such the same way as the human eye reads printed matter. The data is converted into electrical impulses and relayed to the computer system for processing.[14]

---

14. Littlefield and Rachel, *op. cit.*, p. 160.

Disposal of Obsolete Forms: A form no longer in use should be disposed of. Before disposing of, it is necessary to obtain the approval of the head of the department using that form. This approval should be in writing and, if possible, on a copy of the form itself.[15] As soon as a form is declared dead:

(i) Its inventory should be taken out and sold in the market as waste paper, or
(ii) It should be destroyed in the presence of the forms supervisor.

The stock register should be rectified accordingly. The disposal of obsolete forms is advantageous in two respects.

(i) It vacates the storage space occupied by such forms; and
(ii) It relieves the storekeeper of the burden of keeping a record of the forms not in use,

FORM SETS

It is convenient to use sets of forms when more than one copy of any document is required. Form sets facilitate the making of multiple copies by a single writing method. They may be constructed in the following ways:

(i) Sets of Loose Sheets and Carbon Paper: This is the simplest and most commonly used method of making form sets. By this method, the office typist or clerk assembles the forms and carbon paper into the place before typing or writing. But this method suffers from the following drawbacks:

(a) It is time-consuming, for it requires preparatory work for making form sets;
(b) If carbon papers are not used with care, copies may become illegible;
(c) if carbon paper is overused, the copies may be dim;
(d) If the carbon paper is not placed properly, the matter may not be recorded except on the first copy;
(e) Only a limited number of copies can be made.

(ii) Sets in Pads: Identical forms or forms collated into sets may be gathered into pads or bound in such a way that all the copies are perfectly aligned. Carbon paper is usually inserted at the time of use, and the sheets are removed after use. A strip of cloth is also used to hold the sheets firmly in the pad. Where form sets are bound in a book form, the record copy of each form set is retained in the book. When forms sets are gathered in a pad, the record copies can be placed in a lever file, and they may be bound when their number reaches 100 or so;

(iii) Sets in Gangs: The term gang refers to group of two or more identical forms printed on a single sheet which are separated by perforations. Gang sets may be in a loose form; but they are often bound into pads or collated and glued into units sets. All the sheets may by collated and perforated into gangs, or the record copies may not be perforated and used as a register.

(iv) Unit Sets: Under this method, variable lengths and widths of the respective sheets in the sets are used. Unit sets may be constructed in two ways. Unit blocked sets may be made of sheets of variable size. Under this method, individual forms are collated into sets and every single lot is glued. The sets are separated with the help of a paper cutter. Snap sets are prepared by

15. Liffingwelf, *op. cit.*, p. 233.

having a perforated stub portion holding the sheets together. The process facilitates easy separation of copies and removal of carbon paper.

The unit set method has the following features:

(a) Forms of variable length and width may be used;

(b) Papers of different colours, printed in different colours and of different weight and quality can be combined;

(c) Individual copies from the set may be easily removed;

(d) Parts of a set can be separated from each other, and each section remains intact,

(v) Continuous Sets: Continuous sets are also known as continuous stationery, which is discussed in the following paragraphs.

CONTINUOUS STATIONERY

Continuous Stationery may be defined as a device whereby office forms are produced in a continuous strip, and where the separate forms are usually divided from one another by perforations: and whereof several copies are usually detained by the use of various copying methods."[16] It comprises of various forms such as — invoices special accounting forms, etc. — which are printed and supplied in *continuous strip* made up of a series that comes in multiple copy sets separated from each other by perforation. The system implies that various office forms are not bound in a book or pad form, from which they are torn off and interleaved with carbon paper by the clerk typist when he wants to make the desired number of copies. With continuous stationery, several copies are obtained by the use of copying methods without going through the process of tearing off forms and inserting carbon papers.

Fig. 4.1 Continuous Stationery Fanfold

16. Denyer, *op. cit,* p. 226.

Advantages: The use of Continuous Stationery offers the following advantages:

(i) Saving in time in relation to costs is the prime advantage of the use of continuous stationery, for its use avoids the monotonous process of assembling the different copies of a form, interleaving them with carbon paper, feeding separate forms into the machine and detaching them after use.

(ii) It facilitates the optimum use of typewriters, accounting machines etc.

(iii) The user suffers from less fatigue and his efficiency is increased because of considerable saving in time following the elimination of various operations.

(iv) Use of continuous stationery reduces monotony in the office work concerned with the use of multiple forms.

Disadvantages: The disadvantages of Continuous Stationery are:

(i) Corrections and alterations cannot be made with ease, especially when many copies in a set are prepared.

(ii) Forms are spoiled by the pressure or friction of the typing machine rollers on carbon paper.

(iii) Where many forms are interleaved with carbon copies, they may go out of alignment; and in certain forms — for example, invoices — figures may be typed in wrong places in copies. This creates problems for the users.

(iv) Continuous Stationery is rather expensive, and therefore only larger undertakings find its use profitable.

Types of Continuous Stationery

There are three basic types of continuous stationery:

(i) Roll Stationery: In this, the forms are in a continuous roll. Forms printed on a teleprinter, an adding machine, a cash register, etc., are of this type. There are no perforations, and the forms are simply torn off against a metal cutting edge when the message is typed. This type of stationery is generally used on flatbed typewriters which are equipped with rolls of carbon paper moving across the form strips.

(ii) Interfold Stationery: It is the name given to that type of Continuous Stationery where forms are perforated and the stationery is interleaved and folded flat in a concertina fashion. Interfold stationery is also known as flatpack stationery.

(iii) Fanfold Type: In a fanfold or Z-type of Continuous Stationery, separate copies of the forms are joined together end to end and side to side. They are separated from one another by horizontal and vertical perforations. If a number of sets of the fanfold stationery are pulled out, they would open up in the form of a fan; hence its name."[17] This kind of Continuous Stationery is particularly useful:

(a) When forms of different widths are incorporated in a set; and

(b) When pre-punching of filing holes prevent the use of sprocket feeding.

17. J.C. Denyer: *op. cit.*, p. 227.

Factors in Selection of Form Sets

Different types of form sets may be constructed according to specific requirements or the purpose for which they may be used. The following factors may be considered in selecting a particular type of form set:

(i) The number of copies required;

(ii) The method of writing (long-hand or machine);

(iii) The type of carbon paper needed (one-time carbon or carbon backing);

(iv) The method of inserting and removing the carbon paper;

(v) The quality of the paper suitable for each copy;

(vi) The size of each copy in a particular set;

(vii) The filing method adopted for each copy;

(viii) The method of separating and sorting the copies;

(ix) The variable information required to be printed on each copy.

In India, the Continuous Stationery concept is fast gaining popularity, The system of sets of loose sheets and carbon paper is used quite commonly. Sets in pad or book form are the other popular methods of using Continuous Stationery.

Forms File: It is common practice to have two types of forms file. The first is a *numerical file,* which files all forms by identifying numbers on the forms and includes a sample of the form, specifications, and changes that may affect the design or quantity to be ordered at the next printing. The second is a *functional file* in which forms are filed by the function, they serve. The functional file uses classification — forms collected by subject, operation, and function served. These files serve as an excellent tool for indicating the possibility for eliminating or consolidating forms."[18]

Careful analysis of quality, volume and costs should be carried out before deciding on printing of forms and in choosing printing methods.

SUMMARY

Office Forms: Office forms are printed sheets of paper or of cardboard and are used to collect and transmit information. Forms are the basic tools of office work, and they assist in the fundamental functions of receiving, recording, arranging and giving information in the office. The advantages of the use of forms are:

(i) They simplify systems and routines;

(ii) They reduce the cost of office operations;

(iii) They facilitate operations;

(iv) They are useful in the preservation of records;

(v) They make the fixation of responsibility possible;

(vi) They facilitate data processing.

Forms may be single-copy forms or multiple-copy forms. They may be internal office forms or external contact forms.

18. Littlefield and Rachel: *op. cit.*, p. 167.

Forms Control: Forms control is necessary.

(i) For a record of all the forms in use;
(ii) To combine and eliminate as many forms as possible;
(iii) To reduce the size of the forms in use; and
(iv) To prevent an indiscriminate use of new forms.

The steps involved in forms control include:

(i) The establishment of a centralised administration;
(ii) The preparation of forms register;
(iii) The listing of office routines;
(iv) Investigation and analysis; and
(v) Printing and reproduction.

Forms Designing: Forms should be properly designed because a badly designed form is bound to increase the manual labour required to process it and impair efficiency. It may also have an adverse impact on the goodwill and reputation which the organisation enjoys. The principles of form designing are:

(i) The principle of use;
(ii) The principle of standardisation; and
(iii) The principle of centralised control.

Factors Affecting Form Design: These are:

(i) The purpose of the form design;
(ii) Its ease in use;
(iii) Its simplicity;
(iv) Title and numbering;
(v) Proper size;
(vi) Proper type face or printing;
(vii) Use of proper paper;
(viii) Provision for punching, sorting, perforating, etc.

Form Sets: Form sets may be constructed as:

(i) Sets of loose sheets and carbon paper;
(ii) Sets in pads;
(iii) Sets in gangs;
(iv) Units sets; and
(v) Continuous sets.

Continuous Stationery: It is a device by which office forms are produced in a continuous strip, and by which separate forms are usually divided from one another by perforations and the several copies are usually detained by the use of various copying methods.

Advantages of Continuous Stationery are:

(i) Saving in time;

(ii) It facilitates the optimum Use of office machines;

(iii) User suffers from less fatigue and his efficiency is increased.

Disadvantages are:

(i) Difficulty in making corrections and alterations;

(ii) Risk of spoilage of form;

(iii) Problems of wrong alignment of forms; and

(iv) It is expensive.

Types: Continuous stationery may be:

(i) Roll stationery;

(ii) Interfold stationery; or

(iii) Fanfold stationery.

REFERENCES

1. B.H. Walley: *Manual of Office Administration.*
2. Carl Heyel: *Handbook of Office Administration.*
3. G. Mills and O. Standingford: *Office Organisation and Methods.*
4. J.C. Denyer: *Office Management.*
5. Johnson and Savage: *Administrative Office Management.*
6. Leffingwell and Robinson: *Textbook of Office Management.,*
7. Zene *K.* Quible: *Introduction to Administrative Office Management.*

STUDY QUESTIONS

1. What is meant by "forms control"? State briefly its importance in Office Management. *(I.C.W.A. Inter)*
2. Mention the important points one should bear in mind while designing a form. Reproduce a form to illustrate your answer. *(I.C.W.A. Inter)*
3. Write an explanatory note on "Continuous Stationery"? *(Co. Sectt., B.Com., Kolkata) (B.A., (V.S.) Delhi)*
4. The chief executive of your company has decided that too much paper work is involved in administrative procedures. One of the points to which he directs particular attention is the signing of forms when the staff requires stationery, etc. What are the advantages and disadvantages of retaining his control? *(Co. Sectt.)*
5. Discuss the significance of office forms. What are the principles of form designing? *(B.Com., (Pass) Delhi)*
6. Write short notes on:

   (i) Forms Control *(B.Com., Punjab)*

   (ii) Form Control means not to develop forms in future. *(B.Com., Punjab)*

   (iii) Office forms facilitate

   (a) Communication, (b) Control, (c) Co-ordination. *(B.Com., Punjab)*

   (iv) Principles of form designing. *(B.Com., (Pass) Delhi)*

7. What are the various considerations you will keep in mind while designing the office forms. *(B.Com., Punjab)*
8. Describe the various problems faced in designing the office forms, and state various steps that may be taken for the control of office forms. *(B.A., (V.S.) Delhi)*
9. What do you mean by office forms? Discuss their utility and describe the various problems faced in designing the office forms. *(B.A., (V.S.) Delhi)*
10. What do you mean by forms control? Explain the points to which attention should be paid in designing office forms. *(B.A., (VS.) Delhi)*
11. Explain the difference between a well designed form and a badly designed form. What points would you keep in mind in designing office forms. *(B.A., (VS.) Delhi)*
12. Write short notes on:
    (i) Badly Designed Form. *(B.A., (VS.) Delhi)*
    (ii) Continuous Stationery. *(Dip. Corp. Laws)*
13. What do you understand by 'Forms Control'? Describe the steps you would take to initiate a system of Forms Control in a large organisation. *(Dip. Corp. Laws)*
14. What do you mean by the terms 'Forms Design' and 'Forms Control'? Enumerate the principles to be taken into consideration when a form is being designed. *(D.O.O.P. Punjab University)*
15. What are office forms? What should be kept in mind while designing office forms? *(D.O.O.P. Punjab University)*
16. (a) What are the objectives under which Forms Control Programme operate?
    (b) Discuss the functions provided by professional forms service. *(D.O.O.P. Punjab University)*
17. Discuss the essential characteristic features of form design. *(Co. Sectt.)*
18. What is Continuous Stationery? Explain its merits and demerit. *(B.A., (V.S.) Delhi 1992 Supple.)*
19. What is meant by office forms? Discuss their utility. Also state the steps that should be taken for the control of office forms. *(B.A., (V.S.), Delhi), (B.Com., (Pass) Delhi)*
20. What are the essential qualities of a well designed form? How can an organisational control over office forms and stationery be exercised? *(B.A., (V.S.) Delhi)*
21. Write short notes on:
    (i) Principles of form design. (B. Com., (Pass) *Delhi*)
    (ii) Continuous Stationery *(Co. Sectt.)*
    (iii) Forms Control (Co. Sectt.)
22. What is meant by Continuous Stationery? What are its different types? Explain the advantages and disadvantages of Continuous Stationery. *(B.A., (VS.) I Delhi)*
23. "Forms are the basic tools of office." Discuss this statement with reference to the role of forms in office work. *(B.A., (V.S.)Delhi)*
24. State and briefly explain the different parts of an office form. *(B.A., (V.S.) Delhi)*
25. What is the importance of 'forms designing'? What guidelines should be observed in designing the office forms? *(B.Com., (Pass) Delhi)*
26. What do you understand by "Forms Control"? Briefly explain the process of forms control. *(B.Com., (Pass) Delhi)*
27. What is meant by office forms? What is their utility. *(B.Com., (Pass) Delhi 2000)*
28. What do you understand by 'Forms Control'? *(B.Com., (Pass) Delhi 2001)*

29. 'Forms are the tools of all office work.' Comment on this statement explaining the advantages and disadvantages of using office forms. *(B.A., (V.S.), Delhi 2000)*
30. What are office forms? Enumerate the guiding principles which should be taken into consideration while designing a form. *(B.A., (V.S.), Delhi 2001)*
31. What is the importance of form Designing? What guidelines should be observed in designing office forms. *(B.Com., (Pass) Delhi 2001)*
32. (a) What are the principles of form designing?

    (b) What are the types of Continuous stationery? Describe in brief *(B.Com., (Pass) Delhi 2002)*
33. "Forms are the basic tools of office." Discuss this statement with reference to role of forms in office work. *(B.A., (V.S.) Delhi 2002)*
34. Explain the procedure for designing office forms. *(B. A. (Prog.) Delhi April 2005)*
35. What is meant by office forms? What are the advantages and disadvantages of using forms? *(B.A.(Prog.)Delhi April 2006)*
36. Explain the advantages and disadvantages of office forms. *(B.A. (Prog.) Delhi April 2008)*

Chapter 5

COLLECTION OF DATA & PRESENTATION

CONTENTS

Chapter 5

COLLECTION OF DATA & PRESENTATION

> ***"It is not an Exaggeration to say that Modern Society relies much on Statistical Data for its Existence."***

The basic functions of a Modern Office are to receive and collect information, record it, arrange and process it, and **communicate it.** Recently, the term *"information management"* has gained a wider currency than the term *"office management"*. The information in an office is required for preparing various types of reports and surveys, and is collected in the form of facts and figures. This collection of data, *i.e.,* statistical data, is the first and perhaps the most important function of an office. Office reports without their supporting data are nothing more than just statements of opinion. The data may be collected by the office either from *internal* sources—books of records, files, registers and interviews with the personnel in the organisation—or from *external* sources—newspapers, magazines, bulletins, journals, stock exchange directories, financial institutions, management consultants. Government agencies, etc. The accuracy of data is of fundamental importance in all office reporting, for all planning, whether economic or financial, is based on data, and the soundness of business decisions depends largely on the accuracy of the data furnished in business reports. However, it is not possible to achieve a cent per cent accuracy of figures. Nevertheless, a reasonable degree of accuracy should be aimed at. The collected data should also be presented in some suitable format to facilitate their analysis and interpretation. These different aspects are discussed in the following paragraphs.

CONSIDERATIONS IN DATA COLLECTION

The collection of data in an office begins after the following factors have been considered :

(i) Determination of Objectives : The purpose of the objective of data collection should be clearly set out in the beginning. If the object of the enquiry is properly determined and defined, it is easy to decide which data are useful for collection and which are not. For instance, if the purpose of the enquiry is to assess the performance of individual salesmen over a given period, the data relating to the quantity and value of the goods sold by each salesman would be relevant; but data on region wise or district-wise sales would be useless. If the objective of data collection is not clearly set out in the beginning, there would be confusion, duplication of effort and waste of resources. The objective may be determined with reference to the scope of the report. The scope of a report is its coverage in terms of geographical area, the type of information needed and its subject-matter.

(ii) Defining Statistical Unit : Units of collection of data are called statistical units, which are units of measurement in terms of which the data are measured, counted, analysed and interpreted. Before starting on the collection of data the statistical unit should be clearly defined. A statistical unit may be simple or composite. A rupee or a *metric* ton or a *meter* are simple units, while a *tonne, kilometre,* or a passenger *kilometre,* or a *kilowatt hour* is a composite unit. It is not easy to select an appropriate statistical unit, for there may be different criteria out of which one would have to be selected. For instance, if the purpose of the enquiry is to assess the market potential of a particular product, the statistical unit may be the geographical area, the number of customers or the value of expected sales, out of which only one would have to be selected. The statistical unit should be specific, clearly understandable, stable and uniform; and once it is selected it should be followed throughout the enquiry.

(iii) Techniques of Data Collection : Two techniques of data collection are most popular, namely, sampling technique and census technique. The sampling technique implies that a few items are selected at *random* and observations about them are recorded and analysed for the preparation of the report, while the census technique implies that every item has been covered. The decision about the technique to be adopted depends on the following factors :

(a) The time available (if the time available for the preparation of the report is short, the sampling technique would be followed);

(b) The purpose of the report;

(c) The resources (money, staff, etc.), which are available;

(d) The desired degree of accuracy;

(e) The size of the data (if the number of observations is very large, the sampling technique would be preferred).

If the sampling technique is followed, the sample selected should represent the characteristics of the entire data.

(iv) Homogeneous, Complete and Stable Data : A valid comparison of data as between periods and groups is possible only if the basis of compilation is homogeneous. If the data cannot be brought under one heading, they should be divided into small classes or groups to facilitate comparison. For instance, the data on industrial accidents may be divided into a number of classes on the basis of the type of injury and compensation claimed. Further, the data collected should be complete in all details in so far as the nature and scope of the report to be prepared are concerned. To make the data meaningful, the effect of seasonal and cyclical business fluctuations should be eliminated so that a comparison over a long period of time may be facilitated.

(v) Degree of Accuracy Required : As stated above, it is impossible to achieve cent per cent accuracy in statistical data. Absolute accuracy is impossible because :

(a) Statistics are based on estimates;

(b) The tools of measurement are not always perfect; and

(c) There may be an unintentional bias on the part of the investigator enumerator or informant.

Moreover, absolute accuracy may not be desired in certain circumstances. For example :

(a) The time for the collection of data may be short; or

(b) The financial resources may be limited; or

(c) The object of the report is such as would not necessitate accuracy.

However, an attempt should be made to achieve a reasonable degree of accuracy in all cases.

STATISTICAL LAWS

There are two statistical laws which deserve mention here :

(i) Law of Statistical Regularity

When the number of observations to be made is very large, a representative sample of the observations (sampling technique) is selected to represent the entire data. The representative character of the sample is governed by the *law of statistical regularity,* according to which, if a moderately large number of items is chosen at random from a large group, it is almost certain that, on an average, it would have the characteristics of the large group.

(ii) Law of Inertia of Large Numbers

This law states that large numbers are relatively more stable in their properties than small numbers. The reason is that, in large numbers, the chances of compensatory action are greater. For example, if there are variations in one direction, there are likely to be variations in the opposite direction, with the result that the aggregate of the variations would be negligible. If the data on overtime payments to a particular class of employees is collected from one or two firms, they might show wide variations because of the particular situations obtaining in these firms. If on the other hand, the data are collected from all the 50 firms in a particular area, the variations due to the special circumstances prevailing in certain firms may be counterbalanced by the opposite variations in others, so that the aggregate variations would be negligible.

LIMITATIONS OF STATISTICAL DATA

Statistical Data, though of immense utility, have its own limitations. Not only that their accuracy might be doubtful, they also suffer from the following limitations :

1. Only Quantitative Aspects Considered : Statistical data consider only the quantitative aspects of facts and they are incapable of measuring the qualitative aspects directly. For example, the following qualitative traits, though otherwise important cannot he measured directly :

— Honesty of the employee;

— Extra effort put in by the salesman;

— Hard work of the supervisor;

— Intelligence of the executive;

— Politeness of the receptionist, etc.

2. Not Universally True : The conclusions drawn from statistical data are true only 'on an average'. They are not universally true. In other words, the conclusions drawn from statistical data cannot be true for each and every item of study because statistics deal only with averages and extreme values are often ignored.

3. Misuse of Statistics : It is one of the greatest limitation of statistics that it can be misused by the interpreter The interpreter/investigator may use the statistical data in a manner he likes and to prove his point of view. It is rightly said that, *"One of the shortcomings of statistics is that they do not bear on their face the label of their quality."*

4. Condemned Lies. It is commonly said that there are three kinds of lies; 1. *Lies;* 2. *White lies;* and 3. *Statistics.* Lack of subjectivity, lack of trained investigator, Liased approach of the interpreter to the problem can play havoc to the results drawn from the statistical data.

The above limitations of statistics suggest that the statistics collected for the preparation of a report must be interpreted with great care. The user of the statistical data must be well-trained. He should not have a biased mind/approach to the problem. All that is required is a scientific approach to the problem with an open mind free from any kind of bias.

STEPS IN DATA COLLECTION

After taking the initial decisions on the determination of the objective and on the definition of the data, the technique of data collection and the degree of accuracy desired, the office manager should proceed to collect the data. At this stage, the following steps should be taken :

(*i*) *Devising Organisational Set-up :* The first step is to devise an adequate organisational or administrative set-up for the collection of data. This set-up is determined by the purpose of the enquiry. A minor issue may be tackled by a junior executive; but, for a major issue, a senior executive or a director or a committee of experts may be appointed. The set-up should be designed in a manner which facilitates the smooth collection of data.

(*ii*) *Recruitment and Training of Data Collectors :* The next step is to select and train an adequate number of personnel for data collection. This is particularly important when the data are to be collected from external sources. The work of data collectors should be properly co-ordinated and supervised.

(*iii*) *Forms Questionnaire Designing :* Suitable forms or questionnaires for the collection of both quantitative and qualitative data should be prepared and printed. The forms or questionnaires should be simple, brief and easy to understand and fill up.

(*iv*) *Despatch of Forms and Follow-up :* The forms or questionnaires may then be despatched to the informants, or the data collectors may personally visit them and collect the necessary information from them. If these are despatched to the informants and there is no adequate response to them, it becomes necessary to make suitable arrangements for a follow-up action with a telephone call, correspondence or a personal visit, whichever is possible.

(*v*) *Collection and Presentation of Data :* On receipt of the filled-in forms and questionnaires, the data should be statistically analysed. This analysis may be made with the help of ratios, percentages or such other means. Sometimes, the use of calculating machines, computers, etc., may have to be made to analyse the data. The conclusions derived from an analysis of the data should then be presented to the management in a simplified form. Suitable charts, graphs, and diagrams or tables may also be used to depict or highlight the important data.

SOURCES OF DATA

The sources of data collection may be *Primary* or *Secondary*. The primary sources are those sources from which data are collected for the first time through original investigation. By the *collection of data* we actually mean the collection of entirely new data, presumably not already available in a published source. Primary data is collected by means of personal interviews, questionnaires or field surveys. The secondary source of data refers to published data, or the data collected by other investigators, or the records maintained by Government and private agencies, or the data available from research reports, etc. Similarly, all the unpublished records maintained by a business and the published material in different magazines and journals are classified as secondary sources of data. The question whether primary or secondary data should be used depends upon :

(i) The subject-matter under report;
(ii) The time factor;
(iii) The degree of accuracy required; and
(iv) The resources available.

Since published data are now available on a wide range of matters and their reliability has improved considerably in recent years, many business houses consider it very economical and useful to use secondary data rather than primary data, the collection of which entails heavy expenses and is time-consuming.

METHODS OF COLLECTING DATA

Collection of Primary Data

The following methods are commonly used in the collection of primary data :

(i) Observation and Experimentation : Under this method, the investigator collects the information by personally observing a particular fact or situation and noting down his observations or by conducting an experiment to test the effectiveness of a plan or a hypothesis. The effectiveness of observations and experimentation depends largely on the observer's ability, knowledge and experience. The data so collected should be carefully used and analysed.

(ii) Interview Method : Data may also be collected by directly interviewing persons who can provide first-hand information. The objective of an interview is to record hitherto unrecorded information. This is a common method of obtaining information or collecting data. Interviews may be conducted to collect objective data (facts, figures, etc.), or subjective data, such as an individual's opinions, attitudes, preferences, suggestions, etc. Interviews may also be conducted to check the reliability of the data which have been collected by other means—by correspondence or by mailed questionnaires. This method offers the following advantages:

(a) Flexibility;
(b) Adaptability;
(c) Reliability; and
(d) Adequacy of information.

But it also suffers from some drawbacks. These are :

(a) It is time-consuming;

(b) It is costly; and

(c) It offers scope for the personal bias of the investigator.

The effectiveness of the data which have been collected through this method depends largely on the investigator's ability, knowledge and experience, etc.

Essential Qualities of the Interviewer

In order to collect the right type of data by interview method, the interviewer must possess certain qualities which are outlined below :

1. *Proper Education and Training :* The interviewer should have thorough knowledge of all aspects of data collection. He should also be well-trained and experienced for the job.

2. *Tact and Adaptability :* An interviewer has to meet different types of people, therefore, he must have knowledge of human behaviour, be tactful and adapt himself/herself to different environments.

3. *Persistence and Tenacity :* Sometimes it is difficult to obtain information in one meeting. The interviewer should have the qualities of persistence and tenacity to bring results out of his/her efforts.

4. *Ability to Extract The Right Type of Information :* It is an essential quality of the interviewer. Irrelevant information, if collected, proves useless and creates frustration.

5. *Sound Memory :* This trait is of vital significance because at times, the information required is of confidential nature and the informant does not allow the interviewer to take notes. In such circumstances, a good memory will help the interviewer to reproduce the information even after the interview is over.

6. *Personal Qualities :* The interviewer should also possess certain personal qualities of head and heart, such as :

(i) Self-confidence

(ii) Understanding of the subject

(iii) Simplicity of language

(iv) Pleasing personality

(v) Professionally competent

(vi) Accuracy in handling the subject

All these qualities will help the interviewer extract the maximum out of the interview.

(iii) Mailed Questionnaire : A questionnaire, containing a list of questions, is mailed to informants. This questionnaire is generally printed or cyclostyled, and contains questions as well as an adequate space for answers with the questionnaire is sent a letter, explaining the nature and purpose of the enquiry, the method of filling up the questionnaire, and a request that it should be mailed back to the sender. The questionnaire should be drafted with great care, for the success of this method depends upon the kind of questions included in it. This calls for a full understanding of the purpose of the enquiry and the information required as well as the following guiding rules :

(a) Questions requiring lengthy answers should be avoided.
(b) The number of questions should be kept to the minimum.
(c) Questions should be simple and easily understandable, and the language should convey only one meaning.
(d) Questions should be arranged in some logical order.
(e) Questions of personal nature or those affecting personal pride should be avoided.
(f) Questions should be such as call for brief answers—that is, they should be in the form "yes" or "no," or alternative answers should be provided and the informant should be asked to tick off one.
(g) Questions asking the informant to calculate the ratios, percentages, etc., should be avoided.
(h) The necessary instructions should be issued for answers to questions.
(i) Questions should elicit facts and not opinions.
(j) Sufficient space should be provided for questions requiring the expression of personal opinions, etc.
(k) Such questions as suggest answers to the informants should be avoided.
(l) A stamped and self-addressed envelope should be sent with the questionnaire to ensure its return.

Advantages : The main advantages of the mailed questionnaire method are :

(a) It can cover a large number of persons and a wide geographical area;
(b) It is economical when extensive data are required to be collected;
(c) It eliminates the bias which results from personal interviews.

Disadvantages : The limitations of this method are :

(a) It is useful only when informants are literate;
(b) It is not quite certain whether the questionnaire will be mailed back. Generally speaking, the percentage of respondents is very low; it ranges from 5 to 25% As a result, the time, effort and money spent on the enquiry may be a waste;
(c) The information may not be correct or may be difficult of verification.

(iv) Questionnaire Through Enumerators : Instead of mailing the questionnaire to the informants, an investigator may get it filled up through enumerators, correspondents or interviewers. The enumerators or interviewers contact the informants and fill up the questionnaire by asking answers to the questions listed in it.

Advantages : The advantages of this method are :

(i) It is useful when informants are not literate;
(ii) It eliminates the uncertainty of response; and
(iii) It offers greater accuracy of the data collected.

Disadvantages : The disadvantages of this method are :

(i) It is an expensive method;

(ii) It is more time-consuming than the mailed questionnaire method; and

(iii) The data collected are subject to the enumerator's bias.

COLLECTION OF SECONDARY DATA

Secondary data refers to published or second-hand data, *i.e.,* data already collected by someone else. Strictly speaking, the task of collecting secondary data involves merely the compilation of data from various published or unpublished sources. The sources of secondary data are :

(i) Official publications of the Central and State Governments and of local bodies. These may be :

  (a) Regular publications (such as census reports, annual "India" publications, etc.); or

  (b) Irregular publications (such as reports of various committees constituted by the Government, ministerial reports, various legislative enactments, etc.);

(ii) Publications of international agencies—the UNO, the ILO, the IMF, and the WHO;

(iii) Official publications of foreign governments;

(iv) Publications of the Reserve Bank of India and such financial institutions as the LIC, the IFC, the UTI, and the IDBI;

(v) Publications of government undertakings and public corporations in the form of their annual or special reports;

(vi) Annual reports etc., of the private sector companies;

(vii) Technical and trade journals—*The Capital, The Indian Journal of Commerce, The Indian Journal of Marketing; etc.*

(viii) Newspapers and magazines;

(ix) Reports and publications of trade associations, chambers of commerce, banks, co-operative societies, stock exchanges;

(x) Reports submitted by research scholars, university departments and bureau of information;

(xi) Reports of various committees and commissions;

(xii) Unpublished sources of secondary data, such as internal records and office reports, etc.

Secondary data should be used with great caution, for they may not be appropriate for the purpose of the enquiry. Moreover, "it is never safe to take secondary data at their face value without knowing their meaning and limitations" The data collected by others may suffer from many drawbacks. It is, therefore, necessary to scrutinise them thoroughly before making use of them. It should be ensured that the secondary data used in report writing are reliable, adequate and suitable, and that they are reasonably accurate.

Factors affecting the Choice of Sources of Data

Different sources of data provide different set advantages and suffer from peculiar limitations. It is, therefore, necessary that the sources of data to be used for preparation of report should be pre-determined. It would be worthwhile to consider the following factors while deciding about the source of data, primary or secondary, to be collected.

1. Purpose : It is the purpose of the report that in most cases determines the choice of the source. Where the available secondary data does *not* serve the purpose, it becomes necessary to collect the primary data.

2. Reliability : Sometimes, the available secondary data may not be reliable due to many reasons, such as :

(i) Obsoleteness
(ii) Collected by an unreliable agency
(iii) Not comprehensive
(iv) Different purpose of collection of data
(v) Not relevant

Under all such circumstances, data has to be primarily collected.

3. Financial Limitations : Collection of primary data is much more costly than collection of secondary data. Financial or budgetary limitations affect the choice of source of data collection. Where sufficient funds are available, primary data may be collected for more accuracy and reliability. With a shoe-string budget, secondary data is the only choice.

4. Time Factor : Collection of primary data requires long time to organise and complete an enquiry and to compile the results. Whereas, secondary data may be obtained in a ready form. Shortage of time makes the use of secondary data compulsory.

5. Degree of Accuracy : The degree of accuracy of secondary data is a matter of imagination and may fall short of the degree of accuracy required in the compiled data. Therefore, where high degree of accuracy is desired to prepare a report, primary sources should only be used.

Editing the Data

Editing is the last stage in the collection of data. Whether the data have been collected from a primary or a secondary source, it is necessary that they should be edited before they are used in drafting office reports. Editing refers to the process of scrutinising the data. The chief objective of editing is to detect possible errors and irregularities. It is necessary to ensure that the data are :

(i) Adequate and complete;
(ii) Suitable for the purpose of enquiry;
(iii) Reliable and accurate;
(iv) Consistent and not contradictory; and
(v) Homogeneous and have been recorded in the same sense throughout.

Editing involves a standardisation of the units of measurement which are used in the collection of data. Careful editing is necessary for all types of data because any negligence may make the conclusions unreliable and result in a waste of the time and effort spent on collecting the data.

PRESENTATION OF DATA

The data collected from whatever source should be presented in a suitable form to help in their analysis and interpretation. The presentation of the data used in report writing calls for their classification and tabulation in a simple form.

Classification of Data

The classification of data refers to an arrangement of data on the basis of their common characteristics. The objectives of classification are :

(i) To condense the mass of data;

(ii) To facilitate comparison; and

(iii) To focus attention on the more significant aspects of the information.

It may be mentioned here that classified data can be easily statistically treated.

Basis of Classification : Statistical data may be classified on one of the following bases :

(i) Geographical Classification : On the basis of geographical characteristics, *e.g.*, district-wise sales, branch-wise production.

(ii) Chronological Classification : On the basis of time, that is, weeks, months, years, *e.g.*, the number of industrial accidents which occur every month.

(iii) Qualitative Classification : On the basis of some common attributes or qualities, *e.g.*, unemployment of skilled and unskilled labour, males and females.

(iv) Quantitative Classification : On the basis of the quantitative characteristics of the items, *e.g.*, income in rupees, output in units, weight in tonnes, etc. Employees in an office may be classified as those drawing less than Rs. 10,000, those drawing between Rs. 10,000 and Rs. 25,000 and those drawing more than Rs. 25,000.

Tabulation of Data

"A statistical table is the logical listing of related data in vertical columns and horizontal rows with sufficient explanatory and qualifying words, phrases of statements in the form of titles, headings and notes to make clear the full meaning of data and their origin."

Tabulation refers to a systematic arrangement of data in columns and rows. Tabulation follows classification and is necessary for the presentation of the data in a more understandable form. The main object of tabulation is to simplify the study of complex information; and this is achieved by eliminating all the unnecessary details, repetitions, etc., and by putting the numerical data in systematically arranged columns and rows. Tables present the information in a more concise form; they eliminate confusion; they simplify complex data; they are useful for purposes of comparison; and they give an identity to the data. Patterns of information are clearly revealed by giving headings and sub-headings in the statistical table.

Parts of a Table : The number of parts in a table may vary from table to table and depends upon the purpose of tabulation and the nature of the data which have to be tabulated. However, a table usually contains the following parts :

(i) Table number;

(ii) Title;

(iii) Head Note (regarding the unit of measurement, etc.);

(iv) Caption;

(v) Stubs or rows (indicating the types of classification);

(vi) Body of the table; and

(vii) Footnotes (indicating the source of data and other remarks). The format of a table is given below :

Title FORMAT OF A TABLE Head Note

Sub-Heading	Caption	
	Column Headings	Column Headings
Sub-Entries	Body	

Footnotes

Source

Methods of Tabulation : Data may be tabulated manually or with the help of machines.

Manual Tabulation is done by hand without the aid of a machine. A tally sheet is prepared for the counting of the number of observation items to be written in different captions and stubs regarding facts classified in different groups or classes. Tally sheets facilitate counting. For the purpose of counting, small vertical bars are first recorded on the sheet, each bar representing an item; then each group of four vertical bars is crossed out by a diagonal bar, which indicates that the fifth number has been counted. Thus sets of five items are separated and the total number (frequency) under any head or group (class interval) is quickly determined. Manual tabulation is useful when the data are not extensive and when complicated ratios, percentages, etc., have to be worked out; but when the data are extensive, manual tabulation is a costly and time-consuming method.

Machine Tabulation : It involves the use of mechanical devices—punched card machines or electronic computers, etc. Machine tabulation is made use of to process a large mass of data which are of a very complex nature. The whole work of classification, counting, calculation and tabulation of data is done by machines. A tabulating machine consists of three units, each performing a different operation. These are :

Key Punch : For transcribing the data on punch cards by punching holes at pre-determined positions.

Sorter : For the sorting of punched cards into classified groups.

Tabulator : For summarising and tabulating the punched cards. It adds, subtracts, and prints tables in a summary form ready for use.

Electronic computers are also used for the tabulation of data. A programme is prepared and fed into the computer, which does the entire job of tabulation. Machine tabulation offers the advantages of great speed, accuracy, and easy handling of a vast mass of data, it facilitates the handling of the complicated characteristics of data, and ensures economy in the cost of processing and analysing them. But the installation of the computers involves a very high capital outlay and calls for the appointment of trained operators.

GRAPHICAL AND DIAGRAMMATIC PRESENTATION OF DATA

While preparing office reports, it sometimes become necessary to present the data with the help of graphs, charts or diagrams. Tabulated data help one to summarise the collected data; but this may become confusing and may fail to convey the desired information to the reader. It has been said that one picture is worth a thousand words. Hence the importance of the use of graphs, charts, etc., as a means of conveying messages effectively. The following reasons underscore the value and usefulness of charts, diagrams, and graphs :

(i) They give a bird's eye-view of the complete data.

(ii) They leave a lasting impression on the mind and increase the impact of the data.

(iii) They make the data simple and easy to understand. They also appeal to the eye and create a greater interest on the part of the reader in figures.

(iv) They make comparison easier, depict patterns and trends in the data and convey a clear meaning to casual and non-technical readers.

I. Graphs

A graph is the depiction of inter-related data on a graph paper. It generally represents the relationship between two variable factors, *e.g.*, input and output analysis; wages and productivity; revenue and profit; month-wise sales and year-wise sales; and so on. Both the types of data, *i.e.*, the time data and the frequency distribution, can be plotted in points on a graph paper. The points are then joined together into a line or a curve, which gives a picture of the facts. For the plotting of data, two co-ordinates of a graph—the *x*-axis and the *y*-axis—are used, and a convenient measuring scale is chosen for each axis to represent the units of data. Two types of scales—the arithmetic or the natural scale and the semi-logarithmic or the ratio scale—are used. In the arithmetic scale, equal differences are measured in terms of equal distances on the scale. In the semi-logarithmic scale, equal proportional changes are measured by the differences in the scale.

Advantages of Graphs : The advantages of graphs are :

(i) Graphs depict patterns or trends over a period of time and facilitate the comparison of data and forecasting.

(ii) They indicate the relative changes in the time series in the best manner.

(iii) They can be easily prepared and understood.

(iv) More than one kind of information can be depicted on a graph.

(v) Many statistical measures—the mean, the median, the mode, the quartiles, etc.— can be determined accurately on graphs without mathematical computations.

Disadvantages: The disadvantages of graphs are :

(i) The preparation of a graph requires skill in depicting complex information and statistical measures.

(ii) The visual appeal of a graph is much less than that of a diagram.

(iii) The interpretation of graphs pre-supposes some familiarity and understanding of statistical tools or methods.

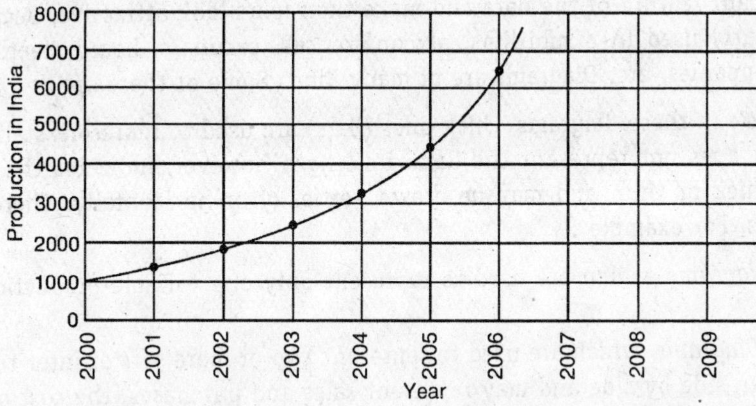

Fig. 5.1 Graphical Presentation of Output (in units) of Product A.

II. Charts

Charts (also known as information charts) are used to convey such information as functional relationships, sequence of operations, movement of materials, etc. Several types of charts are prepared and used by different organisations, the most common being the flow chart and the organisation chart. The following charts, too, may be profitably studied :

(i) Control Chart : It is prepared to control operations in an organisation. Different types of control charts may be prepared for the control of different activities or operations. A control chart may also convey information on the budgeted performance of different departments in terms of production, sales, profit, etc., as well as show the actual performance, calculate the variations and fix responsibility.

(ii) Progress Chart : It is prepared to show the progress of a particular job. Standard performance is shown by a thin horizontal line, while the actual performance is indicated by a thick horizontal line; the difference between the two lines indicates the difference between the standard and the actual work performance.

(iii) Break Even Chart : It conveys the relationships between the sales and costs of a product and the profit made from it, it shows the break-even point (the point of no-profit, no-loss). A break-even point can also be indicated on the graph. Lines are drawn to represent fixed costs, total costs and sales revenue. The point of intersection of the total costs line and the sales-revenue line indicates the break-even point. It can also show the amount of profit or loss at a particular level of output.

(iv) Z-Chart: Known also as a graphic chart, it consists of three lines or curves which together look like the letter "Z", It is prepared to represent weekly, monthly or quarterly returns; cumulative totals of the figures for a particular period; and moving yearly totals of the figures. The line of weekly, monthly or quarterly figures indicates seasonal fluctuations, while the line showing the annual moving totals indicates the trend.

III. Diagrams

A diagram is a pictorial presentation of statistical data. Diagrams are used not only to convey information, but also to make it more attractive to the eye. In business reports, they are used to highlight the significant feature of the data and make the report look attractive. Because of this fact, they are popularly used in exhibitions, at conferences, seminars, board meetings, in the annual reports of companies, etc. Diagrams are of many kinds Some of these are :

(i) Bar Diagrams : In these diagrams, thick lines (bars) are used to represent statistical data. The width of the bar does not represent the data; its length however, indicates the size of the data. Bars may be thick or thin, and may be drawn vertically or horizontally. There are many kinds of bar diagrams. For example :

(a) *Simple Bar Diagrams,* which are used to represent only one variable-production or sales. (See Fig.5.2)

(b) *Multiple Bar Diagrams,* which are used to represent two or more sets of inter-related data. Bars are drawn side by side and may represent sales and purchases, the cost of sales and the selling prices. (See Fig.5.3)

(c) *Sub-divided Bar Diagrams,* which are used to represent parts of a whole. For instance, the total bar may represent the sales value and its division may represent the various components of the selling cost and of profit. (See Fig.5.4)

(d) *Percentage Bar Diagrams,* which are similar to the sub-divided bar diagrams with the difference—that the parts of the whole are shown in percentages. (See Fig.5.5)

(ii) Rectangles : Rectangles are used to convey statistical data. These are two-dimensional diagrams, and the area of each rectangle (which is the product of its length and breadth) represents the data. They are used when two or more variables are compared and when each variable is sub-divided into several components. (See Fig.5.6)

(iii) Squares : Squares, too, are two-dimensional diagrams. They are used instead of rectangle diagrams when the differences in the variables are very wide and the rectangles are difficult to construct. For example, when the sales of three commodities are of the value of Rs. 1.5 lakh Rs. 3.5 lakh and Rs. 4 lakh respectively, the rectangles would look odd because of the wide differences in values. In such cases, squares are drawn. The area of each square is always in proportion to the value it represents and is calculated by finding out the square roots of the values on a suitable scale. (See Fig.5.7)

(iv) Pie Diagrams : In a pie-diagram, circles are used instead of squares. A circular diagram is a hundred per cent graph. The circle is divided into parts, each part representing a percentage break-up of the relevant data. Since a circle has 360 degrees, one per cent works out to 3.6 degrees. An item representing 20 per cent of the total value of the data will be displayed by an angle of 72 degrees $\frac{(20 \times 360)}{100}$ on a pie-diagram. Each part of the circle or pie-diagram is made distinct by using different colours, shades or designs. However, a pie-diagram is not very effective in calculating values or making comparisons, for it is often difficult to grasp quickly the area covered by each part of the circle. (See Fig.5.8)

(v) Pictograms : Pictograms, *i.e.,* pictures, are a very popular and fascinating medium of presenting data. They arouse an intense interest in the reader and are very useful for the presentation of data to non-technical persons. But their limitation is that they do not convey an exact idea of the variables, and are difficult to construct. In a pictogram, the relative values of

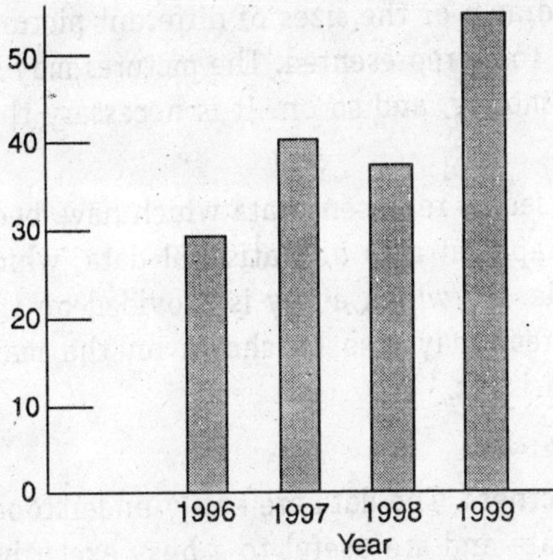

Fig.5.2 Simple Bar Diagram

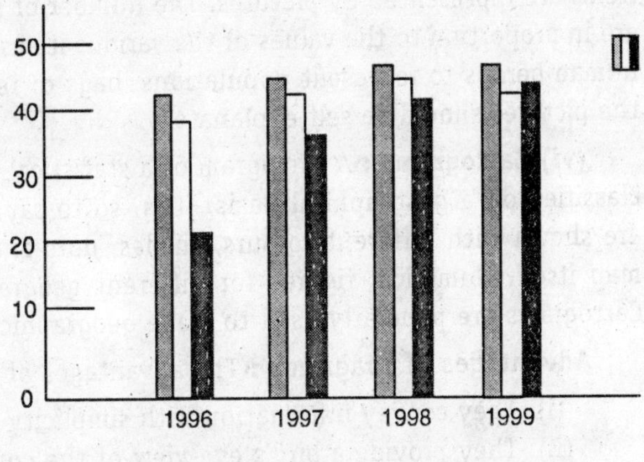

Fig.5.3 Multiple Bar Diagram

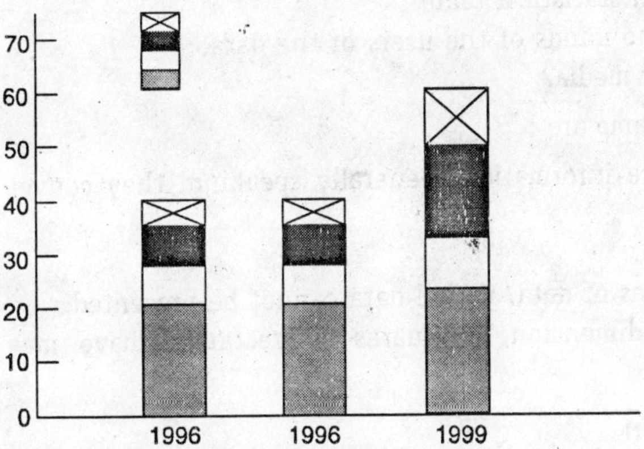

Fig.5.4 Sub-divided Bar Diagram

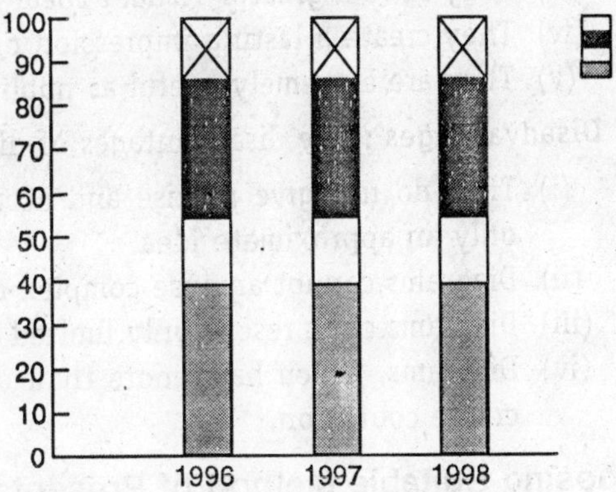

Fig.5.5 Percentage Bar Diagram

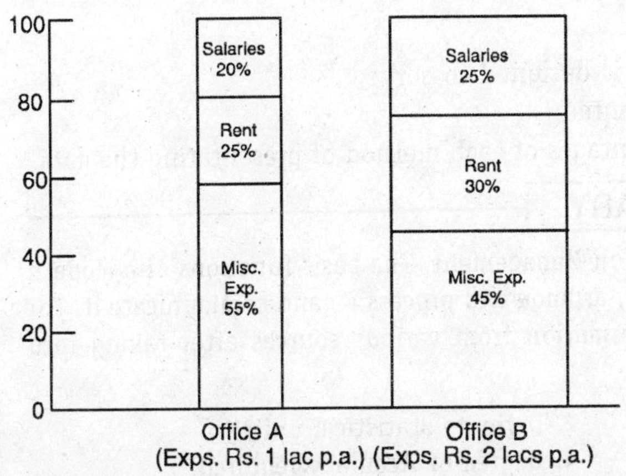

Fig.5.6 Rectangles

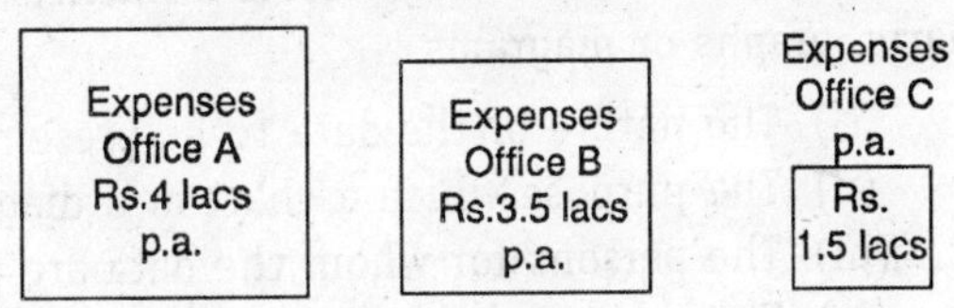

Fig.5.7. Squares

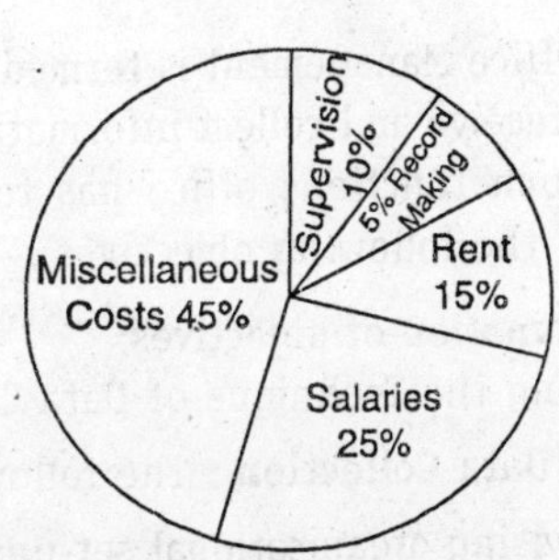

Fig.5.8 Pie Diagram

items are represented by pictures. The number of pictures drawn or the sizes of different pictures are in proportion to the values of the various items that are to be represented. The pictures may be human beings to represent populations, bags to represent money, and so on. It is necessary that the pictures should be self-explanatory.

(vi) Cartograms : A cartogram or a statistical map is used to represent data which have been classified on a geographical basis. It is, so to say, a geographical map of statistical data, which are shown with different colours, shades, dots and symbols, for which a key is provided on the map itself. Numerical figures for different geographical areas may also be shown on the map. Cartograms are popularly used to make geographical comparisons.

Advantages of Diagrams : The advantages of diagrams are :

(i) They convey information with simplicity and directness. The data are easily understood.
(ii) They provide a bird's eye-view of the complete data and are useful to a busy executive as well as a non-technical viewer.
(iii) They have a greater visual appeal than statistical tables.
(iv) They create a lasting impression on the minds of the users of the data.
(v) They are extremely useful as publicity media.

Disadvantages : The disadvantages of diagrams are :

(i) They do not give precise and accurate information. Generally speaking, they convey only an approximate idea.
(ii) Diagrams cannot analyse complex data.
(iii) Diagrams can present only limited types of data. Varied data cannot be presented.
(iv) Diagrams, which have more than one dimension, as squares and rectangles have, may create confusion.

Choosing Suitable Method of Presentation

The choice of a suitable method for the presentation of statistical data is fundamental to its effectiveness. The following factors influence the choice of a particular method of presentation—charts, graphs or diagrams :

(i) The nature of the data to be presented;
(ii) The purpose which a chart or a diagram is designed to serve;
(iii) The persons for whom the data are presented;
(iv) The characteristic advantages and disadvantages of each method of presentating the data.

SUMMARY

Modem Office Management is termed as Information Management. The basic functions of a Modern Office are to receive and collect information, record it, arrange and process it, and communicate it. For performing such functions office has to collect information from various sources after taking into consideration the following objectives :

1. Determination of objectives;
2. Defining statistical unit;
3. Selecting the Technique of Data Collection;
4. Degree of Accuracy required.

Steps in Data Collection : The following steps should be taken in collecting data :

(i) Devising organisational set-up;
(ii) Recruitments and training of data collectors;
(iii) Forms/Questionnaire Designing;

(iv) Despatch of forms and follow up;

(v) Collection and Presentation of Data.

There are two types of Data : (i) Primary and (ii) Secondary. After collecting and editing the data. it is classified on the basis of common characteristics, classified data can be presented in any of the following ways :

(i) Tables; (ii) Graphical; and (iii) Diagrammatic Presentation of Data.

Choice of suitable method of presentation of data depends on variety of factors such as (i) the nature of the data to be presented; (ii) the purpose which it is designed to serve; (iii) the persons for which the data are presented; (iv) the characteristic advantages and disadvantages of each method of presenting the data.

REFERENCES

1. C.B.Gupta : Statistical Methods.
2. D.N. Elhance : Statistics.
3. S.P. Gupta : Statistics : An Introduction.
4. Leffingwell and Robinson : Textbook of Office Management.
5. Zene K. Quible : Introduction to Administrative Office Management.

STUDY QUESTIONS

1. Distinguish between the collection of data by the interview method and the observation method.
2. Write a short note on the principal methods of collecting data.
3. Distinguish between the "Primary Source" and the "Secondary Source" of data. What precautions will you take before using the data from a secondary source ?
4. What are the various methods of collecting data ? Examine the relative merits and limitations of each method.
5. Describe briefly the questionnaire methods of collecting data and state the essentials of a good questionnaire.
6. Compare the relative merits and demerits of the census and the sampling methods of collecting data.
7. What is the procedure for classifying recorded observations ? What points will you take into consideration while tabulating classified observations ?
8. A particular, industrial concern has the following information about its employees :

   (i) Age, (ii) Educational level, (iii) Type of work done, (iv) Family size, (v) Pay, (vi) Length of service, and (vii) Material status, Indicate the nature of the tables to be prepared to bring out the above information.
9. State briefly the purpose of a diagrammatic representation of data.
10. What are different sources of data collection ? Also state methods of data collection. *(B. Com., Punjab)*
11. What is Classification ? State the factors which affect the choice of method of classification. *(B. Com (Pass), Delhi)*
12. You are O & M officer of a large office. What principles would you take into consideration for the O & M work ? *(B. Com. (Pass), Delhi)*
13. What are the objects of O & M department? *(B. Com. Chennai)*

Chapter **6**

ART OF SPEECH MAKING

CONTENTS

Chapter 6

ART OF SPEECH MAKING

Effective Communication is vital to the success of all office activities. Hence it is very important for the office manager and other senior staff to learn the art of speech making. Delivering speech is a part of oral communication. Oral Communication can be divided into two parts, formal and informal. Generally informal presentation communications are made to individuals and formal presentations are made to groups.

Informal Oral Communication : Most of the oral communication in the office is informal, individual to individual. Such communication generally conversational in the form of an instant give and take of information and ideas among the staff working in the office. Some examples of such informal conversations communications include :

(i) Explaining procedures to an employee
(ii) Giving directions to a subordinate
(iii) Discussing about day to day activities of the office.
(iv) Sorting out problems of staff in the office
(v) Providing feedback by subordinate to superiors on office related issues.

Formal Oral Communication : Formal Oral Communication in the office takes the form of public speaking or presentation speaking. Such communication is made to a number of people or a group simultaneously. Some obvious advantages of formal oral communications are :

(i) It avoids duplication of effort.
(ii) It saves time.
(iii) It permits a prepared and polished presentation.
(iv) Sometimes such presentations also allow for question and answer sessions. This facilitates problem solving and clarification and simplification of complex issues.
(v) Oral presentations are generally held in formal settings. This generates a sense of group behaviour and discipline.

* The Author acknowledges the contributions, to the chapter made by Mrs. Shalini Kunwar, Assistant Manager, HDFC Bank, Kamla Nagar, Delhi-110 007.

Formal Oral Communication When necessary. The following are some of the situations which may call for Formal Oral Communication

- Speeches
- Meetings
- Group Discussions
- Oral Reporting
- Lectures
- Conferences
- Orientations classes
- Cocktail meetings
- Presentations
- Seminars
- Symposiums
- Training Sessions
- Banquet meetings etc.

PREPARING FOR A SPEECH

An average office manager/executive may not be an effective communicator or a polished public speaker. Therefore considerable time should be spent in preparing for a good speech. The techniques of speech delivery should be studied, practised and mastered. Most people, particularly introvert, hesitate or get frightened at the prospect of speaking before a group of people. The following steps may be considered in preparing to deliver a speech :

1. Identifying the Topic : It is always recommended that the speaker should identify the topic of speech. If the topic is assigned orally by the superior, he should put it down in writing and get it verified from the seniors. If possible, a written statement of topic from the coordinator or programme director, be received by him. The topic should be clear, understandable and not vague or uncertain. The topic should be subdivided and emphasis marked down on different aspects.

2. Ascertaining the Purpose: After Identifying the Topic, the speaker should try to determine the objectives and purposes of presentation. The purpose may vary, such as :

(i) To transmit information;

(ii) To explain complex issues;

(iii) To describe or narrate methods and procedures;

(iv) To motivate, stimulate or persuade the group;

(v) To give and take feedback on performance, bottle necks, obstacles etc.

(vi) To intimate corporate plans for the near future etc.

After ascertaining the purpose, the speaker should also try to estimate the effect of speech on the audience. The content of the speech should be prepared according to the purpose or intent. For instance, informative speech may consist of factual information in the form of data, graphs, charts, diagrams etc. Similarly, a motivating speech should consist of stimulating anecdotes, quotations etc. of known personalities.

3. Determining the Time Frame : The speaker should find out the time allotted for his presentation. A speech or presentation should neither be too short nor too long. A short speech might miss important points or emphasis required and may also create vacuum in the programme. Similarly, a lengthy speech or presentation may become boring or the audience may lose interest, unless the speaker is competent to make the speech interesting or stimulating.

The speaker may do well to indicate on his notes, at what point he should be at a specific time; one quarter, one half, three quarter, finished. The speaker may have to slow down or speed up according to the time frame. A stop watch or an assistant indicating the time left may be a good help to the presentor.

A speaker who disregards time management may tarnish his personal image and spoils the programme. A speaker who is insensitive to the time allotted to others commits an unpardonable blunder. A good business speaker is brief, to the point and knows what and how much to speak.

4. Observing the Audiance : Since delivering a speech means transfer of ideas, thoughts and information, the speaker should know his/her audiance. He should draw up a profile of audiance. The profile would include the information about :

- average age of audiance;
- Knowledge of language/vocabulary;
- Attitude of audiance;
- Educational background;
- Sex Ratio;
- Level of Interest;
- Social standing;
- Occupation etc.,

of the audiance.[1] He should also know the type of audiance attending the speech/oral presentation *e.g.*, Managers, Accounting staff, clerical staff etc. The size of the audiance and theprevious knowledge of the subject are also important information to be gathered by the speaker/presentor.

The manner of presentation/speech depends on the size of audiance.Speaking before a large audiance may require audio-visual equipment like Projector, screen, amplifiers, sound system etc.

Audio-visual Aids : There are numerous audio-visual aids which may be used by a speaker/ presentor to improve/supplement his presentation. Given below is a list of commonly used audio-visual aids :

- Black boards and chalk
- White Boards
- Flip charts
- Diagrams
- Graphs
- Pictures
- Television
- C.D./D.V.D. Recordings
- Video Tapes and Cassettes
- Overhead Projector
- Magnetic Boards
- Maps
- Models
- Tables
- Film strips
- Slides
- Pemphlets
- Posters
- Transparencies
- Screen.

Audio-visual aids should be liberally used as they enhance on oral presentation, the learning process is more effective when such aids are used. It is generally said that :

"People generally remember 20% of what they hear but 50% of what they see."[2]

The audio-visual aid should be rehearsed before making final presentation.

Precautions before using Audio-visual aids :

(i) The presentor should ensure that the Audio Visual material is visible and heard by everyone in the audiance.

---

1. Nathan Krevin : Communication Systems and Procedures for the Modern Office : Prentice Hall of India.
2. Also see Mary Ellen Guffey : Business Communication : Thomse South Western, 2005 ; Obei : Contemporary

(ii) The aid should be simple, understandable and relevant to the discussion.

(iii) The Printing on the poster or writing on the black board should he clearly visible and legible even from the rear of the meeting/conference room.

(iv) There should he adequate lighting to ensure visibility of material used.

(v) The presentor may request for assistance to operate audio-visual equipments like projector, slides etc.

(vi) The presentor should make sure that he himself does not obstruct the poster or screen used for presentation.

(vii) A Combination of audio-visual aids can be used effectively if well coordinated[3]

5. Researching the topic : The speaker should know the topic/subject thoroughly. Proper homework should be done in this regard. The topic/subject should be researched and its sub-divisions and its main points or issues should be noted carefully. Sources of data information, records or statistics should be properly varified and acknowledged. The information may be collected from one or a combination of the following sources.

- Libraries
- Official records
- Files
- Primary research
- Specialists
- Internet websites
- Magazines, Journals and Newspapers
- Secondary Published information
- Office colleagues

If the speaker does not know the topics/subject thoroughly, he should better decline to accept the invitation to speak on the topic. It is very damaging to speak before an audience who is more knowledgable on the subject than the speaker himself, especially if the questions follow the speech or presentation. The speaker may exhaust the ideas and go stale and may risk being labelled as a bore.

6. Organising the Speech/Presentation : This is the last step for preparing to deliver a speech. The component parts of the speech/presentation should be logically organised and methodically planned. An effective speech should be divided into three component parts :

(i) Introduction

(ii) Body of the speech (main ideas)

(iii) Conclusion (Summary or recommendations).

The purpose of introduction is to state the subject and also to capture the attention of the audiance. The speaker/presenter may give his personal introduction, as well as the introduction of the company/organisation, he is representing. The introduction may also contain historical perspectives and developments, a statement of the topic/issue/problem, an explanatory statement and so on.

The Body of the presentation contains the main part/substance of the speech. It may include ideas, details, factual information, Statistics, graphical or diagrammatical presentation, quotations, reports, analysis of the subject. The speaker may make use of jokes, stories or anecldotes to

3. Natham Krevolin : *op. cit.*, Also see Kitty O. Locker & Stephen Kuo : *Business Communicrtion — Building Critical*

retain the interest of the audiance. Care should be taken that such jokes, stories etc. should relate to the subject matter of the speech/ presentation. Adhering to the time schedule/allotment is also a desireable phenomenon.

The concluding part of the speech/presentation is of utmost importance, since it contains the summary/conclusion/suggestions/recommendations of the speaker. Generally, it is the part which is most often remembered by the listeners. It is always better that the speech should end with a clear summary of the entire presentation.

The summary serves the dual purpose for poor listeners, it repeats and reinforces what has been said earlier. A well drafted summary contains all the important ideas of the speech/ presentation so that a person who listens only to the summary can make out the contents of the speech/presentation.

Sometimes, the speaker is expected to draw conclusions and make recommendations. In such a situation, the conclusion part will contain the decisions, judgements and opinions. The recommendations may also suggest a specific course of action for an effective presentation, the speaker may draw an outline of the speech. The outline may contain the logical sequence of the main ideas. The outline may either be projected on a screen or printed sheets distributed among listeners, or have a personal slip pad to assist during speech presentation.

SUMMARY

Effectively communication is vital for the success of all office/Business activities. Hence every manager and senior staff must learn the art of speech making. Speech making is a part of oral communication which may be (i) formal or (ii) informal.

Numerous situations call for making formal for communication.

Preparing for a speech : Steps include :

1. Identifying the Topic
2. Ascertaining the Purpose
3. Determining the Time Frame
4. Obseruing the Audiance

Audio-Visual Aids : There are numeous audio-visual aids which may be used by a speaker/ presentor to improve his speech/presentation. However, necessary precautions should be taken.

5. Researching the Topic.
6. Organising the Speech/Presentation.

REFERENCES

1. Nathan Krevolin : Communication systems and Procedures Many Ellen Guffy : Business Communication.

2. Ober : Contemporary Business Communication.

STUDY QUESTIONS

1. Distinguish between Formal oral Communication and Informal oral Communication.

2. What steps should be taken while preparing for a speech or presentation?

3. Discuss the various types of audio-visual aids which may be used while delivering a speech.

Chapter 7

THE ART OF LISTENING

CONTENTS

Chapter 7

THE ART OF LISTENING

Listening is a part of Oral Communication. There is a difference between 'hearing' and 'listening'[1]. Hearing is the perception of sound—the aural stimuli. Whereas listening entails hearing with attention, meaning thoughtfulness. We may hear a speaker without listening him.

Office people spend more time in listening than reading, writing or speaking[2]. It is said that White—Collar Office Employees spend nearly half of their time listening. Some employees like interviewers, counsellors, receptionists, telephone operators etc. may spend even higher percentage of their time listening.

Even though listening is the major communicating skill, very few people receive any kind of training in listening. In the present business scenario, where errors can be very costly, training in listening is critical. Marginal or poor listeners are a serious concern to the business, as they may be weakest link in the communication process.

The time spent in listening involves person to person situations. These may be

(i) Private or Interpersonal conversations for rapid exchange of thoughts.

(ii) Formal public listening situations like listening to a lecture or report. During formal public listening the listener plays a less active role.

The listener is the recipient of information, ideas and thoughts. He may not, in some circumstances, contribute to the dialogue by speaking.

The listner must, of necessity, be attentive and receptive. Instructions must be followed precisly : ideas and facts must be transmitted accurately and completely.

Ability to Listen

The Office Manager must make a concerted effort to receive and transmit communications. Since the manager is in the position of a leader, he has to issue directions and orders frequently. The office must listen to the manager. It is equally important that the manager should also be a

1. *Communication Systems & Procedures for the Modern Office* : Nathan Krevolin : Prentice Hall Inc. USA.
2. Paul T. Rankin, *"Listening Ability : Its Importance, Measurement and Development"*, Chicago School Journal.

good listner if upward communication is to take place in the office. The ability to listen is an important communication tool of the effective manager. If manager is not a good listner, he may be deprived of some vital information concerning the office.

Listening: The Key to Understanding[3]

The rushed, never-listening manager will seldom get an objective view of the functioning of the organization. Time, empathy, and concentration on the communicator's messages are prerequisites to understanding. People want to be heard, want to be taken seriously; want to be understood. Thus, the manager must avoid interrupting subordinates and putting them on the defensive. It is also wise both to give and to ask for feedback, for without it, one can never be sure whether the message is understood. To elicit honest feedback a manager should develop an atmosphere of trust and confidence and a supportive leadership style, with a de-emphasis on status (such as barricading oneself behind an extrawide executive desk).

Active Listening

On average, people spend 45 per cent of the total communications time in listening (Nichols and Stevens). It is important, therefore, that managers learn to listen effectively. Yet most people only prove the saying 'in one ear, out the other!' The problem is often developed from a young age. After all, many years are spent in school in learning to read, but very little time is devoted in learning to listen.

Effective listening requires active listening, being responsive and not sitting passively without any sound or reactions. The receiver of a message must not only hear but also listen. Hearing is the process by which auditory sensations are received by the ears and transmitted to the brain. Listening, on the other hand is the psychological process of interpreting and understanding the significance of the sensory process. Therefore one can hear without listening.

Active listening is very important since it improves the quality of the information being sent by the speaker. Also it is difficult for the listener to sit for any length of time without doing something, as required by active listening.

There are a few simple ways to improve active listening:[4]

- Show interest in what is being said and indicate that the message is being understood. One can respond by word and also by gesture and facial expression. Give undivided attention. Listen with understanding (Rogers and Roethlisberger, 1991).
- Pay attention. The mind can absorb information about five times faster than the speaker can deliver it. Therefore make sure that attention does not wander. Concentrate on other aspects of active listening, such as watching for visual communications,
- See the communications from the sender's frame of reference. Try to feel the sender's feelings. Ask the question to yourself: 'What does the speaker feel when saying that?'
- Show empathy with the sender's feelings. About 80 per cent of all communications is non-verbal, so watch out for body language. Much of the sender's feelings can be

3. Koontz etc. : Principles of Management
4. Wells *Communication in Business* : Wadsworth Publishing Co., Belmont California, USA. 2nd Ed.

determined from this. Further a large part of the feedback that a listener provides must also be non-verbal.

- Listen without interruptions to start with, so as to get the full story. Don't lead the speaker with questions.
- Adopt the correct posture. Lean forward slightly towards the speaker; have an open position (legs and arms uncrossed); use movement, but be careful of distracting movements or appearing to be nervous. Eye contact is important, but don't stare. No one likes talking to someone whose eyes roam all over the room but do not look at him.
- Paraphrase and provide reflective responses. A paraphrase is a concise response which summarizes the essence of the message from the sender. In a reflective response the receiver restates the feeling or content of the message from the sender in a form which indicates to the sender that the message is being understood and accepted.
- A sender will often code messages without knowing that this is being done. The receiver must therefore evaluate the message carefully to determine whether coding has been applied before decoding it.
- Often the sender will have difficulty in identifying, handling or conveying feelings. The sender may also 'beat around the bush' and not get directly to the main aim of the message. The listener must be prepared to help and encourage by active listening.

According to Kitty O.Locker and Stephens Kyo :

"**In active listening,** receivers actively demonstrate that they've heard and understood a speaker by feeding back either the literal meaning or the emotional content or both. Other techniques in active listening are asking for more information and stating one's own feelings.

Five strategies create active responses :

- **Paraphrase the content.** Feed back the meaning in your own words.
- **Mirror the speaker's feelings.** Identify the feelings you think you hear.
- **State your own feelings.** This strategy works especially well when you are angry.
- **Ask for information or clarification.**
- **Offer to help solve the problem."**

Active listening takes time and energy. Even people who are skilled active listeners can't do it all the time. Furthermore, as Thomas Gordon and Judith Gordon Sands point out, active listening works only if you genuinely accept the other person's ideas and feelings. Active listening can reduce the conflict that results from miscommunication, but it alone cannot reduce the conflict that comes when two people want apparently inconsistent things or when one person wants to chance someone else.[6]

5. Business Communication : *Building Critical Skills* : Kitty O. Locker & Stephens Kyo : McGraw Hills : Ed. 2004.
6. *Ibid.*

PRACTICES GOOD LISTENERS SHOULD FOLLOW :

Good listeners follow following four[7] practices :[7]

1. Pay Attention

Good listening requires energy. You have to resist distractions and tune out noise whether the rumble of a truck going by or your own worry about whether your parking meter is expiring.

Some listening errors happen because the hearer wasn't paying enough attention to a key point. "After a meeting with a client, a consultant waited for the client to send her more information that she would use to draft a formal proposal to do a job for the client. It turned out that the client thought the next move was up to the consultant. The consultant and the client had met together, but they hadn't remembered the same facts".

To avoid listening errors caused by inattention :

- Before the meeting, anticipate the answers you need to get. Make a mental or paper list of your questions. When is the project due? What resources do you have? What is the most important aspect of this project from the other person's point of view? During a conversation, listen for answers to your questions.
- At the end of conversation, check your understanding with the other person. Especially check-who does what next.
- After the conversation, write down key points that affect deadlines or how work will be evaluated.

2. Focus *on* the Other Speaker(s) in a Generous Way.

Some people listen looking for flaws. They may focus on factors other than the substance of the talk "What an ugly tie." "She sounds like a little girl." "There's a typing error in that slide." Or they may listen as if the discussion were a war, listening for points on which they can attack the speaker. "Ah! You're wrong about that!"

Good listeners, in contrast, are more generous. They realize that people who are not polished speakers may nevertheless have something to say. Rather than pouncing on the first error, they hear and tuning out the speaker while they wait impatiently for their own turn to speak, good listeners weigh all the evidence before they come to judgement. They realize that they can learn something even from people they do not like. To avoid listening errors caused by self-absorption, a good listener.

- Focus on the substance of what the speaker says, not his or her appearance or delivery.
- Spend your time evaluating what the speaker says, not just planning your rebuttal.
- Consciously work to learn something from every speaker.

3. Avoid Making Assumptions

Many listening errors come from making faulty assumptions. In 1977, when two Boeing 747 jumbo jets ran into each other on the ground in Tenerife, the pilots seem to have heard the control towers instructions. The KLM pilot was told to taxi to the end of the runway, turn around, and wait for clearance. But the KLM pilot assumed he didn't need to follow the order to

7. Adopted : *Ibid.*

wait. The PanAm pilot assumed that his order to turn off at the "third intersection" meant the third *unblocked* intersection. He didn't count the first blocked ramp, so he was still on the main runway when the KLM pilot ran into his plane at 186 miles an hour. The planes exploded in flames; 576 people died.[8]

In contrast, asking questions can provide useful information. Magazine advertising account representative, a Real Estate Agent received a phone call from a client who wanted to cancel the space he had bought. The Agent, saw the problem as an opportunity; of "Instead of hearing 'cancel,' I heard, "There's a problem here—let's get to the root of it and figure out h6w to make the client happy.' " met with the client, asked the right questions, and discovered that the client wanted more flexibility. The Agent changed some of the markets, kept the business, and turned the client into a repeat customer.

To avoid listening errors caused by faulty assumptions a good listener

- Should not ignore instructions he thinks are unnecessary.
- Consider the other person's background and experiences. Why is this point important to the speaker? What might he or she mean by it?
- Paraphrase what the speaker has said, giving him or her a chance to correct your understanding,

4. Listen for Feelings as Well as Facts

Sometimes, someone just needs to blow off steam, to vent, Sometimes, people just want to have a chance to fully express themselves; "winning" or "losing" may not matter. Sometimes, people may have objections that they can't quite put into words.

To avoid listening errors caused by focusing solely on facts :

- Consciously listen for feelings.
- Pay attention to tone of voice, facial expression, and body language
- Don't assume that silence means consent. Invite the other person to speak,[8]

Most of us do our worst listening when we are in highly charged emotional situations, such as talking with someone with whom we really disagree, getting had news, or being criticized. At work, you need to listen even to people with whom you have major conflicts.

At a minimum, *good listening* enables you to find out why your opponent objects to the programmes or ideas you support. Understanding the objections to your ideas is essential if you are to overcome those objections.

Good Listening is crucial when you are criticized, especially by your boss. You need to know which areas are most important and exactly what kind of improvement counts. Otherwise, you might change your behaviour in a way that wasn't valued by your organization.

Listening can do even more. Listening to people is an indication that you're taking them seriously. If you really listen to the people you disagree with, you show that you respect them. And taking that step may enable them to respect you and listen to you.[9]

---

8. *Ibid.*
9. *Ibid.*

BECOMING AN EFFECTIVE TEAM LISTENER[10]

A vital part of every successful team is high-quality communication. And three quarters of high-quality communication involves listening. In addition to helping you interact with teams, listening skills are important in getting along with colleagues, managers, family, and friends. Although our discussion centers on business and employment needs, many of the listening tips you learn will be equally effective in your personal life.

Most workers spend 30 to 45 per cent of their communication time listening, while executives spend 60 to 70 per cent of their communication time listening.[19] Although executives and workers devote the bulk of their communication time to listening, research suggests that they're not very good at it. In fact, most of us are poor listeners. Some estimates indicate that only half of the oral messages heard in a day are completely understood. Experts say that we listen at only 25 per cent efficiency. In other words, we ignore, forget, distort, or misunderstand 75 per cent of everything we hear.'

Such listening inefficiency may result from several factors. Lack of training is one significant reason. Few schools give as much emphasis to listening as they do to the development of reading, speaking, and writing skills. In addition, our listening skills may be less than perfect because of the large number of competing sounds and stimuli in our lives that interfere with concentration. Finally, we are inefficient listeners because of the slowness of speech. While most speakers talk at about 150 words per minute, listeners can process oral communication at over 400 words per minute. This lag time causes daydreaming, which in turn reduces listening efficiency.

Tips for Better Team Listening

Team listening in Business Communication is more difficult and challenging than attending a Seminar or lecture where experienced speaker present well organised lectures and focus on important point. In Business however, information within a team is often exchanged casually. It may be disorganised, unclear, and cluttered with extraneous facts. Moreover, team members are usually colleagnas and friends. Because they are familiar with each other, they may not be as polite and courteous to each other as they are with strangers. Friends/colleagues may tend to interrupt, jump to conclusions, and take each other for granted. They must however remember that their job is to *listen* carefully and to understand what is being said so that they can perform well. The following suggestions[11] can help one improve his/her listening effectiveness, both as a team member and as a business communicator in general :

1. Control External and Internal Distractions. Move to an area when you can hear without conflicting noises or conversations. Block out surrounding physical distractions. Internally, try to focus totally on the speaker. If other projects are on your mind, put them on the hack burner temporarily. When you are emotionally upset, whether angry or extremely happy, it's a good idea to postpone any serious listening.

2. Become Actively Involved. Show that you are listening closely by leaning forward and maintaining eye contact with the speaker. Don't fidget or try to complete another task at the same time you are listening. Listen to more than the spoken words. How are they said? What implied meaning, reasoning, and feelings do you hear behind the spoken words? Does the speaker's body language (eye contact, posture, movements) support or contradict the main message?

---

10. *Business Communication : Process & Product* by Mary Ellan Guffey : Thomson South Western : 2005

11. Adapted from *Business Communication : Process & Product;* By Mary Ellan Guffey : Thomson South Western : Ed. 2005.

3. Identify Important Facts. Team members may intersperse critical information with casual conversation'. Unrelated topics pop up—ball scores, a customer's weird request, a computer glitch, the boss's extravagant new sports utility van. Your task is to select what's important and register it mentally. What step is next in your project? Who does what? What is your role?

4. Don't Interrupt. While someone else has the floor, don't interrupt with a quick reply or opinion. And don't show nonverbal disagreement such as negative head shaking, rolling eyes, sarcastic snorting, or audible sighs. Good team members let speakers have their say. Interruptions are not only impolite, but they also prevent you from hearing the speaker's complete thought. Listeners who interrupt with their opinions sidetrack discussions and cause hard feelings.

5. Ask Clarifying Questions. Good team member wait for the proper moment and then ask questions that do not attack the speaker. Instead of saying, "But I don't understand how you can say that," a good listener seeks clarification with questions such as, "Please help me understand by explaining more about ... ." Because questions can put you in the driver's seat, think about them in advance. Use open questions (those without set answers) to draw out feelings, motivations, ideas, and suggestions. Use closed fact-finding questions to identify key factors in a discussion. And, by the way, don't ask a question unless you are ready to be quiet and listen to the answer.

6. Paraphrase to Increase Understanding. To make sure you understand a speaker, rephrase and summarize a message in your own words. Be objective and non-judgmental. Remember that your goal is to understand what the speaker has said—not to show how mindless the speaker's words sound when parroted. Remember, too, that the rest of the team will also benefit from a clear summary of what was said.

7. Take Advantage of Lag Time. While you are waiting for a speaker's next idea, use the time to review what the speaker is saying. Separate the central idea, key points, and details. You can also use lag time to silently rephrase and summarize the speaker's message in your own words. Most important, keep your mind focused on the speaker and his or her ideas—not on all the other work waiting for you..

8. Take Notes to Ensure Retention. Don't trust your memory. A wise person once said that he'd rather have a short pencil than a long memory. If you have a hallway conversation with a team member and don't have a pencil handy, make a mental note of the important items. Then write, them down as soon as possible. Even with seemingly easily remembered facts or instructions, jot them down to ease your mind and also to be sure you understand them correctly. Two weeks later, you'll be glad that you did. Be sure you have a good place to store notes of various projects, such as file folders, notebooks, or computer files.

Checklist for Improving Listening[12]

- **Stop talking.** Accept the role of listener by concentrating on the speaker's words, not on what your respouse will be.
- **Work hard at listening.** Become actively involved; expect to learn something.
- **Block out competing thoughts.** Concentrate on the message. Don't allow yourself to daydream during lag time.

12. *Ibid.*

- **Control the listening environment.** Move to a quiet area where you won't be interrupted by telephone calls or visitors. Check to be certain that listeners can hear speakers.
- **Maintain an open mind.** Know your biases and try to correct for them. Be tolerant of less-abled and different-looking speakers. Provide-verbal and non-verbal feedback. Encourage the speaker with comments such as "Yes," "I see," "OK," and "Uh huh," and ask polite questions. Look alert by leaning forward.
- **Paraphrase the speaker's ideas.** Silently repeat the message in your own words, sort out the main points, and identify supporting details. In conversation, sum up the main points to confirm what was said. Take selective notes. If you are hearing instructions or important data, record the major points; then, verify your notes with the speaker.
- **Listen between the lines.** Observe nonverbal cues and interpret the feelings of the speaker: What is really being said?
- **Capitalize on lag time.** Use spare moments to organise, review, anticipate, challenge, and weigh the evidence.

Requirements of Effective Listening

According to experts, "Almost everyone in business is a talker. The problem is getting them to listen." The following may he enumersted[13] as the requirements of efective listening :

1. Listening for Purpose as Well as Details Obviously, as a good listener, you listen for facts—whether you intend to respond to them immediately, or to store them in mind for future reference. And listening for facts is more than just listening to details, as important as those details may be.

You want to listen, as well, for a sense of where the speaker is going. He may state his purpose clearly and openly as he begins to talk to you— but not always. He may not wish to reveal his purpose right away, or may just assume you can see it. in such case, you have to interpret the direction of his remarks and infer his purpose from them. He may simply be unorganized, forcing you to work hard mentally to get a sense of the direction in which he's moving,

As soon as you're sure what his purpose is, you're in a position to aid or hinder him in achieving it (whichever you wish) by how you respond. And you know how long to let him speak before you offer a reply. Knowing his purpose, you not only hear the details he's stating, but you're able to weigh those details as the instruments with which he's attempting to achieve his purpose. And you're able to see what kinds of details, if any, he's leaving out or ignoring.

2. Listening for Bias. Careful listening requires that you listen for connotations, as well as for literal meanings. The words a speaker chooses to transmit his information will very quickly reveal any biases he feels about that information. This is probably even truer for speakers than writers, for writers have chance to reconsider their words in a rough draft, while speakers (at

13. *Engineering Management* by Fraidoon Mazda : (Pearson Publishing Co.).

least those who are speaking extemporaneously, or "off the cuff") generally use the first words that come to mind. Or. they'll evidently fumble around for substitute words, in either case, their bias shows.

3. Encouraging the Speaker to Open Up. The good listener isn't merely a sensitive receiver of details and a perceiver of biases and purposes. He also encourages a speaker to express himself or herself more freely and more fully, thereby learning as much as possible from the speaker. When someone is talking to you, give him or her your complete attention. That's what the speaker wants, and he'll be flattered to have it. Establish eye contact with the speaker and maintain it as best you can. Bé sure that your posture and facial expression imply that what you're hearing is important to you: you may, in fact, be able to listen very well from a slouch or with a blank look on your face, but the speaker will feel that such a manner betrays a lack of interest on your part—and be more likely to "clam up" than "open up."

In addition to the above requirements, the listener must also try to avoid the following pitfalls. These may be termed as negative requirements for effective listening and are disscussed in the same sequence;

4. Preconceptions. You may have some preconceived opinions or biases regarding the matter being put to you by a speaker. Your opinions may even be more valid than the speaker's (or at least seem to be at the outset). However always hold open the possibility for it's very real-that the speaker has a new slant on the matter, or has some new information that nasn't yet reached you. Hear him out as though he does. Set aside your preconceptions while he speaks, and make yourself as free of your own biases as you possibly can.

5. Getting Turned Off by Dryness or Dullness. Many people, when confronted by a speaker, listen carefully for a minute—then, if the subject seems dry, or the speaker clumsy, they get "turned off". They continue listening, if at all, though a filter of their own disapproval. And through such a filter, you don't hear very well. Good listeners, when they find themselves "trapped" by dry subjects or dull speakers, remind themselves that even the driest presentations can yield some fertile facts or ideas. They also remember that there is little relationship between the quality of a person's mind and the fluency of his tongue; the most tongue-tied speakers can put forth valuable information and insight.

6. Becoming Distracted. Because we can think, and hence receive information, at a much faster rate than a speaker can give it to us, there is always the risk that we'll allow something else to enter our field of attention and distract us from what a speaker is saying. You've got to protect yourself against this. Work hard to improve your power of concentration. Shut the door or the window, if necessary. Turn off the mobile or the intercom. Move closer to the speaker. Use that faster thinking rate to anticipate where the speaker is going, to mentally summarize where he's been, to assess his nonverbal signals and to measure his motives and purposes.

7. Note-Taking as a Pitfall. Though you can think more quickly than a speaker can speak, you cannot (unless you're a master of shorthand) write as fast. As a consequence, listeners who take notes when a speaker speaks—and who try to get down *everything* the speaker says—usually fall behind and lose track of the central idea being developed. Tests have shown that only one out of four people listening to formal speeches are able to grasp the central idea. (And people speaking extemporaneously to you are usually even less organized than formal speakers!) in spite of good intentions, therefore, the copious note-taker often distracts himself more than he helps himself by trying to get everything down on paper. If you do take notes, put down only major ideas and direction signals. Listen carefully and jot down statements of purpose, patterns of idea development, and recapitulations—

8. Fatigue. Listening, like most other human activities, consumes vital energy. Careful listening is actually marked by a faster heartbeat, quickened pulse, even a small rise in body temperature. The lesson is clear then: when you've got to be at your listening best (in an important conference or during an interview) do anything you can to avoid entering the situation in a state of fatigue or divided interest.[14]

The Listening Process[15]

While talking of listening, we think primarily of the act of sensing sounds. In human communications, the sounds are mainly the spoken words. Viewed from a business communication standpoint, the listening process involves the following *four* stages :

1. Perception. The listening process begins when you hear sounds and concentrate on them. Stop reading for a moment and become conscious of the sounds around you Do you notice the hum of an electrical appliance, background sounds from a TV programme, traffic noise, or the murmur of distant voices? Until you 'tuned in" to them, these sounds went unnoticed. The conscious act of listening begins when you focus on the sounds around you and select those you choose to hear. You tune in when you (1) sense that the message is important, (2) are interested in the topic, or (3) are in the mood to listen. Perception is reduced by impaired hearing, noisy surroundings, in-attention, and pseudo-listening. Pseudo-listening occurs when listeners "fake" it. They look as if they are listening, but their minds are wandering far off.

2. Interpretation. Once you have focused your attention on a sound or message, you begin to interpret, or decode it. Interpretation of a message is coloured by your cultural, educational, and social frames of reference. The meanings you attach to the speaker's words are filtered through your expectations and total life experiences. Thus, your interpretation of the speaker's meaning may be quite different from what the speaker intended because your frame of reference is different.

3. Evaluation. After interpreting the meaning of a message, you analyse its merit and draw conclusions. To do this, you attempt to separate fact from opinion. Good listeners try to be objective, and they avoid prejudging the message. In a study of college students, one researcher determined that closed-mindedness and opinionated attitudes functioned as major barriers to listening. Certain students were not good listeners because their prejudices prevented them from opening up to a speaker's ideas. The appearance and mannerisms of the speaker can also affect a listener's evaluation of a message. Thus, to evaluate a message accurately and objectively, you should (1) consider all the information, (2) be aware of your own biases, and (3) avoid jumping to hasty conclusions.

14. Fraidoon Mazda : *op. cit.*

15. Adapted from : *Basic Business Communication : Skills for Empowering the Internet Generation* : Lesikar & Flatley : Tata McGraw Hill ed. 2007.

4. Action : Responding to a message may involve storing the message in memory for future use, reacting with a physical response (a frown, a smile, a laugh), or supplying feedback to the speaker. Listener feedback is essential because it helps clarify the message so that it can be decoded accurately. Feedback also helps the speaker to find out whether the message is getting through clearly. In one-to-one conversation, of course, no clear distinction exists between the roles of listener and speaker—you give or receive feedback as your role alternates.

Barriers to Listening

Before attempting to improve listening skills, listners should be aware of the major barriers to listening. Barriers to effective listening may be outlined below :

1. Speaker-Related Barriers :

(a) The speaker may speak too slow or too fast and in either case clarity may be compromised.

(b) Some speakers speak in a very soft voice (often inaudible) whereas others may be too loud to hear. In both the cases, listener feels disturbed or distracted.

(c) Some speakers may take long pauses frequently during their speech whereas other speak non-stop without taking a pause. In both the cases, there will be distraction and the message gets diluted.

(d) With mannerisms, the speaker may be either too active or inactive. In either way, it is a barrier to oral/verbal communication.

(e) The speaker may be more intelligent/literate than the audiance and discussion may go above their head (beyond the level of understanding of the listeners) or in a reverse case the discussion may go down their head (below the level of understanding). This results in a barrier.

(f) If the listeners are not familiar with the medium of expression used by the speaker, the entire exercise may be wasteful.

2. Listener Related Barriers :

(a) Lack of Interest : The listener may not be fully interested in the conversation or speech as he may he interested somewhere else due to mental preoccupations.

(b) "I know it all" attitude : If the listener assumes that he knows the subject and does not require further discussion on it, such an attitude is certainly going to affect his listening.

(c) Psychological Rejection : A listener may reject a person on an emotional or psychological level or, he may have a general dislike about the speaker, which has nothing to do with the subject matter of discussion. In such cases, the attention of the listener takes the beating.

(d) Listener's State of Mind : Many a times, the listeners mental state acts as a barrier to listening. If the listener himself, or any of his family members are unwell, his mental state may not be fully receptive to the message.

(e) Bias or Wrong Perception : If the listener does not have any interest in the subject matter due to an underlying bias or wrong perception, speakers effort may go waste.

(f) Ambiguity of Purpose : If the purpose of the speech is not clear or it does not serve any purpose, the listener may not listen.

(g) Physical Appearance or Defective Delivery : Sometimes the speaker's looks, dress, manners, age or speech defect may distract the listener from the subject matter. This could turn out to be a common barrier to effective listening.

(h) Dificulty in understanding : Level of understanding of difficult topic varies with individuals. Sometimes, when the topic is difficult, the listener's turns off his listening skills, thus creating a barrier in the communication process.

3. Environmental Barriers : Many a times, distractions are caused due to the following trivial matters, such as :

(a) Poor seating arrangement which is uncomfortable to the listener.

(b) Extreme hot or cold conditions (A.C. not working) at the venue ;

(c) Odd timings of the presentation;

(d) Noise made by doors, windows, fans, tables, chairs etc

(e) Poor lighting or ventilation.

(f) External noise or distractions

(g) Coughing, chatting, attending mobile phone by next person.

4. Other Barriers

(a) Barriers due to *differences in individual perception* about the subject matter;

(b) *Poor or high expectations* of the listener due to past experiences in similar situations.

(c) *Relationship with speaker* may determine listeners' perception about him/her.

(d) Individual *attitudes and beliefs* create positive or negative mental perceptions about the subject matter as well as the speaker in the mind of the listener. This creates barriers to listening which are hard to overcome.

(e) Many listeners *fake attention*. They show to be listening when they are actually hearing only.

(f) Some listeners fake note of the facts only, while ignore the overall massage of the speech, thus making the whole exercise futile.

(g) Distractions such as day dreaming (about unrelated subjects) or detouring (travelling with their own thoughts), debating (arguments against what is said) or planning (thinking of what to say when his turn comes) also create barriers to listening.

(h) Since listening is a *passive activity*, the listener has to sit for long. Though a speaker can move during speech, a listener can't move while listening*[16]

(i) Other factors such as (i) Physical or Mental tiredness of the listener, (ii) closed mind of the listener; (iii) status consciousness of the speaker; (iv) boring, unrelated or unnecessarily lengthy speech also creates barriers to listening.

DO'S OF LISTENING

For a better listening experience, the listener must :

- Observe silence while listening.

16. Adapted : *Business Communication* : M.K. Sehgal and Vandana Khetrapal : Excel Books : First Ed. 2006.

- Focus on what the speaker says instead of his appearance or looks.
- Listen first and take notes later
- Let the speaker finish first
- Control and minimise distractions
- Be friendly towards the speaker.
- Observe the non-verbal signals, body movements face expressions and gestures to get the total message.
- Try to find an area of interest in the speech
- Look interested in the speech.
- Keep your mind open to every subject & speaker
- Communicate feedback to the speaker.
- Ask questions related to the subject matter only
- Reach before scheduled time of lecture, talk or meeting.
- Empathise with the speaker by trying to understand his opinions, views and expressions.
- Try to enrich vocabulary for better understanding of the subject.

DONT'S OF LISTENING

The listener should not do the following :

- Interrupt the speaker while speaking.
- Reach late at the place of meeting or lecture.
- Show impatience while listening (towards speaker)
- Show the state of excitement or emotional outbreak
- Show lack of interest in the speech.
- Show close-mindedness.
- Show hesitation to give oral or non-verbal feedback.
- Attend mobile phone calls or reading e-mails while simultaneously listening a speech.
- Distracting the speaker by contradicting his statements or by pointing towards petty grammatical mistakes.
- Avoid daydreaming.
- Focus on the appearance and looks of the speaker.[17]

---

17. Adapted from *Business Communication* : M.K. Sehgal and Vandana Khetrapal : Excel Books : First Ed. 2006.
18. As quoted by Lesikar & Flatley in *Basic Business Communication : Skills for empowering the Internet Generation* : Tata McGraw Hill : Ed. 2007.

"THE TEN COMMANDMENTS OF LISTENING"

Keith Davis and John W. Newstrom proposed ten guides to improve listening. These are summarised below :[18]

1. Stop talking. Unfortunately, most of us prefer talking to listening. Even when we are not talking, we are inclined to concentrate on what to say next rather than on listening to others. So you must stop talking before you can listen.

2. Put the talker at ease. If you make the talker feel at ease, he or she will do a better job of talking. Then you will have better input to work with.

3. Show the talker you want to listen. If you can convince the talker that you are listening to understand rather than oppose, you will help create a climate for information exchange. You should look and act interested. Doing things like reading, looking at your watch, and looking away distracts the talker.

4. Remove distractions. The things you do also can distract the talker. So don't doodle, tap with your pencil, shuffle papers, or the like.

5. Empathize with the talker. If you place yourself in the talker's position and look at things from the talker's point of view, you will help create a climate of understanding that can result in a true exchange of information.

6. Be patient. You will need to allow the talker plenty of time. Remember that not everyone can get to the point as quickly and clearly as you. And do not interrupt. Interruptions are barriers to the exchange of information.

7. Hold your temper. From our knowledge of the workings of our minds, we know that anger impedes communication. Angry people build walls between each other. They harden their positions and block their minds to the words of others.

8. Go easy on argument and criticism. Argument and criticism tend to put the talker on the defensive. He or she then tends to "calm up" or get angry. Dale Carnegie has aptly said, "You may win an argument, but lose a friend". Rarely does either party benefit from argument and Criticism.

9. Ask questions. By frequently asking questions, you display an open mind and show that you are listening. And you assist the talker in developing his or her message and in improving the correctness of meaning.

10. Stop talking. The last commandment is to stop talking. It was also the first. All the other commandments depend on it.

From the preceding review it should be clear that to improve your listening ability, you must set your mind to the task. Poor listening habits are ingrained in our makeup. We can alter these habits only through conscious effort,

INFLUENCE/IMPACT OF PERSONAL CHARACTERISTICS ON LISTENING

Several researches on the Impact of personal characteristics (Age, sex, physique, nature of the person, intelligence level etc.) on the listening capability of a person have revealed that some characteristics don't influence whereas some other characteristics have a definite impact on their listening competence. These characteristics are discussed below :

1. Sex : Research has shown that gender differences does not impact listening capability of a person. It is an accepted fact now that listening capability is not inherent in sex differences.

2. Personality : personality or physical characteristics have no relation with listening ability. According to research analysis, a good listener may not possess a certain type of physique or personality.

3. Intelligence : Intelligence of the listener may have a positive impact on his listening capability. Generally speaking, higher the level of intelligence, higher is the listening or comprehension capability. At the same time, intelligence alone can't produce best listening skills. Other aspects are equally important.

5. Hearing Ability : It is a general belief that people who suffer some hearing loss are not good listeners. However, researches have time and again proved that the reverse is true. It is an established fact that those with moderate hearing loss are generally better listeners as they try to conquer their disability by being more attentive and so on.

6. Practice and Usage : Writing skills often improve with usage. To a lesser extent, speaking skills can also be improved with practice and usage. However, the same can't be said about listening skills. Listening skills can't he learn easily. It requires high degree of patience, preseverance and recognising the importance of listening.

7. Interest in the Topic: Listening capability improves, if the listener has an interest in the topic/subject matter. Capability improves considerably if :

(i) The topic is of listener's interest before the speech;
(ii) The interest is created during the speech; or
(iii) If the listener is to be tested after the speech.

Listening capability is also influenced by ways which help create a positive mindset among the listeners. Similarly, if the speaker indicates the critical nature of the speech, the listener is apt to give more attention.

In short, the interest in the topic, the positive mindset and attitude may improve the listening capability of the listener.

8. Verbal Competence : It means an adequate knowledge of the language and its vocabulary. If the verbal competence is high, the listening comprehension will be high and *vice versa.*

9. Organised and Structured Speech : An unorganised or unstructured speech negatively impacts the listening capability of the listener. The more well organised speech is, the better the level of comprehension. This applies both to speakers and listeners.

---

19. See also *Business Communication* : M.K. Sehgal and Vandana Khetrapal : Excel Books : First Ed. 2006.

10. Environmental Distractions : Environmental distractions like poor lighting, ventilation, temperature, external noises, movement of people, mobile ringtones etc., affect the listening capability negatively. By overcoming these distractions, the listening capability of the audience may be positively enhanced.[19]

"TECHNIQUES FOR IMPROVING LISTENING SKILLS"

1. Concentrate : Listen actively, attentively, alertly, critically. Concentrate on the speaker's message, not on the speaker. Do not take mental excursions-day dreaming is particularly hazardous. A boring speaker may require more attentiveness than usual. Your mind is capable of racing ahead more rapidly than the speed of words being received.

2. Take Notes : Jot down the key ideas, facts, conclusion, and recommendations of the speaker. Do not attempt to write verbatim the entire presentation or every detail. This effort will bog you down, so that you miss important concepts. If possible, formulate an outline of the speaker's presentation.

Is there a logical sequence or flow of ideas? Written notes are generally better than mental notes, especially if the subject is complex.

3. Listen with An Open Mind : Preconceived notions can cause a listener to resist or reject new ideas. Listen for content.

4. Observe the Speaker's Nonverbal Communication: Notice if the speaker's gestures body language, and facial expressions are attuned to what is being said. Remember, the message conveyed nonverbally may be more significant and convincing than what is being stated.

5. Analyse the Motives of the Speaker : Is it to convince, convey information, motivate action, persuade, or provide solutions? Is the speaker sincere, rational, objective, emotional, omitting facts? A Flamboyant delivery may be masking the meaning of a message. Discern the motives of the speaker.

6. Be Wary of Distractions : Distractions such as the speaker's accent, command of English, physical appearance, or manner of delivery may cause a listener to tune out. For example, a speaker has an unusual tie. This visual distraction interferes with listening. Attention is focused on the tie, not on what is being said.

7. Be Alert To Language Barriers : The level of language used by the speaker may be above or below the level of understanding the listener. Listen for meaning, stated or implied. Your understanding of words may differ from the speaker's.

8. Create A Good Listening Environment : Try to create a good physical environment conducive to listening, an environment free from distractions. The radio blaring in the background can be switched off; windows can be closed to shut out noise. Many business offices have conference rooms that provide a pleasant physical environment for listening : comfortable chairs, sound proofing, pads for note taking, and so on.

9. Avoid Distracting the Speaker : The listener can inadvertently distract the speaker and create a disjoined presentation. A question asked at the wrong time, an inappropriate siege of coughing, or other distractions can disrupt the logical transition of ideas. The listener should look alert and listening. Nothing is as disconcerting to a speaker as a yawning listener! Basic courtesy is a pre-requisite to good listening. Eye contact is desirable. Feedback to the speaker in the form of a smile, frown, or nod, may help the speaker improve the impact being made by the talk and thereby, aid in structuring remarks.

10. Be Mentally Prepared : Preliminary preparation may be necessary for effective listening, especially if the subject is complex. Research the topic as well as you can. For example, if the talk is about the automated office, the listener should familiarise yourself with terms such as coded keyboards, electronic blackboards, electronic circuits, and high-speed printers.

11. Be Physically prepared : One should be in good physical condition to listen effectively. It may be physically taxing to attend a long oral presentation. Don't skip lunch and attend a conference. A drink before a lecture can cloud the listener's mind.

12. Recapitulate : After hearing the speaker, immediately review your notes. If there are any discrepancies or inaccuracies, it may be possible to check with the speaker. Assess the value of the presentation by making your own value judgements. Recapitulation will help to reinforce what has been said and facilitate retention. It is interesting to note that about half of the message is generally lost immediately after it has been transmitted![20]

12 Rules of Effective Listening

By Geoffrey Nightingale

President : Syner Genics

1. Listen for ideas, not facts — ask yourself what they mean.
2. Judge Content, not delivery — *i.e.;* what they say, not how they say it.
3. Listen optimistically — Don't lose interest straightaway.
4. Do not Jump to conclusions.
5. Be flexible — adjust your note taking to the speaker.
6. Concentrate — Don't start dreaming — and keep an eye contact.
7. Don't think ahead of the speaker- you will lose track.
8. Work at listening — be alert and alive.
9. Keep emotions under control — when listening.
10. Open your mind — practice accepting new information.
11. Breathe slowly and deeply.
12. Relax physically, get comfortable.

SUMMARY

Listening is a part of oral communication. It is different than hearing. listening entails hearing with attention office/Business people more time in listening than speaking, reading or writing. Some

20. Adapted from : *Communication Systems and Procedures for the Modern Office* : Nathan Krevolin : Prentice Hall : New Jersey : Pages 282-284.

employees like Receptionists, Telephone operator, Interviewers, Counsellors spend more than 50% of their time in listening.

Active listening : On average, people spend nearly 45% of their communication time in listening. Therefore, Managers must learn to listen effectively. Effective listening requires active listening, being responsive and not sitting passively. The receiver of a message must not only hear but listen. There are simple ways to improve active listening.

Good listeners should follow the following practies :

1. Pay attention
2. Focus on the Speaker
3. Avoid making assumptions
4. Listen for feelings as well as facts

Requirements for effective listening include :

(a) Listening for purpose as well as details, (b) listening for bias, (c) encouraging the speaker to open up; (d) Preconceptions; (e) Getting turned off by dullness, (f) Becoming distracted, (g) Note-Taking as a pitfall, (h) Fatigue

Barriers to listening are of the following types :

1. Speaker related Barriers
2. Listener related Barriers
3. Environmental Barriers
4. Other Barriers

Following personal characteristics influence listening :

- Sex
- Personality
- Intelligence
- Hearing Ability
- Practice & usage
- Interest in the Topic etc.,

Techniques for Improving listening skills :

1. Concentrate, 2. Take notes, 3. listen with an open mind, 4. Observe the speaker's non-verbal language, 5. Analyse the motives of the speaker, 6. Be wary of distractions, 7. Be alert to language Barriers, 8. Create a good listening environment, 9. Avoid distraction, 10. Be mentally prepared, 11. Be physically prepared. 12. Recapitulate.

REFERENCES

1. Nathan Krevolin : Communication System and Procedures for the Modern Office.
2. Paul T. Batkin : Listening ability.
3. Koontz etc. : Principles of Management
4. Wells : Communication in Business
5. Kitty O. Locker & Stephen Kyo. : Business Communication : Building Critical Skills.
6. Mary Ellan Guffy : Business Communication : Process and Product.
7. Fraidoon Mazda : Engineering
8. Lesiker & Flatley : Basic Business Communication : Skills for Empowering the internet generations
9. M.K. Sehgal & Vandana Khetrapal : Business Communication.

STUDY QUESTIONS

1. Define 'active listening'. How it helps in effective listening.
2. What practices a good listener should follow ? Dissuss in detail.
3. What are the requirements for effective listening? Discuss.
4. Discuss in detail, the defferent types of barriers to effective listening. How can they be overcome?
5. Explain how personal characteristics can influence effective listening?
6. Discuss the techniques for improving listening skills.
7. Discuss the importance of listening and silence in communication.

   (B.Com. (Hons.) I Paper VII (a) Delhi 2005 B)

8. Write short note of about 50-60 words :

   (i) Body language *(B. Com. (Hons) I Paper VII (a) Delhi 2006A)*

   (B. Com. (Hons) I paper VII (a) Delhi 2008A)

   (ii) Sign language *(B. Com. (Hons) I Paper VII (a) Delhi 2007A)*

Chapter 8

OFFICE ETIQUETTE

CONTENTS

Chapter **8**

OFFICE ETIQUETTE

Etiquette : Meaning and Definition

Etiquette is a code that governs the expectations of social behaviour, according to the contemporary conventional norm within a society, social class or group. Usually unwritten, it may be codified unwritten form. Etiquette usually reflects an underlying ethical code or it may grow more as a fashion statement. Like 'culture', it is a word that has gradually grown plural, especially in a *multi-ethnic society* with many clashing expectations' A few definitions quotes of etiquette may be noted :

"Etiquette means the forms required by good breeding, or prescribed by authority, to be observed in social or official life, observance of the properties of rank and occasion, conventional wisdom, ceremonial code of polite society." — *Prescott*

"Etiquette has to do with good manners. It is not so much our own good manners, but making other people feel comfortable by the way we behave. So it is more or less thinking of others and how others perceive us: so that everyone knows the rules for doing things and everyone is in a very comfortable position in society". *Naomi Polson*

— www. essortment.com

"The high point in civilisation is that you can hate me and I can hate you but we develop an *Etiquette* that allows us to deal with each other because if we acted solely upon our impulse, we'd probability go to war." — *Stanlay Crouch*[2]

"Etiquette means and include the forms, manners and ceremonies established by convention as acceptable or required in social relations, in a profession, or in official life."

—*Free English Dictionary (Google Search)*

Built up over hundreds of years; worthless ones are continuously being discarded and those proven to be useful are kept and improved upon."[3]

1. From wikipedia, the free encyclopedia
2. www.brainyquotes. com/words/et/etiquette
3. Funk & Wagnell : *The Emily Post Book of Etiquette for Young People*".

Many people feel that Etiquette is simply showing respect for others and yourself at the same time. So even though aspects of good manners may vary from place to place and some rules may be added or 'tweaked' to keep up with technology and life-styles — the foundation of *Etiquette*, its meaning, will forever remain strong.

Lillian Eichler[4] in her book, "Today's Etiquette" writes : "In social and business life we seek the people with whom we can be at ease, the people whose manners do not offend us and in whose company we feel entirely comfortable. There is, indeed, nothing that costs less and at the same time is of more value to you than good manners... However, it must be remembered that.. Just as words die from our language and others are born into it, just as skirts soar to the knees one season and tumble to the ankles the next, so do the formalities and outward gestures of etiquette vary according to the times. Although the spirit of etiquette remains always essentially the same, the expression of etiquette — the rules of conduct which govern social life and our associations with one another — is forever adjusting itself to new conditions..."

History of Etiquette Codes

Etiquette is dependent on culture; what is excellent etiquette in one society may shock another. Etiquette evolves within culture[5]. Etiquette is a topic that has occupied thinkers and writers in all sophisticated societies for centuries and even millennia. A brief history of the evolution of the etiquette codes follows

- **2414-2375 B.C. :** A behaviour code devised by *Ptahhotep, a vizier in ancient* Egypt's old Kingdom during the reign of the *fifth dynasty* King *Djedkare Isesi.*
- Ancient *Greece* and *Rome* and all known literate civilisations, developed rules for proper social conduct, confucius included rules for eating and speaking along with his more philosophical sayings.
- **1630 :** Dutch paintings of the *Middle Ages,* portrayed a bonding experience that reinforced the comparative ranking of two people, one ground the other groomer and portrayed the rules of conduct and representation.
- **1780 :** In the late 18th Century, *Adolph Freiher Knigge* wrote a book called the *Knigge,* on high rules of conduct which became the unofficial code of conduct in Germany.
  The code of conduct is still used primarily in high society in Germany, and commands high respect.
- **1789 & 1797** in U.S., Benjamin Franklin and *George Washington* wrote codes of conduct for young gentlemen. The immense popularity of *Advice Columns* and books by *Letitia* and *Miss Manners* shows the currency of the Topic.
- **1900 :** Early modern conceptions of what behaviour identifies a 'Gentleman' were codified in the sixteenth century, in a book by *Baldassare,* "The courtier." Its codification of expectations remained in force until World War I in Italy.
- **1920 :** King louis XIV established an elaborate and rigid set of rules for stylish eating and fastidious behaviour at dining, in Italy, called galateo (or etichetta).

4. Lillian Eichler : *'Today's Etiquette' : Double Day Doran* : Ed. 1941 (Google Internet Search).
5. Andries Both : *Hunting Lice by Candlelight.* (Google Internet Search)

- **1950 :** Debrett (U.K.) is considered by many to be the arbiter of etiquette. His guides to manners an form have long been the last word among, polite society. His publication *'correct form'* has lately been updated and new titles, *'Etiquette for Girls'* and *'Manners for Men'* act as guides for those who want to combine a modern life-style with traditional values.
- **2000 :** Recently, the rise of the internet, has necessitated the adaptation of existing rules of conduct to create *'Netiquette'*, which governs the drafting of e-mail, rules for participation online forum etc. and so on.

General Office Etiquette

While different offices have different policies, there are a few universal truths about etiquette that must be observed at all times. These may include the following :

- **Ask before you borrow anything.** There's nothing worse than being branded the office thief because your stash of 'borrowed' rulers or pens is discovered by the cleaning lady. **Wash your mug after you've used it.** Don't expect the cleaners to wash up for you. Clean it yourself
- **Any release of bodily gases is highly frowned upon.** Farting may have been okay back in High School, but you won't be taken seriously if you perform a rendition of Flight of The Bumble Bee at the workplace.
- **Don't fall asleep at your desk.** And if you do, make sure you're at a desk that faces away from everyone else and you don't snore[6].
- **Open doors for your colleagues.** It is a good gesture to open doors for your colleagues visiting your cabin, particularly the women colleagues.
- **Monitor your speaking volume.** People always tend to speak louder than necessary when on Mobile. Make sure to lower the volume or go into the corridor.
- **'Printer Etiquette'** is a term popular in Australia. It refers to giving preferential treatment to workers printing one page only, ahead of others using half an hour and half a rim to print out large documents.
- **Be sensitive about smells :** Avoid or limit the use of strong perfumes, excessive body odour or very fragrant flowers, as they may offend others.
- **Keep your music to yourself :** Not everyone at the office would be keen to listen to your favourite music. So, keep to listen to your favourite music. So, keep the volume low or use head-phones.
- **Stay home during sickness :** Do not turn up for work while experiencing cough, flu or fever symptoms to avoid the risk of spreading injection to others. If you must appear, be considerate and use tissues and wash hands frequently to minimise the spread of germs.
- **Be punctual :** A British survey has revealed[7] that two out of three people regularly turn up late for meetings. Avoid (*i*) being late; (*ii*) cancelling the meeting at short notice or (*iii*) chatting with others while the meeting is on.

---

6. Adapted from the *Ultimate Office Etiquette Guide* : Posted on 10th March, 2008 : Google Internet Search.
7. *Office Etiquette.* tips posted on 24.12.2007 (Google Internet Search)
8. This Sinha Phira. *Money Control.com* posted on 7.10. 2006.

• **Stay away from Office Gossip :** There is, one virus which generally flouts all office etiquette[8]. That is Gossip. Avoid the risk of "getting caught in the firing range of all the back stabbing and never ending office gossips.

• **Don't Treat Office Phone as a PCO :** Calling everyone and anyone you know, making personal calls on office phones for hours, talking to your boy/girl friend for hours, chatting with your buddy endlessly on office phone during office time is absolutely not right.

• **Tell about your Whereabouts :** To those who should know about it or leave a note on your desk before leaving.

And if you find yourself not following these general tips, you surely need a refresher course in Office Etiquette.

Verbal Communication Etiquette

The way one communicates with fellow employees is very important to one's career. Here's what one need to know about verbal Office Etiquette.

• **Being formal is a necessity in the workplace.** You'll be speaking to people you've never met before, customers, other departments and so on. Answering the phone in a causal or informal manner is not considered business like.

• **If someone gives you their name, remember it.** Especially, if you're in a role where clients regularly come to the office. Using their name to address them throughout the meeting makes it more personalised and makes them feel more relaxed and willing to engage in conversation with you.

• **Leave the bad habits at home.** Don't swear and don't chew gum when speaking to someone. Even over the phone. They can hear it and it is annoying.

• **Make sure you listen when people are speaking to you.** Looking around and wondering what time you're meeting the guys in the bar later while your boss briefs you on a new campaign is poor form and when you can't remember what he's said, you'll look incompetent and unprofessional.

• **In an initial meeting play it safe and keep conversation solely on work matters.** You must not be telling the I.T. Manager about the bedroom antics of the hot girl in Accounts.

• **End your meeting with a hearty handshake,** thank them for their time and exchange business cards if necessary.

• While in a group or at a meeting, cell phones should either be shut off or put in a silent mode/vibrator mode, placed in either the bag or the pocket, out of sight.

Colleague Relationship Etiquette

It's important to always be respectful of your colleagues and avoid burning your bridges with them. You never know when you may rely on their help to get you out of a tricky jam. Here are a few things you should be aware of :

• **There's nothing more annoying that a ringing phone that goes unanswered.** If you don't want to answer your phone put it on silent or divert calls to your answer phone. Also, keep your cell phone on vibrate because "if I hear another rendition of the Crazy Frog ring tone, I *will* kill someone".

• **Office politics is unavoidable.** Don't let people undermine you or draw you into arguments. Let your achievements do the talking for you and make sure that the right people are aware of what you have accomplished without you needing to brag about.

• **If you're going to take lunch at your desk, keep it simple.** A sandwich is best. Don't go bringing in a homemade spicy chicken and pasta dish that's going to stink up the office and annoy people. Make sure you don't disturb people with work-related problems when they're on their lunch. They won't thank you for it and you'll be repaid in kind at a later date.

• **Always offer to make tea and coffee for your colleagues.** If you do take these but do not contribute in the expense kitty, you will be called 'names' in your absence. Evil eyes and anonymous hate e-mail will surely follow.

• **Avoid making sex with your colleague in your office cabin.** If you really must have sex with a colleague in office place, be a gentleman. "If you love her and leave her, you better believe the office will be rife with talks about your lack of stamina and incompetence." Also you will look unprofessional to your bosses and forfeit all future chances of making relationship with other colleagues.

• **Most offices have some sort of Friday 'ritual'.** Where everyone may come in jeans/t-shirt etc. If there is such a ritual, observe it to avoid looks fool.

• It is common practice in the workplace to use high decibels when using the phone, in most case deliberately (to catch the boss' attention) and in some cases intentionally, which in any case disrupts the work environment and is a total violation of office etiquette.

• Another familiar workplace irritant is the **constant complainer.** The complaints are generally about work, facilities, boss, health, kids, maids etc., The **control freak** is yet another nuisance at the workplace.

• And *'Sexual Harassment'* should come in 'No Tolerance Zone' in every company's policy.

• *Don't comment on personal appearance* or clothes of colleagues in a negative way. If you cannot appreciate or compliment your colleagues, donot say anything at all.

Etiquette and manners at workplace are about putting others before you and treating them with respect and courtesy at all times. As such, observe the following :

- Don't try and find 'best friends' among your colleagues.
- Don't try and get up, close and personal with your boss.
- Don't try and seek audience from the next cubicle when talking on the phone.
- Don't keep ringtones of your mobile very loud when at work.
- Don't peep over your colleague's shoulders to read their emails
- Don't entertain jokes that have sexual overtones
- Don't comment on people's sense of dressing.
- Don't try and seek unnecessary attention be constantly talking about your achievements.

What you Must do

- Do reply to office mails and try to use lower cases while typing as bold letters signify a scream.
- Do keep you voice low while talking.
- If you have a problem that may force you to stay away from work, keep your boss in the loop.
- Do congratulate a colleague on his/her achievements, even if you do not approve of his/her ways.
- Do not forget to shut you mobile phone during meetings.

Visitor's Etiquette :

While visiting other offices as part of the work schedule, one should follow these simple yet effective etiquette rules.[9]

- Be punctual and if you are 5 minutes early, even better. This indicates that you respect other people's time.
- Don't stroll into a place as if it's your own.
- Be polite to everyone you meet irrespective of if it's the receptionist or the CEO.
- If the office that you are visiting needs you to sign in, and take a visitor card, comply with the protocol. You could supply the receptionist with your visiting card.
- While waiting, don't try to chat up the receptionist, in case you're feeling bored!
- While waiting in someone's office, don't touch anything on his/her desk or around his/her room. Similarly, his/her reading material is his/her own, and is not there for you to kill time with.
- Carry your own pens and note pads; it looks very unprofessional when you ask to borrow theirs.
- Get your work done and leave. This is not a social visit so don't grab every opportunity to chitchat.
- On your way out, remember to thank the receptionist !

Outside the Office Etiquette

Office etiquette extends beyond the walls of your workplace and into any venue that involves work. This is where it gets tricky because, as they say, you should never mix business with pleasure. *Apparently.*[10]

- **If you've got a business lunch, then get there on time.** Leave early if you need to but do not be late because it isn't a lunch per se, it's a meeting in an informal location.

9. "Your manners are always under examination, and by committees little suspected, awarding or denying you very high prizes when you least think of it."
10. *Ibid.*

- **Turn your phone off during any business lunch you go to.** Nobody wants to look inconsiderate while taking a call during an important meeting.
- **Keep your greeting short and sweet with the aforementioned handshake.** Proper business meeting etiquette allows for a few minutes of small talk but keep it simple.
- **If you invited your guest to the lunch, you're the one who should be paying for the meal.** You can of course discuss splitting the bill when arranging the meeting but don't leave it till the bill arrives as some people see this as a sign of professional weakness. Don't forget to tip the restaurant staff.
- **When networking at business conferences you should make the first move to approach people wherever possible.** Remember that first impressions count so dress to impress and keep the conversation formal.
- **You can build your business contacts by networking with the speakers at conferences.** Do your research and find out who is speaking and what they are about. This will give you some good topics to discuss with them if you get the chance.
- **Set yourself a target to meet during a conference.** Say, five new contacts through networking. Using the amazing etiquette tips you've learnt so far, it should be easy.
- **Don't get too drunk at the office party!** How many people have lost respect, pay rises and even their job from drunken antics over the years. Keep your alcohol consumption in moderation and avoid flirting with the boss' wife, wherever possible.[11]

Business Meeting Etiquette

While attending or going to attend Business meeting, the following etiquette tips may be of help :

- Confirm your appointment to know any cancellation at short notice.
- Keep your schedule flexible so that it can be adjusted for last minute rescheduling of meeting.
- Arrive at the meeting venue in time, preferably a few minutes early.
- Generally meetings start with a great deal of introduction talks. Be ready for late conclusion of meeting.
- Always send a detailed Agenda in advance. Send back-up materials, data and charts etc. as well to allow others to know and review the material prior to the meeting.
- Follow up a meeting with an overview of the discussions held and the next action programme.
- If the meeting is to continue for long hours, provide breaks for tea/coffee, lunch or driver, whichever is appropriate, at proper intervals.

Cellphone Etiquette

The basic guide to the use of the cellphone is not to offend the people around you. The cellphone etiquette would include the following :

11. Ralph Waldo Emerson : Google Internet Search.

• **Don't talk loudly in public :** The cellphone is meant to promote your privacy, without disturbing the privacy of everyone around you. No body wants to know if your child missed the school bus or the tailor ditched at the last moment or what medicine to take for that problem, God knows what.

• **Don't call people as and when you want :** The cellphone is meant for the convenience — of its owner. But you should also care for the appropriateness of the timings for the person you call. Calling at odd hours should be avoided as far as possible.

• **Cover your mouth :** While talking on the phone in public.

• **Know your cellphone :** Know the features of your phone so that you can use them when required. Some basic features include caller ID, Ringtones, Memory, Phone book, Calender, Calculator, Alarm, one touch dialling etc. Use the features, when required.

• **Follow the Rules :** Rules about where you can use the cellphone. Some people say, the phone menace is worse than smoking.' Talking loudly on cellphone in the Cinema Halls, Seminars or Conference rooms or at the hospitals may be very irritating to others.

• **Cellphone as health hazard :** Don't talk too much on your cellphone. Several studies say that it can be injurious to health. What could also be dangerous in where you keep the phone. Keeping the cellphone in the shirt pocket could cause a heart attack. Similarly, keeping it in the front pocket of the pants will risk the chances of the person having children[12].

FAX(ing) Etiquette

Faxing is a very important aspect of office communication. Certain etiquette tips[13] should the followed :

- When sending fax, always include a cover page specifying whom the message is being sent for.
- Preferably type your message.
- If you have to write out the message, use capital letters
- Corrections, if made by correction fluid show up as dark patches. Better, make a photocopy and use it to fax the message.
- Many offices receive faxes on a computer, so make sure the paper is inserted the Right side up, otherwise the message can't be read unless it is printed out.
- Fax paper is very expensive. Avoid sending unnecessary long messages.
- Call and check if the timing is convenient for the receiver to receive the fax message.
- If confidential information is to be taxed, call ahead and inform the recipient so that he/she can retrieve it personally.
- Don't use office Fax machine for sending personal message or office Gossip etc.

12. Also see *"Learn the Art of Calling"* By Insiya Amir, Times of India, New Delhi, 7th Dec. 2008.
13. See also *Office Etiquette* : Google Internet Search.

Gifting Etiquette

On certain occasions or during festive season, it is customary to exchange greeting cards and gifts while celebrating. Some offices do have a protocol on making or receiving gifts by the employees. Here are a few tips :

- If office Protocol prohibits the giving or accepting of gifts above a certain monetary limits, it should be strictly followed.
- Avoid sending intimate gifts to colleagues or clients.
- If you receive anything inappropriate, return it immediately with a *polite but firm* note of refusal.
- While sending out cards, add a small line of greeting, wishes or appreciation.
- When a large number of cards have to be sent, they may be sorted into 'personal note' and 'Signature only' categories.
- If you can't sign the card, don't send it.
- Always promptly acknowledge greeting cards and gifts received by you. Acknowledgement must contain your appreciation or thank you notes etc.
- Greetings sent by e-mail must be personalised.
- Make sure that Cards and Gifts must reach the recipient before or at the appropriate time/event and never later. Carefully plan the timings.
- It is not the value of the gift, but the sincerity with which it is given. That is important to the recipient.

E-mail Etiquette

E-mail etiquette is also called *Netiquette*. The following is a list of top e-mail Etiquette Rules, which need to be followed :[13]

1. Be concise and to the point. Do not make an e-mail longer than it needs to be. Remember that reading an e-mail **is** harder than reading printed communications.

2. Answer all questions, and pre-empt further questions : An e-mail reply must answer all questions, and pre-empt further questions — If you do not answer all the questions in the original e-mail, you will receive further e-mails regarding the unanswered questions, wasting, time of both sides and causing frustration.

3. Use proper spelling, grammar and punctuation : This is not only important because improper spelling, grammar and punctuation gives a bad impression of your company, it is also important for conveying the message properly. E-mails with no full stops or commas are difficult to read and can sometimes even change the meaning of the text.

4. Answer swiftly : E-mails are sent as people wish to receive a quick response. Each e-mail should be replied to within at least 24 hours, and preferably within the same working day.

5. Do hot attach unnecessary files : By sending large attachments you can annoy others and even bring down their e-mail system. Wherever possible, try to compress attachments.

6. Use proper structure & layout : Since reading from a screen is more difficult than reading from paper, the structure and lay out is very important for e-mail messages. Use short paragraphs and blank lines between each paragraph. When making points, number them or mark each point as separate to keep the overview.

7. Do not write in Capitals : If you write in Capitals it seems as if you are shouting. This can be highly annoying and might trigger an unwanted response in the form of a flame mail. Therefore, try not to send any email text in capitals.

8. Read the e-mail before you send it. Reading the e-mail before sending it, relieve it of the grammatical and spelling mistakes. Moreover, reading your e-mail through the eyes of the receiver will help you send a more effective and appropriate message.

9. Do not overuse Reply to All : Only use Reply to All if you really need your message to be seen by each person who received the original message.

10. Do not use e-mail to discuss confidential information : Sending an e-mail is like sending a postcard. If you don't want your e-mail to be displayed on a bulletin board, dont send it. Moreover, never make any libelous, sexist or racially discriminating comments in e-mails, even if they are meant to be a joke.

11 Use cc: field sparingly. Try not to use the cc: field unless the recipient in the cc: field knows why they are receiving a copy of the message. Using the cc: field can be confusing since the recipients might not know who is supposed to act on the message.

12. E-mail Etiquette is commonly flouted when sick jokes are sent to everyone in the address book. Almost everyone opens the mail to read at least the first few lines before deciding to go ahead or skip it.

Cross-cultural Etiquette[14]

Editors of Publication International, Ltd. have compited several example of good and Bad Manners Around the World. These and other matters of Etiquette are listed below :

Manners that may be good in one country may not be in other parts of the world. Cross-Cultural Etiquette may differ widely.

"Sit up straight. Say please and thank you. Don't put your elbows on the table." Most of us were taught from an early age in proper manners and etiquette. But once you leave your home country, things get a bit complicated. Here are some examples of how other cultures do things differently.

1. In China, Taiwan, and much of the Far East, belching is considered a compliment to the chef and a sign that you have eaten well and enjoyed your meal.

2. In most of the Middle and Far East, it is considered an insult to point your feet (particularly the soles) at another person or to display them in any way, for example, by resting with your feet up.

3. In most Asian countries, a business card is seen as an extension of the person it represents;

14. "Office Etiquette" : Adapted (Google Internet Search).

therefore, to disrespect a card — by folding it, writing on it, or just shoving it into your pocket without looking at it is to disrespect the person who gave it to you.

4. Nowadays, a bone-crushing handshake is seen as admirable in the United States and U.K., but in much of the East, particularly the Philippines, it is seen as a sign of aggression — just as if you gave any other part of a person's body a hard squeeze!

5. Orthodox Jews will not shake hands with someone of the opposite sex, while a strict Muslim woman will not shake hands with a man. To confuse matters, a Muslim man will shake hands with a non-Muslim woman. People in these cultures generally avoid touching people of the opposite sex who are not family members.

6. When dining in China, never force yourself to clear your plate out of politeness - it would be very bad manners for your host not to keep refilling it. Instead, you should leave some food on your plate at each course as an acknowledgement of your host's generosity.

7. In Japan and Korea, a *tip* is considered an insult, rather than a compliment, and for them accepting tips is akin to begging. However, this tradition is beginning to change as more Westerners bring their customs with them to these countries.

8 The "okay" sign (thumb and forefinger touching to make a circle) is very far from okay in much of the world. In Germany and most of South America, it is an insult, similar to given someone the finger in the United States, while in Turkey it is a derogatory gesture used to imply that someone is homosexual.

9. Similarly, in the U.K., when the two-fingered "V for victory" or "peace" salute is given with the hand turned so that the palm faces inward, it is considered extremely rude, having a meaning similar to raising the middle finger to someone in the United States.

10. In Greece, any signal that involves showing your open palm is extremely offensive. Such gestures include waving, as well as making a "stop" sign. If you do wish to wave good bye to someone in Greece, you need to do so with your palm facing in, like a beauty pageant contestant or a member of the royal family.

11. In many countries, particularly in Asia and South America, it is essential to remove your shoes when entering someone's home, while in most of Europe it is polite to ask your host whether they would prefer you to do so. The reason, as anyone who's ever owned white carpet will attest is simple hygiene and cleanliness.

12, Chewing *gum* might be good for dental hygiene, but in many parts of the world, particularly ' Luxembourg, Switzerland, and France, public gum-chewing is considered vulgar, while in Singapore most types of gum have been illegal since 1992 when residents grew tired of scraping the sticky stuff off their sidewalks.

13. In most Arab countries, the left hand is considered unclean, and it is extremely rude to offer it for a handshake or to wave a greeting. Similarly, it is impolite to pass food or eat with the left hand. If you must know why, let's just say that, historically, people living in deserts didn't have access to toilet paper, so the left hand was used for "hygienic functions," then cleaned by rubbing it in the sand.

14. What is rude in Japan may be perfectly acceptable in Latin America. However, you will be excused for not knowing the rules of an alien culture. But you will not be excused for being

careless in your own country. In any case, always remember the principle of not making other uncomfortable.

15. Etiquette may be enforced in pragmatic ways : "No shoes; no shirt; no service" is a notice commonly displayed outside shores and cafes in North America.

16. In China, a person who takes the last item of food from a common plate or bowl without first oppering it to others at the table may be seen as a glutton and insulting the generosity of the host. In America, a guest is expected to eat all of the food given to him, as a compliment to the quality of the cooking.[15]

Etiquette may be regarded as a social weapon. The outward adoption of the superficial mannerisms of a group, in the interests of social advancement rather than a concern for others, is a form of *snobbery,* lacking in virtue.

Bad Office Etiquettes

The examples are : —

1. Taking personal (or very personal calls) or on speaker phone with door open.
2. Refusing to toss trash in his own wastebasket. Instead throwing his trash away in everyone else's wastebasket.
3. Speaking in a really loud tone of voice that can be heard from everywhere in the office.
4. Barging into another's office without knocking.
5. Sniffing the nose without using a handkerchief
6. "Some people in the office smack their lips, snack their teeth or make any kind of audible annoying sound."
7. People who crack jokes on other colleagues or call them names.
8. Clipping of nails during work.
9. Taking long lunches or tea breaks.
10. Coming late, going early
11. Spending all day finding mistakes of others.
12. Borrowing and not returning or stealing other's stationery articles.
13. Leaving important/confidential papers on the fax machine.
14. Viewing pornographic or adult sites during office time on office computers.
15. Doing phone interview with other companies while at work.
16. Making conference calls with the door open.
17. Constantly ridiculing the clothing or dress sense of other co-workers.
18. Changing 'My setting' or 'uninstalling' the programmes installed by others.
19. Using dirty words for subordinates.

---

15. Adapted from "*13 Examples of Good and Bad Manners Around the World.*" By the Editors of Publications International Ltd. 28th Oct. 2008.

20. Flirting with every person of the opposite sex during office work time.
21. Forgetting names of Juniors or subordinates showing that they are not so important for him/her to bother about their names.
22. Female staff wearing low-cut-shirts and distracting male colleagues by flaunting their assets.
23. Attending the office while sick and wasting other's time in telling the details of Doctor's diagnoses to each and every co-worker.
24. Discussing personal extra-marital affairs with co-workers during working time.
25. Wearing the same shirt or suit two or three days in a row. (Part of Office Decorum).
26. Pinching other colleagues for wearing new, everyday in the morning at the office.[16]

Dining Etiquette (Buffet)

Most office Dining is in the form of Buffet Dining. The following rules of etiquette should be followed while at an office Dining :

1. Resist from heaping a mountain of food on your plate, instead make additional trips to the buffet.
2. Leave the line when coughing or sneezing, to prevent contamination of the food.
3. Roll up your sleeves, mind your tie, sari, dupatta etc.
4. As a rule, take what you touch on the Buffet counter.
5. In a paid-for buffet, like a restaurant, feel free to change you plate every time you visit the Buffet counter, leaving your old plate at the table for the waiter to clear away.
6. In a Banquet party, hotels count the number of dinner plates picked up at the Buffet counter when billing the host. So, if you pick up a plate every time, the host ends up paying for it.
7. In a stand-up buffet, rice and pasta and other snacks are easier to eat than rotis or bread, as they donot mess the fingers.
8. Small boneless pieces of meat are easier to eat, as tearing the meat away from the bone with the plate in one hand and no knife can be tricky.
9. In a paid-for buffer in a restaurant, where waiters serve the drinks, bring snacks or hot food etc. a 5% of the total bill is a good tip.[17]
10. As a Guest, you should stick to your own dietary preferences.
11. If you donot or cannot, as laid down by caste, cread, religion or personal choice, take something, you should feel free to refuse. If you are served, say beef or pork, and you donot eat it, say so politely.

16. Compiled from different sources through Google Internet Search and blogs like www.yelp.com/topic/bad office Etiquettes, Beach front office wordpress.com etc.
17. Also see *Q & A Buffet Etiquette* : Shital Kakar Mehta, The Economic Times 22nd August, 2008.

12. The same attitude should be shown towards drinks. If you are a teetotaler, decline the offer to drink politely. Do not elaborate on the harms of drinking.
13. Although it is considered best to avoid drinking at office dinners, but, if you do accept the drink, avoid drinking too much.
14. After eating, make it a point to clean up the space, use tissue papers to clean the dining space used by you. Put all wrappers and wastes in the bin. after finishing your meal.

Table Manners

Office dinners are formal occasions. So the manner of using forks, knives and a spoon indicate how cultured and well groomed you are. Most Indians prefer to eat food with their hands. The only cutlery used by them could be a spoon. Some General[18] tips of correct use of cutlary are given below :

Cutlery set for a formal serving

Placed from Left to Right

- A Butter Knife placed on Butter & Knife plate.
- Dessert spoon and Dessert fork.
- Water Glass, wine/beer glass
- Coffee cup & Saucer

Placed from Right to Left

- Cocktail fork
- Soup Spoon
- Tea Spoon
- Dinner Plate
- Dinner Napkin

Using Knife and fork at the Dinner Table

- Always use the knife for cutting the food and the form for placing it into the month.
- Use Knife for cutting food into small pieces such as vegetables, meat or any other food. Knife should never be placed into the month.
- The fork is first held in the left hand with knife in the right hand, to cut food into small pieces. Then the knife is kept on the plate and in its placed the fork is held in the right hand to place the food into the mouth.
- When you are not using them, both knife and fork should be placed on a side plate, but never on the table.
- If you are accustomed to eating with hands, use a spoon instead.
- Table spoons may be used for eating rice, vegetable etc. while tea spoons may he used for taking sauces, vinegars, ketchup etc., or for making tea or coffee after dinner.
- Instead of shouting or loudly calling the waiter, the best way is to try and establish eye contact. If necessary, move a little towards the waiter to draw his/her attention. The best thing to do is to say, "Excuse me".

18. *Business Communication* : M.K.Sehgal, Vandana Khetarpal, Eagle Books, ed. 2006 (Adapted).

Workplace (Office) Washroom Etiquettes

The ground rules for etiquette in the office are endless. Similarly, etiquette in the office washroom (toilets) is also equally important, if not more. The following Do's and Dont's must be observed for impeccable washroom etiquette :

- **Be Sanitary :** Don't leave your mess for others to clean. Throw away your trash (into the bin only), wipe up excess water on the counter tops and don't leave the seats wet.
- **Flush :** Always flush after using the toilets. Save others from the trauma of flushing the toilets used by you.
- **Wash your Hands :** Imagine the feeling when you have to respond to a colleague's filthy, germ ridden, unwashed hands extended to give you a hand shake. Save others from similar feelings when you do the same with them.
- **Care other's time :** If people are waiting outside to use the washroom, don't take your time admiring yourself in the mirror or talking on mobile to someone special. Do your thing and come out of there.
- **Don't Comb your Hair :** And, if you must comb your hair, make sure you don't leave behind strands of your hair around the place.
- **Don't Gossip :** Washrooms are the best place to have gossip sessions about colleagues of opposite sex or the complaints about the boss. But not only this leads to inconveniencing the people waiting outside but their is always a risk of being caught.

In short, whenever you step into your office washroom, make it quick and keep it clean.

B 2 B Etiquette

Companies are represented by individuals. The norms of behaviour/conduct that apply to person to person communication apply also to Business-to-Business (B 2 B) communication. Every individual who is representing a company should know the essential norms of behaviour (etiquette). Good B 2 B Etiquettes include the following :

1. Never to criticise your organisation before your friends from other companies.
2. Defend your colleague's action without offending the complainant. Promise remedial action on your company's/colleague's behalf.
3. Always speak well of your company and stand up for the policies pursued by the company.
4. Be positive about your company. Keep yourself well informed of the achievements and prospects of your company. Highlight the positive gains and avoid discussing the short comings.
5. Also, do not over defend your company. Your objective assessment and sense of proportion should be visible.
6. Don't discuss confidential matters of the company with others, not even with your colleagues. The information may be used against the interest of the company.
7. Protect the records of the company in your possession from leakage of information to anyone.

8. Respect hierarchy. While dealing with persons from other companies, inform them of your position through your business card and similarly know host's position in his/her company. Give due respect to the hierarchy/position of the person you are calling.

B 2 C Etiquette

Business image of a company is best seen in the dealing and behaviour of its employees with its suppliers and customers. Business-to-customer (B 2 C) Etiquettes are as important as Business-to-Business (B 2 B) or Interpersonal ones. An employee who is representing a company to its clients and customers must observe the following norms of conduct/behaviour :

1. Appropriately welcome all step-ins (People entered) into office everyday.
   (a) Handle even the poorest of customers well.
   (b) A Company's image is best built on how the employees treat company's ordinary customers and clients
2. Be prompt in your service/supply to the customers.
3. Keep in mind that, 'a satisfied customer tells at least 5 others, whereas a dissatisfied/ harrassed customer tells at least 20 others.
4. Keep record of all complaints and a track of their redressal etc.,
5. When you have to take a decision that will affect the interest of the company, adopt a balanced approach so as to minimise loss to the company, while at the same time gaining customer's satisfaction.
6. Keep your cool while dealing with angry/annoyed customers.
7. Keep your seniors informed about unusual/difficult to handle complaints and follow their instructions religiously.

SUMMARY

Etiquette is a code that governs social behavioural expectations of a society/social class or a group. It may be codified or in unwritten form. These are built up over hundreds of years, continuously discarded, transformed or invented.

History of Etiquette is around 4500 years old (2414 B.C.) Ancient Greece and Rome and all known civilisations developed rules for proper social conduct, including for eating and speaking etc., Debrett (1950) UK is consideredly many as Arbiter of Etiquette. Recently (2000) internet has invented 'netiquette' which governs the drafting of e-mails, participating in online forum etc.,

Types of Etiquettes :

1. General Office Etiquettes
2. Verbal Communication Etiquette
3. Colleague Relationship Etiquette
4. Visitors Etiquette
5. Office Etiquette
6. Business Meeting Etiquette
7. Cellphone Etiquette

8. Fax(ing) Etiquette
9. Gifting Etiquette
10. E-mail Etiquette (Netiquette)
11. Cross-cultural Etiquette
12. Bad Office Etiquette
13. Dining Etiquette
14. Table Manners
15. Workplace (Washroom) Etiquette
16. B 2 B Etiquette
17. B 2 C Etiquette

REFERENCES

1. Funk & Wagnell : The Emily Post Book of Etiquette for young people
2. www.brainyquotes.com/words/et/etiquette
3. www.wikipedia.org./
4. Lillian Eichlar : 'Todays' Etiquette'
5. Andries Both : Hunting lice by candlelight.
6. The Ultimate Office Etiquette Guide(Google Search)
7. This Sinha Phira : Money Control.com. (7-10-2006)
8. Ralph Waldo Emerson : (Google Internet Search)
9. Insiya Amir : Learn the Art of Calling (Times of India : 7th June 2008)
10. Editors of Publications International : 13 Examples of Good and Bad Manners around the world.
11. Shital Kakar Mehta : Q & A Buffet Etiquette (The Economic Times 22nd August, 2008)
12. M.K. Sehgal & Vandana Khetarpal : Business Communication (2006)
13. M.K. Sehgal and Vandana Khetarpal : Business Communication (2006).

STUDY QUESTIONS

1. What do you mean by Etiquette? How is it defined?
2. How old are Etiquettes? Give the historical background and the Contemporary Scenario of Etiquettes ?
3. Write Short notes on :
   (i) Netiquette
   (ii) Dining Etiquette
   (iii) E-mail Etiquette
   (iv) Cell-phone Etiquette
4. Give examples of cross-cultural etiquettes with reference to Indian Traditions.
5. Write notes on :
   (i) B 2 B Etiquette
   (ii) B 2 C Etiquette
   (iii) Bad Office Etiquette
   (iv) Fax(ing) Etiquette

Chapter 9

MISCELLANEOUS TOPICS

CONTENTS

Chapter 9

MISCELLANEOUS TOPICS

A. PUBLIC RELATIONS

Modern Office has undertaken to perform a number of non-traditional functions. One such important function is called public relations, also known as "PR" function. The purpose of public relations in business organisations, is to create a favourable image of a company and thereby create and maintain goodwill. Therefore, several activities are undertaken to enhance the reputation of a company by managing external relations effectively. These activities are performed by or through the office.

Important facts and ideas about an organisation are communicated through appropriate channels of communication, such as the press, radio, television and films. Arthur W. Pearce[1] lists the following recipients of this information;

1. The community where the business operates;
2. Present and prospective employees;
3. Customers;
4. Suppliers;
5. Share holders;
6. The financial community, and
7. The general public.

In the broadest interpretation, a public relations programme consists of a broad spectrum of activities ranging from advertising and sales promotion to employee relations. However, the discussion in this chapter is restricted to external activities associated with public relations such

1. Handbook of fousiness Administration (McGraw Hill Book Co. New York).

as news releases, press conferences, executive speeches, video appearances, special publications and interviews.

Press Releases

Business Houses release news items to various media : newspapers, magazines, trade publications, radio and television (also on the internet). These news releases are commonly known as 'Press Releases'. These contain newsworthy (1) information about the business organisation, (2) its personnel (3) its activities (business and community), (4) sales, (5) financial standing, (6) dividend declarations, (7) products and services, (8) new launches, (9) plans, (10) amalgamations, (11) mergers, (12) lockouts, (13) new inventions, (14) donations for a social cause, (15) appointment of a chief executive/president, (16) Receiving a new/big contract, (17) Receiving ISO 9001 /9002 certification etc. All of these stories warrant media coverage. At times, graphs and photographs are also submitted along with the press releases as a means of illustrating the story.

Administration of Press Releases

In most large business houses, the issuance of press releases is the responsibility of public relations department. In some organisations, public relations firms are employed for this propose. In smaller organisations, this responsibility may be delegated to the director of managerial communications or to a manager familiar with publicity.

Press-releases are either hand-delivered, mailed or electronically, transmitted (E-mail, fax, internet, etc.) to various news media. Press releases offer the following distinctive advantages :

1. Information from the releases are printed without charge in the business/finance sections of newspapers and magazines or in other special sections, depending on the nature of the story.
2. Press releases are an excellent communicative device. They can be more effective than paid advertisements.
3. Press releases enhance goodwill of the organisation in the community, provide free publicity for the company and are generally more informative than the advertisements.

Administration of Press Releases requires that all such releases be reviewed and approved by appropriate company sources. One executive should control all press releases from the initial drafting stage to the actual communication to the media. If press releases are distributed indiscriminately, pre-mature news might be released or incorrect/misleading information might be disseminated-creating a credibility problem and adversely affecting the image of the organisation.

Writing Press Releases

Nathan Krevolin in his book *'Communication Systems and Procedures for the Modern Office'* suggests two methods for writing press releases :

1. *Journalistic Formula.* The beginning (or lead) of a typical press release starts with the traditional 5 W's of Journalism: *who, what, when. where* and *why.* At times, if appropriate, an H is added : *how*

When writing a press release, jot down the five W's and H and fill in the necessary information. The five W's can be in any order, and the H is optional.

Who? TATA MOTORS

What? Launch of a new car

When? 23rd March, 2009

Where? At Mumbai and Delhi

Why? To accept bookings for the new car

How? Two models (petrol and diesel version)

The lead paragraph of the press release will state;

> *TATA MOTORS will launch the first 'People's Car' 'NANO' on 23rd March 2009 at Mumbai and Delhi. The company will accept bookings for 'NANO' from 6th April 2009 to 20th April 2009 and the deliveries will start from July 2009.*

2. Inverted Pyramid Press releases are usually written in an inverted pyramid form. The most important elements appear first. Details and less critical information follow. Each paragraph of the article should be so written that it can stand alone without losing the total impact of the story.

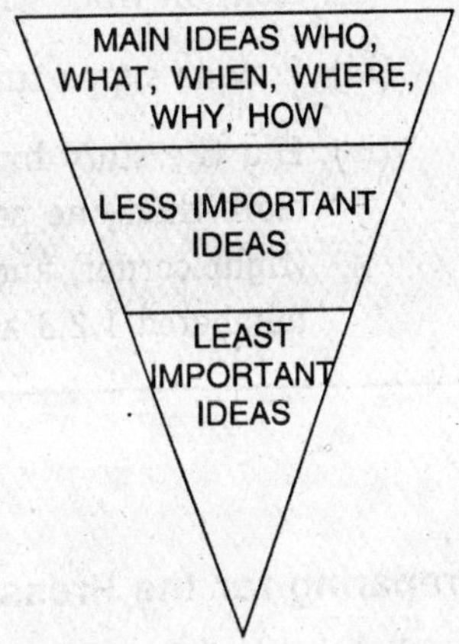

Fig. 9.1. Inverted Pyramid form of Press Release.

Due to media space limitations, the editor might delete parts of a press release. The cutting is done from the bottom upward. If the press release is writte in inverted pyramid form, deletion of one or the other part would not make the press release senseless, because each paragraph is so written that it can stand alone without losing the impact of the story.

Precautions

Press releases should be carefully written. These should be factual, concise correct and straight forward. Long, subjective or editorial details should be avoided. Only news worthy or typical information should be induded in a press release. Superlatives or editorial comments should not be used unless these can be attributed to a specific person. Most editors are flooded with unsolicited press releases and competition for space is always keen. It is therefore necessary that the releases should be news worthy. Also, to facilitate editing by the media the body of the story should be typed in double space. Adequate top and side margins should be provided.

Press Release Format

Press releases should be so drafted that they require little editing. They should follow prescribed journalistic format and style so that chances of publication increase. Some organisations have pre-printed press release forms while others type out their releases. The format of a press release is as follows :

1. The information contained at the top of the press release should include :

(i) The words **"Press Release"** in Capital Letters;

(ii) The name, address and telephone number of the sender; and

(iii) The suggested publication or release date.

2. The 'heading' should be brief. It is usually typed in capital letters. Some companies prefer not to use headlines, feeling that the editor would be forced to read the story.

3. The 'Body' should :

(i) Include a dateline consisting of the city of origin and date.

(ii) Mention Who, What, Where, Why, When and How in the lead.

(iii) Provide supporting details in descending order of importance.

(iv) End the story by using the printer's terms: (END), -end-, # # #. If the release is in more than one page, the words, *'to be continued' is typed* at the bottom of the page (right corner) and 'continued' is typed at the top of the next page. The pages can be numbered 1,2,3 and so on.

B. PRESS CONFERENCES

Preparing for the Press Conference

Certain situations may arise in an organisation when special treatment should be given to important news items. A conference is called where members of the press and other media are invited. The invitation is usually extended by telephone or hand delivered letters. The letter contains standard information about the press conference such as topic, date, time and place of the conference.

Convening the Conference

At the press conference, one or more company executives appear before the media representatives and, either

(i) read out a pre-prepared detailed announcement; or

(ii) make the important announcements and discuss and clarify the questions or queries raised by the press or media people; or

(iii) make visual or audio-visual presentations regarding the important topic or event; or

(iv) distribute copies of the notification or announcements containing the biographical sketches, tables, pictures, figures, photographs, excerpts reviews, etc.

It is expected that the news item announced at the press conference will receive substantial coverage and perhaps be a major news item in the forthcoming issue of the newspaper/magazines/journal, etc.

Press conferences should be held discriminately and only for major/important newstimes. If they are called indiscriminately for minor news items, members of the press/media will avoid to attend the future press conferences.

Press conferences are usually held for following purposes :

1. Launch of a new product
2. Announcement of a technical/technological breakthrough (a new invention/innovation)
3. Announcement of amalgamation/merger/ reconstitution of the company.
4. Announcement of a social welfare project by a company.
5. Announcement of annual returns, issue of bonus or right shares,
6. Announcement of public issue by the company.

Other Public Relations Activities

Though press releases and press conferences are considered to be the main public relation activities, certain other communicate activities are undertaken by business organisations to ensure better public relations. These include the following:

1. *Executive speeches:* Company executives are invited to speak before various forums/ groups of people. This provides an opportunity for direct communication with other business people or the public. It is also common for business executives to attend various seminars. Conferences and group meetings and to exchange views on subjects of common interest. ;

2. *Media appearances:* Radio, television and films provide an opportunity for business executives to communicate to large audiences. Nowadays many business organisations sponsor several kinds of sports events,-social welfare projects and/ or T.V. serials, programmes, contests through financial grants. This fosters goodwill and creates a positive image for the company, Some examples of such sponsorships, etc. are cited below:

(a) Femina Miss India Contest.

(b) Graviera Suitings Mr. India Contest

(c) ITC's/Wills World Cup for Cricket

(d) Four Square's White Water Challenge

(e) Colgate Top Ten

(f) Close Up Antakshari

(g) DLF IPL 2009

(h) Amul — Voice of India

(i) Red & White Bravery Awards

(j) Manikchand — Filmfare Awards

(k) Vodafone — Garnier Dus Ka Dum

TATA NANO CREATES HISTORY

Fig. Tata Nano

Mumbai : History was created in Mumbai on 23-04-2009 when Tata Motors launched the world's least expensive car — NANO — a car that can redefine personal transportation in Modern India.

Described as 'People's Car' by Tata Group Chairman Ratan Tata, Nano's commercial launch will mark a milestone in a journey which was replete with controversies, hurdles and criticism from competitors.

As far as customers are concerned, they can expect to own a car at a price between Rs. 1.20 lakh and Rs. 1.70 lakh depending on the version of Nano. According to Dealer sources, if TATA keeps the ex-factory price of Rs. 1 lakh as promised, then the base model could easily have an on-road price of Rs. 1.20 lakh after adding excise duty, road tax and IT cess alongwith transportation changes, local taxes, Insurance and Registration fees and lifetime parking fees (wherever applicable).

Fig. : Newsitem based on Company's Press Conference.

3. *Interviews:* At times, top company executives grant special interviews to reporters working for newspapers or magazines. It is important that the executive should prepare for the interview and speak only the policies of the company and refrain from speaking out his personal views and opinions. It is imperative that only authorised executives grant interviews (usually CEO, MD, Chairman or President of the company) This is important because giving interviews requires a great deal of experience and expertise and information to respond intelligently and convincingly to probing questions by reporters.

4. *Special public issues :* Several companies publish inhouse journals, magazines or newsletters, such as corporate reports and company magazines. At times such magazines are distributed externally to promote goodwill and good public relations. A company may also submit articles for publication in respective/professional trade journals. Such coverage also gives some mileage to the company in public relations activities. Companies, annual reports, prospectus, etc. also contain financial performances, future plans, bonus/right/public issue of shares, debentures, etc. and such other topics. These create awareness about the companies' financial standing and prospects and thus help in making good public relations.

B. FLEXIBLE WORKING HOURS

Flexible working hours or flexitime is a system by which the staff is allowed to start and finish work as they choose, provided that:

(i) they work within the earliest and latest times laid down;

(ii) they are present during the 'core' time when everyone in the staff is expected to be at work, say 11 am to 2 pm;

(iii) they work an agreed total number of hours within a specified period eg. a week or a month.

The flexible working hours is a variation of the application of single shift working hours of 10 am to 5 pm working with everyone working the same hours It provides a change in work pattern that is being successfully applied in some of the western countries.

With the relaxation in strict adherence in office discipline and a greater awareness of differences in individual psychology, the apparent need to work a rigid 10 am to 5 pm pattern is being superseded by flexibility in working hours. Experiments have been made and in some instances formal changes have also fallowed in allowing flexibility in attendance at the office. A standard scheme stipulate core hours say, form 11 am to 2 pm when everyone should be present.

On either side of these times, individual arrangements are negotiated, for example 8 am to 3 pm or 9 am to 4 pm or 10 am to 5 pm or 11 am to 6 pm and so on. Variations on this scheme to suit particular circumstances are also seen operating in some European countries.

The 'core' time is the time when everyone has to be at work, say 11 am to 2 pm, so that customers can be dealt with, discussions held, workload planned and results discussed. Outside 'core' time, staff is allowed to opt for an extension or reduction hours at either end of the normal working day. They can also take a shorter or longer lunch break. They can also be allowed to take time off for extra hoursworked. Thus even though the employees' starting times are flexible, they must work the required number of hours per day or per week. In most cases, restrictions are imposed on the degree of flexibility allowed. A starting time and a closing time is fixed within which the employee can decide about his working hours. To facilitate scheduling, some organisations also specify, that employees must report to work at the same time each day for a weeks duration. Some organisations may also have policies against the participation of certain employees or departments in the flexible programme, if their output provide input for other employees Normally a time recording unit is also used to ensure that employees do not abuse the system.

Most flexitime systems have a settlement or accounting period, covering a period of time, say a week or a month at the end of which employees must settle their account either by taking compensatory time off or putting in additional hours to make up for any deficiencies in the number of working hours.

With flexitime the employees have greater freedom and with it often demonstrates a corresponding sense of responsibility. The employee does not feel guilty about being late for work or having time off for personal reasons. The married women in particular are able to coordinate their work with domestic and family responsiblities without having to watch the clock too closely. Employees with travel related difficulties can avoid the rush hours. In some circumstances flexitime may be better suited to the workload and result in a reduction in overtime outside normal working hours.

Whenever flexitime has been put to work, it appears to be popular among the employees and in other cases a more even flow of work is obtained.

Impact on the organisation

Studies have been made in western countries that reveal the following impact of flexitime on the organisations :

(i) By permitting individual employees to exercise freedom in the choice of working hours, the authority and discipline traditionally considered so essential in running offices is diluted. A change in management behaviour and style is often necessary when flexitime is introduced.

(ii) Flexitime requires improved delegation. If superior and subordinate have opted for defferent working hours, then it is necessary to establish co-ordination and delegation which can cope with the change.

(iii) The improved delegation might contemplate need for training supervisors in participative management.

(iv) Similarly, training maybe required for employees who have opted for flexitime but find that they are unable to plan their work appropriately.

(v) Some categories of employees might not be allowed to have flexible working hours such as the receptionist, the telephone operator, the cashier or the billing clerk etc. This may create frictions among employees.

Benefits of Flexible working hours

Flexible working hours offer a large number of advantages, most of which accrue to the employees. W.H. Walley outlines the following benefits of flexible working hours :

1. Flexible working hours provide a positive contribution towards job enrichment and self respect by helping participants to meet their social ambitions. This in turn, will provide a powerful motivator in achieving organisational as well as personal objectives.
2. To accommodate the idea of flexible working hours, team work has to improve considerably. A freer and more open relationship between manager and their staff often emerges. This in time could lead to improved performance which is beneficial to the organisation
3. By extending flexible working hours, it is likely that staff who would not otherwise work at all will be attracted to administrative work. Women with young children, for example, want to be at home when their children arrives back from school.
4. Flexible working hours are often seen as a valuable fringe benefit and in many organisations, it has been used to recruit a variety of personnel-secretaries, computer programmers etc. Absenteeism is lessened.
5. In an era when flexibility is a growing and essential part of the success of any organisation, the use of flexible working hours aids the generation of a flexible approach to work, job design, work teams and even work location.
6. Peak hour travelling can be avoided by many employees.
7. Many organisations which have a flexible workload would be better served by having flexible working hours.

8. Metabolism of people tends to differ. Some are bright and more active in the morning, others later in the day. Flexible working hours provide a situation where people can work at the time of the day that suits them.
9. Many people prefer to have a part of the day when they can sit quietly and carry out 'quiet work'. Flexible working hours provide this opportunity.
10. Women who often need to be able to alter the length of their working day to suit their personal situation, are usually more in favour of flexible working hours than men. Consequently organisations with a high proportion of women in their workforce might best be suited to flexible working arrangements.

Zene K. Quible lists the following distinct advantages :

11. Flexitime greatly decreases the rate of absenteeism and almost totally eliminates tardiness.
12. Levels of production increase because employees are responsible for a full working day no matter when they arrive on the job.
13. Because flexitime helps fulfil some of the human needs of employees, they experience greater job satisfaction.
14. Employees experience less frustration in going to and from work because public transportation facilities and highways are less congested.
15. Employees whose leisure activities require several hours of daylight have the flexibility to plan their work schedules accordingly.
16. Flexitime provides employees with the opportunities of easily accumulating overtime hours in order to take time off later.
17. Employees can use their own time to schedule doctor and other kinds of appointments.

Drawbacks

1. Increased costs will be incurred. There will be the cost of using the time recording mechanisms, plus the cost of administrating the scheme. If the day is lengthened, then increased lighting, air conditioning or heating will be required.

2. Where the company provides transport or has arrangements with local transport authorities to have transport for its staff, the problem of rearrangement could be considerable and might inhibit the scheme totally.

3. Employees may tend to abuse the system by wrong recording of hours worked.

4. Where the organisation has commitments to outsiders eg. giving a service to the public, the service maybe guaranteed only by providing extra staff.

5. In the event of failure, it may be difficult to revert back to a normal hours system.

6. Employee's whose output becomes another employee's input may not be permitted to participate in the flexitime programme. In some instances, larger inventories are maintained so that the work process is not hampered when employees utilise variable starting hours.

7. Planning work schedules may become cumbersome, especially in organisations that utilise multiple shifts.

8. Employees who ride in carpools with other employees of other organisations find flexitime to be impractical.

In Indian context the need of flexible working hours stems more importantly in view of certain peculiar circumstances. In Indian metroes, the following problems have been surmounting in gigantic proportions since long :

(i) bottlenecks in transportation of staff, during fixed office hours;

(ii) dangerous levels of pollution during peak hours (office times);

(iii) bottlenecks in services like communication, electric supply etc., during peak hours and underutilization of these during non-peak hours;

(iv) Delays due to traffic jams, overcrowding in public transportation systems etc.

In India, flexitime may be gainfully employed in the metroes by a large number of organisations such as the following:

(i) Accounting staff, mail receiving staff, correspondents, data analysts may have working hours starting earlier than the normal working hours.

(ii) Despatch staff, filing staff and recordkeeping staff etc. may have working hours finishing later than normal working hours so that they can finish the work done by the office staff during normal working hours.

(iii) Computer operators, Receptionist, Telephone operator, cashiers, subordinate staff, sales staff, invoices/billing clerks, correspondents etc. may have normal working hours to carry out routine business activities during normal working hours.

(iv) Supervisory and administrative staff should either have working hours similar to their subordinates or may learn to delegate in an improved manner in the style of participative manner.

(v) Managers and senior executives may follow different time schedules on different days so that they can check the working of the staff during different hours; This ensures moral check on the staff.

The advantages of flexible working hours outweigh the disadvantages of the same. It is need of the hour that organisations think in terms of flexible working hours for their staff and provide relief to the social system in terms of decongestion, peak hour bottlenecks, traffic related problems and peak hour load on communication and infrastructural facilities.

SUMMARY

A. Public Relations : Public Relation or PR is an important function of Modern Office/Business. Its purpose is to create a favourable image of the company and thereby create and maintain goodwill.

Public Relations may be performed by issuing press releases to various media like newspapers, magazines, trade publications, Radio & T.V., Internet etc., A Press release may contain information about the business, products, new launches, plans, mergers, lackouts, new inventions, appointment of senior/management cadres, receiving any certification or award etc.,

4. George R. Terry, *op. cit.*
5. Littleield & Others *op. cit.*
6. George R. Terry, *op. cit.*
7. B.H. Walley : Handbook of Office Management (z/e).

Press releases are either hand-delivered, mailed or electronically transuitted by e-mail, Fax, Internet etc., The offer following advantages :

(i) They are printed without charge

(ii) They are excellent communicative device

(iii) They enhance goodwill of the company

(iv) They provide free publicity

(v) They are generally more informative than Advertisements.

B. Press Conferences : A conference is called where members of the press and other media are invited by Telephone or hand delivered letters.

In the conference, the company executive or executive generally appear and

(i) read out a pre-prepared draft statement, or

(ii) make an important announcement, or

(iii) make visual or audio-visual presentations, or

(iv) distribute copies of the notification or announcement etc.

The purposes of press conference may be similar to those of press release.

Other Public Relations Activities

1. Executive Speeches
2. Media Appearances (on Radio or TV) though sponsorships of sports/fashion/social event.

REFERENCES

1. Nathan Krevolin : Communication Systems Procedures for the Modern Office
2. Handbook of Busianess Administration : (McGraw Hill Book Co. New York)

STUDY QUESTIONS

1. What are the methods of Writing Press Releases Discuss ?
2. What information is generally contained in the Press releases ? Give examples.
3. Write short notes on :
   (i) Press Release Format
   (ii) Public Relation Activities.
4. Draft a Press release for announcing the launch of a T.V. cum D.V.D. Player cum Home Theatre (Three-in-one) by Sony India Ltd, announcing the features and price of different models of the new launch.

APPENDICES

Appendix-I

SMS ABBREVIATIONS (Popularly used Internet Acronyms)

With the advent of e-mail and Messaging service on mobile and Internet, a new language in abbreviated from has been developed. These are variously described as Internet Acronyms, E-mail shorthand, chatting shorthand, shorthand for newsgroups.[1] These have gained popularly because it is easier and takes less time to type than typing the full expressions. Many of these are also used in office communication through e-mail etc. Some of the most popular acronyms are listed below:

AFAIK	:	As far As I Know
AKA	:	Also Known As
AMBW	:	All My Best Wishes
ASAP	:	As Soon as Possible
AUP	:	As You Please
BBAIB	:	Be Back In A Bit.
BBL	:	Be Back Later
B2B	:	Business To Business
B2C	:	Business To Customer
BBN	:	Bye Bye Now
BCNU	:	Be Seein' You
BFN	:	Bye For Now
BIF	:	Basic In Fact
BITD	:	Back In The Day
BM	:	Byte Me
BRB	:	Be Right Back

1. Adapted: The Hindustan Times.

BTW	:	By The Way
CID	:	Consider It Done
CIO	:	Check It Out
CULR	:	See You Later
F2F	:	Face To Face
FWIW	:	For What It's Worth
FYI	:	For Your Information
GL	:	Good Luck
GMTA	:	Great Minds Think Alike
GR&D	:	Grinning, Running And Ducking
GTG	:	Got To Go
GTGB	:	Got To Go Bye
GTSY	:	Glad To See Ya
HAND	:	Have A Nice Day
HAGO	:	Have A Good One
HTH	:	Hope This (That) Helps
IAE	:	In Any Event
IC	:	In Character
ICE	:	Information Technology, Communication and Entertainment
IDKY	:	I Don't Know You
IDST	:	I Did't Say That
IDTS	:	I Don't Think So
IMHO	:	In My Humble Opinion
IMNSHO	:	In My Not So Humble Opinion
IMO	:	In My Opinion
IOH	:	I'm Outta Here
IOW	:	In Other Words
IOU	:	I Owe You
IRL	:	In Real Life
KIT	:	Keep In Touch
LR	:	Later
LOL	:	Laughing Out Loud or Lots of Love
LTNS	:	Long Time No Seen
MOF	:	Male or Female
MOTD	:	Message Of The Day
MOTSS	:	Members Of the Same Sex
NBIF	:	No Basis In fact

NP	:	No Problem
NRG	:	Energy
NRN	:	No Reply Necessary
OIC	:	Oh, I see
OOC	:	Out Of Character
OTOH	:	On The Other Hand
PLS	:	Please
PMFJI	:	Pardon Me For Jumping In
POV	:	Point Of View
ROTFL	:	Rolling On The Floor Laughing
RSN	:	Real Soon Now
RTM	:	Read The Manual
SITD	:	Still In The Dark
SUYF	:	Shut Up You Fool
SWG	:	Scientific Wild Guess
SWDYT	:	So What Do You Think
TIA	:	Thanks In Advance
TIAIL	:	Think I Am In Love
TIC	:	Tongue In Cheek
TTFN	:	Ta Ta For Now
TTT	:	To The Top
TTYL	:	Talk To You Later
TX	:	Thanks
TYVM	:	Thank You Very Much
WG	:	Wild Guess
WB	:	Welcome Back
WCA	:	Who Cares Anyway
WDYS	:	What Did You Say
WE	:	What Ever
WTG	:	Way To Go
WYRN	:	What's Your Real Name?
WYS	:	Whatever You Say
WYT	:	Whatever You Think
YA	:	Yet Another
YDKM	:	You Don't Know Me
YGTBK	:	You've Got To Be Kidding
YSYD	:	Yeah/Sure You Do.

Appendix-II

A MANAGEMENT GUIDE TO OFFICE TERMINOLOGY

Many terms and abbreviations are used in the day-to-day working of an office. These have been explained below:

TERMS EXPLAINED

Acknowledgement	: To make known the receipt of.
Affidavit	: To attest the truth of.
Agreement	: An offer and acceptance in writing.
Application	: A request for something.
Authorisation	: To permit an action.
Budget	: A Financial plan of the activities of the organisation for a particular period.
Budgetary Control	: The process of using the budget by comparing the actual results with the budgetary targets in order to correct either the estimates or the causes of differences.
Centralisation (of authority)	: Concentration of decision-making.
Certification	: To attest the truth of.
Claim	: To demand as due.
Committee	: A body of persons entrusted with the resposibility of discharging some assigned functions collectively as a group-permanent or ad hoc.
Communication	: Exchange of facts, ideas, opinions or emotions by two or more persons.
Contract	: A valid agreement.
Control	: Measurement and correction of the performance of the work force to ensure the attainment of organisational objectives.
Correspondence	: Communication in writing on subjects of mutual interest either within the organisation or with an outsider.

Decentralisation (of authority) : Selective dispersal and concentration of authority.
Delegation : A process of entrusting a part of the work to subordinates.
Departmentation : The process by which the activities or functions of an enterprise are grouped homogeneously into different sections.
Directing : Process of guiding and supervising the subordinates.
Estimate : To forecast or calculate approximately.
Filing : The process of classifying, arranging and sorting records so that they may be readily available when needed.
Flow of work : The way work moves from one operation to another.
Follow-up : Reminder of uncompleted action.
Form : A standardised record used to accumulate and transmit information for reference purposes.
Form Letter : A standardised letter which is used to answer all correspondence of a similar and recurring nature or to give the same information to a number of correspondents.
Identification : To name.
Indexing : A method of making reference to the records which have been filed.
Inspection : Testing an item to find out if it does or does not satisfy the standard shape, colour or other factors previously determined.
Instruction : To explain 'How'?
Inventory : Recording a periodical count of stock in hand on a certain date.
Job Analysis : A method by which the facts about each job are secured, organised and combined.
Job-Description : To accurately describe the work and responsibility of a particular position.
Job-Grading : Determination of relative levels of various jobs.
Leadership : Ability to enthuse, to inspire and guide subordinates.
Mail : Written communication that passes through a messenger or a post office.
Method : Manner in which a clerical operation or task is performed.
Microfilming : A method of copying records on safety-base film.
Morale : A feeling of friendliness, an air of cheerfulness, a spirit of co-operation, and a relaxed attitude which permeates a group or department.
Motivation : Inducing subordinates to work with zeal and gusto.
Notice : To communicate an unsolicited statement of action.
Office Layout : The arrangement of furniture and equipment within a given floor area.
Office Management : Planning, organising, controlling and actuating office work and performing it so as to achieve the desired objectives.
Office Management Audit : A careful analysis of office activities. A thorough examination of the planning, organising and directing which goes on in a firm.
Office Manual : A handbook containing written information, instructions, rules and regulations of the organisation and employment conditions of its employees.
Order : To order purchase of materials, work, etc.
Organisation : A management process by which the activities of a group of persons are co-ordinated to achieve a desired goal.
Organisation Chart : A diagrammatical presentation showing important aspects of an organisation, including its major functions and their relationships.
Pass : A permit or licence to pass, or to go.
Permit : Permit or licence to perform a specific act.

Procedure	: A series or sequence of related operation designed to standardise the performance of various steps which make up a major operation.
Questionnaire	: To ask questions for the purpose of obtaining data.
Receipt	: To acknowledge delivery or payment given by the recipient.
Record	: To retain an account of facts or data.
Records	: All forms of information processing media used by a business, office, whether, these are in the form of correspondence, cards, tapes, or microfilms.
Report	: A communication that contains factual information, organised and presented in clear, correct and coherent language.
Request	: To ask for.
Requisition	: To formally request.
Roster	: The list of personnel.
Routing Slip	: To send an attachment along a circuit of persons or places
Schedule	: To outline regularly recurring events or write plan of future events.
Scientific Management	: "Knowing exactly what you want men to do and seeing that they do it in the best and cheapest way". —F.W. Taylor
Selection	: Choosing one object from several.
Staffing	: Recruitment, selection, compensation, training, promotion and retirement of subordinates
Stock Record	: A record of stock in hand.
Supervision	: "Watching over the activities of others."
System	: A complex of related procedures designed according to an integrated scheme for the purpose of running a major activity of a company.
Typing Pool	: A central typing place which looks after the typing work of all the departments.
Work Measurement	: A technique used to determine the time necessary for the performance of a certain task.
Work Standard	: A measure or level of accomplishment in a specified activity under specific conditions.

Appendix-III

ABBREVIATIONS OF WORDS

Abbreviation	Word
Acct	Account
Add	Additional
Admn	Administration
Admv	Administrative
Advt	Advertisement
Advtg	Advertising
Agcy	Agency
Agt	Agent
Anx	Annexe
Assn	Association
Asst	Assistant
Auto	Automobile
Ave	Avenue
Bch	Branch
Bdg	Boarding
Bk	Book
Bkg	Booking
Bldg	Building
Bldr	Builder
Bnk	Bank
Bnkg	Banking
Bros	Brothers
Bzr	Bazar
Cabt	Cabinet
Cntn	Canteen
Cent	Central
Cert	Certified
Ch	Chief
Co	Company
Com	Commission
Consult	Consultant
Contr	Contractor
Constn	Construction
Corp	Corporation
Coun	Council
Cl	Clause
Crcl	Circle
Dept	Department
Dy	Deputy
Dir	Director
Dist	District
Distrib	Distributor
Div	Division
Dupl	Duplicating
Elec	Electric
Empl	Employment
Eng	Engineer
Engg	Engineering
Exp	Export
Extn	Extension
Est	Estate
Estab	Establishment
Exch	Exchange
Exec	Executive
Fcty	Factory
Fed	Federation
Fgn	Foreign
Fin	Financier
Furn	Furniture
Gds	Goods
Gdw	Godown
Gen	General
Govt	Government
Hdqrs	Headquarters
HO	Head Office
Hon	Honourable
Htl	Hotel
Hydr	Hydraulic
Imp	Import
Imptr	Importer
Inc	Incorporated
Ins	Insurance
Inst	Institute
Instl	Instalment/ Installation
Instmt	Instrument
Int	Interior
Internal	International
Lab	Laboratory
Ldg	Lodge
Litho	Lithographic
Ltd	Limited
Ltg	Lighting
Mach	Machine/ Machinery
Mech	Mechanic/ Mechanical
Med	Medicine/

	Medical
Merc	: Mercantile
Merch	: Merchandise
Mfg.	: Manufacturing
Mgr	: Manager
Mgt	: Management
Mg	: Managing
Mkt	: Market
Mortg	: Mortgage
Opp	: Opposite
Opr	: Operator
Mtr	: Motor
Mun	: Municipal
Mt	: Metre
Nws	: News
Off	: Office
Optg	: Operating
Pat	: Patent
Pbc	: Public
Photog	: Photographic
Pl	: Place
Plg	: Planning
Plmbr	: Plumber
PO	: Post Office
Ppr	: Paper
Pres	: President
Priv	: Private
Pvt	: Private
Prof	: Professor
Prod	: Product
Prop	: Proprietor
Prov	: Provision
Ptnr	: Partner
Pubg	: Publishing
Qty	: Quanitity
Reg	: Regional
Regd	: Registered
Regr	: Registrar
Regy	: Registry
Reps	: Representative
Res	: Residence
Resh	: Research
Ret	: Retail
Retlr	: Retailer
Retd	: Retired
Rly	: Railway
Rprs	: Repairers
Rstnt	: Restaurant
San	: Sanitary
Sci	: Scientific
Secy	: Secretary
Ser	: Service
Shpg	: Shipping
Shrm	: Showroom
Offr	: Officer
Sht	: Sheet
Shthd	: Shorthand
Soc	: Society
Spl	: Special
Solr	: Solicitor
Spts	: Sports
Sq	: Square
Supr	: Supervisor
St	: Street
Stge	: Storage
Stk	: Stock
Stn	: Station
Steno	: Stenographer
Stnr	: Stationer
Stny	: Stationery
Supt	: Suprintendent
Tech	: Technical/ Technician
Teleg	: Telegraph
Tel	: Telephone
Ter	: Terrace
Trans	: Transport
TV	: Television
Typw	: Typewriter
Undtkr	: Undertaker
Up	: Upper
Vdr	: Vendor
Veg	: Vegetable
Vntlg	: Ventilating
Vstr	: Visitor
Wks	: Works
Wkshp	: Workshop
Wldg	: Welding
Wldr	: Welder
Wndw	: Window
Wr	: Warn
Yd	: Yard

Appendix-IV

ABBREVIATIONS OF TERMS

A/C	:	Account
A/D	:	Acknowledgement Due
ADP	:	Automatic Data Processing
ANS	:	Alpha Numerical System
AO	:	Administrative Officer
BASIC	:	Beginners' All-Purpose Symbolic Instructions Code
B/E	:	Bill of Exchange
B/L	:	Bill of Lading
BMTS	:	Basic Motion Time Study
C/A	:	Current Account
CENTREX	:	Central Exchange
COBOL	:	Common Business Oriented Language
COD	:	Cash on Delivery
CP	:	Charter Party
CPC	:	Computer Process Control
CPM	:	Critical Path Method
CPU	:	Central Processing Unit
COM	:	Computer Output Microfilm
CR	:	Confidential Report
CRT	:	Cathode Ray Tube
7c's	:	Clarity, concisencess, completeness, courtesy, consideration, correctness and concreteness (used in business writing)

D/A	:	Documents Against Acceptance
D/P	:	Documents Against Payment
DACOM	:	Datascope Computer Output Microfilmer
DLO	:	Dead Letter Office
DP	:	Dynamic Programming
DGS&D	:	Directorate-General of Supplies and Disposals
EAM	:	Electronic Accounting Machines
EDP	:	Electronic Data Processing
EOQ	:	Economic Order Quantity
ESI	:	Employees State Insurance
FC	:	Flow Chart
FIFO	:	First-In, First-Out
FT Calls	:	Fixed Time calls
GIGO	:	'Garbage-In, Garbage-Out'. (An Input Warning)
GPD	:	General Purpose Data
GPO	:	General Post Office
FORTRAN	:	Formula Translating Language for Scientific Computations
HO	:	Head Office
HQ	:	Headquarter
IDP	:	Integrated Data Processing
IBM	:	International Business Machines World Trade Corporation
I/O	:	Input-Output
IR	:	Information Retrieval
ISI	:	Indian Standards Institute
IST	:	Indian Standard Time
Intercom	:	Intercommunication System
JCC	:	Joint Consultation Committee
LIFO	:	Last-In, First-Out
MCD	:	Master Clerical Data *(Quible)*
MICR	:	Magnetic Ink Character Recognition
MIS	:	Management Information System
MTA	:	Motion Time Analysis
MTM	:	Methods Time Measurement
NCR	:	No Carbon Required (Carbonless Copy Paper)
O&M	:	Organisation and Methods
OMTC	:	Organisation and Methods Training Course
OR	:	Operations Research
P&T	:	Post and Telegraphs Department
PAX	:	Private Automatic Exchange

PABX	:	Private Automatic Branch Exchange
PCO	:	Public Call Office
PAYE	:	Pay As You Earn (A System of Tax Collection)
PERT	:	Programme Evaluation Review Technique
PFC	:	Process Flow Chart
PMBX	:	Private Manual Branch Exchange
P/N	:	Promissory Note
PO	:	Post Office
PP	:	Particular Person Call
PSALI	:	Permanent Supplementary Artificial Lighting of the Interior
QMS	:	Quick Mail Service
RBI	:	Reserve Bank of India
RPG	:	Report Programme Generator
3R's	:	Reading, Reference and Revision
SDA	:	Source Data Automation
SQC	:	Statistical Quality Control
SPS	:	Symbolic Programming System
STD	:	Subscriber's Trunk Dialing
SFT	:	Subscription Fixed Time Calls
TCCS	:	Telex Computer Communication Service
TELEX	:	Teleprinter Exchange
TWI	:	Training Within Industry
TMUS	:	Time Measurement Units
UPC	:	Under Postal Certificate
VEP	:	Variable Factor Programming
VPP	:	Value Payable Parcel
WATS	:	Wide Area Telephone Service

BIBLIOGRAPHY

A.R. Robert : Effective Business Communication

Allen Lovis A. : The Art of Delegations.

American Management Association : Effective Communication on the job.

Appley Lawrence A. : Management in Action

Austin J.L. : How to do things with words.

Baird J. K. etc. : The Dynamics of Organisational Communication.

B. F. James : Make your Business letters, Make friends.

B. J. Francis : Practical Communication

Bell R.W. : Write What you Mean.

Berlo D.K. : The Process of Communication

Bright J. S. : Precis Writing.

Brown L. : Effective Business Report Writing

Bunker L. : Fundamentals of Office Methods & Forms Design.

Burns T. : Non-verbal Communication

Chappel R.T. : A Text Book of Business Communication

Chappell & Read : Textbook of Business Communication

Chrissie Wright : A Handbook of Business Communication

Carl Heyel : Handbook of Office Administration

Covey, Stephen R : The Seven Habits of Highly Effective People.

Crane W.G. etc. : How to think & write

Douglas P : Communicating Through Reports.

Dubin Robert : The World at Work.

Flesch R. : The Art of Readable Writing.

Fox, Sue & C. Perin : Business Etiquette for Dummies
Fraidoon Mazda : Engineering Management
Gaum Greaves and Hoffman : Report Writing
Gibbons, D : 'Using E-mails'.
Guffy. M.E. : Essentials of Business Communication.
Hamphill & McCormick : Business Communication
Harcourt J. : Business Communication
Havland C.L. : Communication and Persuation.
Jepson, R.W. : A new Guide to Precis Writing
Kitty O. Lecker & Stephen Kyo : Business Communication : Building Critical Skills.
Koontz etc. : Principles of Management
Lawsche C.H. : Communication in Organisations
Lee, I. : How to talk with people
Lesiker & Flattey : Basic Business Communication : Skills for Empowering the internet generation.
Lesiker, Raymond & Lyons : Report writing for Business
Leskiar & Flatley : Basic Communication skills.
Little Peter : Communication in Business.
L.G.S. Menon : Organisation Charts
M.K. Sehgal & Vandana Khetrapal : Business Communication.
Mary Ellen Guffy : Business Communication
Maslow A.H. : Motivation and Personality
Namita Gopal : Business Communication; Oral and Written
Nathan Krevolin : Communication Systems & Procedures
Ober : Contemporary Business Communication
Paul T. Rankin: Listening Ability. Its Importance, Measurement and Development
Partridge Eric : Precis Writing
Paul T. Batkin : 'Listening Ability.
Persing B. S. : Business Communication Dynamics
Penrose : Advanced Business Communication
Pollock N.C. & Others : Form Design
R.R. & W. Kees : Non-verbal Communication
Rasberry R.W. etc. : Effective Management Communication
Redfield, C.E. : Communication in Management.
Robinson David : Business Etiquette

Schramm, W.L. : The Process & Effects of Communication.

Shearing H.A. etc. : Talks & How to give them.

Shurter, L.H. : Written Communication in English

Sturart, C : Effecting Speaking.

Taylor H.M. etc. : The Right way of Conduct Meetings, Conferences & Discussions

Theilbert, P.R. : Business Writing for Busy People

Thill, John & Bovee : Excellence in Business Communication

Treece, M : Successful Business Communication

Walton, Donald : Are you Communicating?

Wells : Communication in Business.

Whalan. J.E. : E-mail@ work

Zane K. Quible : Introduction to Administrative Office Management

Zelany, Gene : The Executive Guide to Visual Communication.

INDEX